The
Boomer Book
of
Christmas Memories

ISBN: 978-0-9853973-4-0

Library of Congress Control Number:
2014919343

Published by

K
kalambakal
press

Rancho Palos Verdes, CA

Editing and book design by Stacey Aaronson

The BOOMER BOOK of CHRISTMAS MEMORIES

Vickey Kall

K
kalambakal
press

The author in her favorite dress,
circa 1960.

For Kalani, Nathan, and Ezra

Contents

Chapter 4: Yuletide Entertainment

Part One

Everything But Toys

Chapter One

Christmas Trees & Decorations

* * * * * * * * * *

Christmas trees date back to Ye Olde Europe, but that doesn't have much to do with the Baby Boomer generation. The idea of dragging a tree indoors and decorating it is relatively new. Our Founding Fathers never bothered; you wouldn't find a Christmas tree at Mount Vernon or Monticello when George Washington or Thomas Jefferson lived there.

Indoor Christmas trees did not become popular with Americans until a century before the Boomer Era. Back then—around 1850—*Godey's Lady's Book,* the *Good Housekeeping* of its day, circulated pictures of Queen Victoria's decorated tree in Windsor Castle. The image showed the royal family, including five skirted children (two of whom were boys), before a table that held a heavily ornamented tree.

Even in those halcyon days before Photoshop, pictures could be altered—and this one was. The original engraving printed up in London showed Victoria wearing her crown, with a mustachioed Albert sporting a military-style sash. Those fancy trappings were "erased" from the *Godey's Lady's Book* photo, which was widely copied. Apparently, editors figured Americans would warm up to the royal couple more if they looked less formal and regal. And danged if the editors weren't correct.

The royal family looked warm and loving, just like American families. The picture was so popular that it made Christmas trees popular. Suddenly, everyone wanted one to prop up and decorate.

For a hundred years, we cut down or bought spruce, fragrant balsam fir, and other evergreens, despite warnings from conservationists that we risked destroying our national forests. Bit o' trivia: Franklin Delano Roosevelt, the president our parents remember best, farmed Christmas trees at his Hyde Park home.

During the 1930s, people embraced a new type of tree: Scotch pine. It had longer needles, but they stayed on the tree longer too. If you're an early Boomer, that's probably the tree you remember from childhood. Those who grew up in the 1960s most likely had Douglas firs, but by the '70s, Scotch pine was back on top. Today, it's still the best seller.

Although fake trees got lots of publicity in the Boomer Era, around three-fourths of the trees we had in our living rooms were real back then. Not until the 1990s did fake trees outsell real ones.

Still, there's no denying that the coolest homes had glittery fake trees, preferably in designer colors not known to Mother Nature. Salesmen spread the word that they were safer and fire retardant, and fake trees shed no needles onto the carpet. In 1957, the Frostee-Glow Company wanted everyone to know that Elvis used their white nylon tree in his new, palatial home: Graceland. It sat behind the north window in the dining room and was decorated with red ornaments.

In 1965, the 135-foot tall "city tree" erected at Pershing Square in Los Angeles for the holidays was a vinyl faux spruce (formerly, real trees from the Angeles National Forest had been brought in).

If you had a fake tree in the 1950s or '60s, it could've been made of almost anything—nylon, Lucite, vinyl, spun glass, plastic—but the material that defined the Boomer Era Christmas tree was aluminum.

Aluminum Christmas Trees

The first big fad in fake trees hit around 1959, lasted for a good ten years, and became an iconic image of mid-century modernism . . . or kitsch. Of course, we're talking about the aluminum Christmas tree.

Evergleam aluminum trees, made by the Aluminum Specialty Company of Manitowoc, Wisconsin, set the standard for the trendy new look.

Who was this prescient company, sitting on the cutting edge of modernity?

Founded in 1909, the Aluminum Specialty Company turned out cookware—everything from Jell-O molds to electric frying pans—as well as rowboats and other goods. Locals called it "The Specialty" and almost everyone in Manitowoc had a family member who worked there. Like many firms, it's gone now, but people remember the place and its most famous product, the Evergleam Tree.

How did the Evergleam line get its start?

First, to be clear, aluminum trees had been used before—a 1953 description of Hollywood's Santa Claus Lane Parade mentions "100 giant aluminum Christmas trees" lining the boulevard. But those were outdoor decorations.

A vintage aluminum tree, restored and in the permanent collection of The Children's Museum of Indianapolis.

No one thought of making metal trees for *home use* before. The closest thing to that would be a very short-lived and nearly forgotten fad of having a cut tree "painted"—silver aluminum paint went on quite easily.

Furthermore, Evergleam did not produce the first aluminum trees, not even the indoor models. That honor belongs to Modern Coatings of Chicago. Their tree was shiny and big, but too heavy and expensive for the mass market. In 1958, Tom Gannon of The Specialty visited one of his customers, a Ben Franklin store, and saw the Modern Coatings tree. He bought one and brought it to a Specialty engineer named Richard Thomsen. An eight-foot prototype was created and a patent was applied for.

Modern Coatings had patented their tree as well, so the two companies entered into a partnership to make and market aluminum trees under the Evergleam name. They took their tree to the New York Toy Fair in spring 1959, where it was a big novelty hit. Although it was risky—no market research or reports indicated that Americans wanted aluminum trees—Evergleam went into full-scale production and by the autumn of that year, tens of thousands of trees hit the stores.

Evergleam's success was immediate. Soon, the trees were part of the Sears Wish Book at around $20 apiece. Smaller vendors were selling six-foot aluminum trees for under $8. They were sleek and Space-Agey, shiny like chrome, but simple too. Display trees were either bare or hung with ornaments in a single style and color, so consumers would buy boxes of ornaments in one color for their new trees. To clutter the tree with old-fashioned or homemade gewgaws would be gauche.

Aluminum trees were made by hand at The Specialty. For a decade, three shifts—ten women in each—would wind and glue strips of frilled aluminum foil onto the wire rods that served as branches, over and over again, one rod at a time. Meanwhile, men drilled holes for the rods into the wooden trunks of the faux trees (those trunks would eventually be covered with aluminum too).[1]

By 1961, an addition had been added to the factory just for tree production, and the warehouses were full by the time the holidays neared. The next year, The Specialty introduced a new feature: pom-pom aluminum trees. Each branch ended in an explosion of curled bits of metal, catching the light like a little firework.

More than one million aluminum trees were sold in the 1960s, and The Specialty continued to manufacture them into the early 1970s. Imitations sprang up too—there's no telling how many millions were sold over the years.

Aluminum trees were not as hardy as you might think. Their "needles" bent easily and left them looking frowsy after a couple of seasons. They were quick to catch fire as well, and the boxes warned consumers NOT to decorate the tree with strings of lights, because any short could start a fire, melting the tree and spreading to the home.

This was the catalyst for the popularity of color wheels and projectors. Rotating color wheels carried the same name as the most favored tree brands—like Evergleam, although there were plenty of knockoffs—and lit the tree without touching it. The Specialty came out with a Santa Lite—a plug-in, rotating, four-color screen that cast an ever-changing light over the tree.

Evergleam and its parent companies are now history. Ironically, the appeal of this once ultra-modern decoration is the fuzzy-warm nostalgic feeling we all get when we see an aluminum tree.

Flocked Christmas Trees

Flocking simply means spraying cellulose and water mixed with something sticky (like wax) onto an object. Fabrics, for instance, can be flocked and so can trees. On fabrics, you'd probably want a stenciled pattern—say, snowflakes or a poodle. On a tree, flocking just looks like snow. That was the original idea, anyway. But somehow, in our era, the fake snowy look turned pastel.

Home-flocking kits date back to the 1940s and used the family vacuum cleaner to apply flocking, a messy method that never caught on. Buying a pre-flocked tree became the Boomer way.

White and powder blue were the first options available in professionally flocked trees. White, obviously, looked like snow. But blue? No one can quite explain that. By 1950, pink was an option as well. In fact, any color, natural or not, could be applied. In 1962, Liberace had six flocked trees, each a different color, in his living room.

Gold, lilac, lavender, even black—though we suspect that was reserved for the Addams Family or the Munsters—all colors were possible. And flocking is one Boomer trend that never completely disappeared. You can still get your tree flocked today.

Themed Christmas Trees

One more tree tradition started in the Boomer Era: the themed tree, introduced by the Kennedy White House. But before going into that, here's a paragraph of Christmas trivia about the president's home, where yuletide traditions flourish.

The otherwise forgettable President Franklin Pierce gets the credit for the first White House Christmas tree in 1856, complete with flaming candles on the branches. Teddy Roosevelt, a conservationist, forbade Christmas trees in his White House at the beginning of the 20th century. He believed that cutting trees for every family in America would destroy our forests, but it was an open secret that Teddy's children had a decorated tree hidden from their father. And in the 1920s, Calvin Coolidge was the first to flip a switch and illumine a huge tree outside on the Ellipse—and ever since, the lighting of the National Christmas Tree has been a newsworthy event.

Themed Christmas trees were introduced by style goddess Jacqueline Kennedy. As First Lady, she decorated the White House Christmas tree with miniature nutcrackers, tin soldiers, birds, and angels, creating a Nutcracker Tree. It stood in the Blue Room, one of several oval rooms in the White House.

After her 1961 Nutcracker Tree, Jackie settled on a Children's Tree for 1962. She reused many of the Nutcracker ornaments and added something more: ornaments made by the disabled and by senior citizens. These included candy canes, gingerbread cookies, little wrapped packages, and straw ornaments. Stuffed animals and tiny reindeer were also on the branches. The tree stood in the Grand Foyer for all to see, although the Kennedys spent that Christmas in Palm Beach, Florida.

In 1963, Lady Bird Johnson was suddenly the First Lady, and during her tenure she chose nostalgic themes harkening back to early America. Her Christmas trees had garlands of popcorn, wood roses from Hawaii, and tiny ornaments made from fruit and seedpods, as well as later additions of silver balls, stars, and little mirrors. In 1968, she added gingerbread.

Then came Pat Nixon. Disabled workers in Florida made velvet and satin balls, each decorated with a state flower for her American Flower Tree in 1969.

President and Mrs. Kennedy in the White House Blue Room, before the Nutcracker-Themed
Christmas Tree. December 13, 1961; photo by Robert Knudsen.

The tradition of a themed tree in the White House continues to this day. Here are some other White House trees you might have seen on television:

.... 📺 ....

1970

Pat Nixon

Disabled workers in NY made between 50 and 100 gold paper replicas of fans—the kind used by ladies in the early 1800s—to be added to the American Flower ornaments of 1969. The fans—called Monroe fans—anchored gold garlands on the tree.

1971

Pat Nixon

Gold foil angels were added to the decorations.

1972

Pat Nixon

Two White House collection paintings by Severin Roesen provided inspiration for a tree decorated with 3000 pastel satin-finished balls, 15 gold federal stars, and the flower balls from 1969. That year, the National Christmas Tree—the one in the Ellipse—caused controversy because it was topped not with a star, but with an atomic symbol. That tree was designed by GE, however, so no one can hold the Nixons responsible for *that*.

1973

Pat Nixon

Gold-beaded strings and gold ornaments honored
James Monroe, the president in 1817 who brought
gilded gold tableware to the White House.

1974

Betty Ford

To promote recycling and economy, the tree featured
crafts, including handmade ornaments from Appalachia and
from senior groups. Patchwork garlands circled the tree.

1975

Betty Ford

An "Old-Fashioned Children's Christmas" was the theme,
and artisans from Colonial Williamsburg made ornaments
of paper snowflakes, cookies, acorns, dried fruit and
veggies, straw, and yarn. Nothing made of plastic or foil
hung on the tree.

1976

Betty Ford

To express the "love that is the spirit of Christmas," the
tree was filled with natural ornaments made by members of
the Garden Club of America.

Over the years, a preponderance of gold themes emerged, along with a periodic reference to Monroe—as in James Monroe, our fifth president. There's a good reason for that: the Blue Room, where the White House Christmas tree is displayed, is always painted in light blue with gold trim, and the furnishings follow this pattern too so the room always looks as it did during the Monroe Administration.

Lynda Bird Johnson Robb in the Blue Room of the White House with children Patrick Lyndon Nugent and Lucinda Robb, in 1968. The tree was a testimonial to Flower Power!

Ornaments

Glass and tin ornaments decorated trees in the 19th century, and most came from Germany.

Do you remember Woolworth stores? They're gone now, but these original five-and-dime emporiums were a big part of Main Street America for over a century. Today, through many changes and acquisitions, Woolworth survives as the Foot Locker. But the original Woolworth store and chain shared a long and close history with Christmas tree ornaments.

Just before Christmas in 1880, Mr. F. W. Woolworth of Lancaster, PA, who had opened his first store only one year earlier, imported $25 worth of bright, blown-glass German ornaments. He wasn't enthusiastic about them but bought the case because a salesman kept pestering him.

All 144 ornaments sold in *one day*, leaving Woolworth shocked because the ornaments were expensive and broke easily. But he wasn't stupid; he ordered more for the next Christmas, and the next. In fact, between 1880 and 1939—the year Woolworth stopped importing from Germany—an estimated *five hundred million ornaments* were sold through his chain.

Though you probably don't need to be told why imports from Germany stopped just before World War II, you may not know that over the years leading up to that war, a few non-German companies produced blown-glass trinkets for trees too.

Shiny Brite ornaments with stenciled Christmas scenes, from the 1960s.

The first American company to get in on the ornament action was Corning Glass, thanks to a gentleman named Max Eckardt. He imported ornaments from his native Germany to his new home of America in the 1920s and '30s. Because of his many trips to Deutschland before and after the rise of Adolf Hitler, he feared that Germany would soon go to war. Whatever personal pain that caused, Eckardt didn't let it shake him as a businessman.

Eckardt visited the Corning headquarters in (where else?) Corning, NY. That firm had patented a process called ribbon glassblowing, which they used to turn out 2,000 electric light bulbs a minute. Eckardt's idea was that they use their light bulb-making technology for glass globes—the basis for ornaments.

Eckardt paid a visit to the Woolworth headquarters as well. Then he set up his own factory to decorate the glass globes produced by Corning, and that factory business eventually took the name Shiny Brite. The Woolworth chain agreed to buy the output, and by Christmas 1939, stores took delivery of 235,000 American-made ornaments.

War or not, the German ornament-making industry was doomed. Germany was still turning out the decorations by hand, and Corning could make more in one minute than an old-fashioned glassblower could make in a week. Not only that, but after the war the major ornament-making centers ended up in East Germany, behind the Iron Curtain.

It's no surprise that by our Boomer Era, Shiny Brite was the biggest producer of Christmas tree ornaments in the world. They even hit on the idea of using a box with cellophane windows on the top so shoppers could see the ornaments.

Shiny Brite used mercury glass for its ornaments after the war. The material is also called silvered glass, but neither silver nor mercury go into it. Shiny Brite's product was simply glass molded in a double layer, with silver nitrate between, a substance that could be tinted different colors. Combine that with the fact that the outside of the ornament could be decorated too, and the possibilities were endless.

Between Shiny Brite and other companies, our parents bought sets of ornaments in gold, silver, red, green . . . and turquoise, orange, raspberry, purple, and lime. Spaceship silver was favored over gold. Some bulbs had horizontal stripes—like latitudinal lines—of magenta and silver. Others were striped in ripples or silk screened. Each year brought new variations: clear ornaments with bands of glitter or color, or balls with recessed sections in silver to reflect the lights.

Families used the decorations over and over again, scraping off sprayed snow as they brought them out of the box each year. But by the 1960s, glass ornaments fell victim to a new trend: plasticization. Christmas fads come and go (this book will prove that many times over!), and consumers went crazy for unbreakable plastic ornaments.

So, Shiny Brite's glass decorations—now eminently collectable and often reproduced—fell out of favor and the company closed its doors. Today, the Christopher Radko Company of North Carolina creates reproductions of many Shiny Brite ornaments, using that brand name.

And let's not forget icicle ornaments. Remember those strips of tin, maybe an eighth of an inch wide and four or five inches long, curling like a single strand of DNA and catching the light as it hung from a branch? Those originated in Germany as well, then were made in the US. Later, plastic icicles that were a bit longer were sold in clear, white, or blue.

Tinsel

Tinsel has been around for many generations, and like so many decorations associated with Christmas trees, it came from Germany—Nuremberg, in this case. At first it was made of silver foil, so only the rich could afford it. Back in the days when candles lit the tree, and then later when electric lights replaced candles, the silver reflected and enhanced the light.

Tinsel took off in America about the same time smoking became popular—around World War I—and a problem developed: the silver tarnished when the room filled with cigar and cigarette smoke. And back in those days, the homes of the rich and poor alike were often filled with smelly tobacco smoke.

Inventive folks found that strands of tinsel could be made of lead. It was just as pretty and sparkly and it didn't tarnish when exposed to smoke, so from the 1920s up through the 1960s, tinsel was fabricated from lead.

The manufacturing moved from Europe to the US, thanks to the entrepreneurial spirit of one Mr. Wilmsem, who supplied Christmas tree ornaments to the Woolworth stores for decades. After World War I, Wilmsem set up his own tinsel-making factory, and Woolworth was his primary—but not his only—customer.

Woolworth had tinsel made into garlands too, going back to the days when the stuff was imported. Garland manufacturing switched to America, and in the early 1950s cellophane garlands began replacing the colored tinsel ones, because cellophane was cheaper. But cellophane could not be used to make lead tinsel.

Many Boomers remember the feel of "real" tinsel—although we probably thought it was made of tin. Our parents were careful to the point of obsession over it:

"Only take two or three strands at a time!"

"Don't grab so much!"

"Layer it gently on a branch; don't throw it!"

And how many of us had to collect the tinsel from the dead tree after Christmas and drape it back over the cardboard holder to be used again next year? Was tinsel really all that expensive, or were our parents—raised in the Depression—just averse to seeing anything usable being thrown out?

Can you imagine anyone reusing the plastic stuff that passes for tinsel today? And whatever happened to lead tinsel, anyway?

Well, remember the lead poisoning scare of the 1960s? We were inundated with the news that lead was bad; it was hazardous to babies and pets who might eat it. In fact, as a gesture of respect, let's pause right now to remember all the innocent hamsters who will wheel no more because of an indigestible strand of tinsel that somehow looked too tasty to pass up.

The powers-that-be got lead out of paint and toys—and, though no law specifically mentions it—they extracted the lead from tinsel. Manufacturers tried other materials with mixed results. Spun glass, for instance, made people's fingers itch, and aluminum didn't hang right. Today's tinsel is usually made of Mylar.

 *Lights*

New York City, 1882: the biggest city in the US gets electricity! This is huge news—after all, the electric light bulb has only been around for three years. People experiment, pushing the new innovation to its limits. And toward the end of that year, a Christmas tree with electric lights appeared!

A reporter called it "most picturesque and uncanny." The tree stood in the home of the Edison Electric Company's VP, Edward Johnson, who kindly invited members of the press in to view it and his showcase home, fully wired with electrical power.

Eighty red, white, and blue lights—"about as large as an English walnut"—blinked off and on, color by color, as the large tree turned on a pedestal, propelled by an electrically-powered crank under the floor. It's a good guess that the reporter who saw this was dazzled; likely he'd never seen a home lit by electric lights before, let alone a Christmas tree.[2]

The marvelous Christmas tree lights remained expensive for decades. Ever-Ready sold a "festoon" of 28 strung lights for twelve dollars in 1903. The set included four red and four frosted bulbs along with the white bulbs, but twelve dollars was a week's salary for many working men.

Christmas tree lights went through many styles and innovations. Even before the 20th century, back in the 1890s, people could buy lights made to look like pine cones—from Germany, of course. Lights that looked like fruits and nuts followed, and finally animal lights were available by the 1920s. These "figural lights" or "fancy lamps" soon featured Disney cartoon characters, cowboys and Indians, angels, snowmen, and Santas. And that's still back before World War II.

In those days, Germany and Japan vied with GE for sales in the USA. Surprisingly, many Japanese firms survived the war to sell strings of lights, or individual painted bulbs in the shape of fruit, birds, Santa, snowmen, lanterns, nursery rhyme characters like Humpty Dumpty, and more. As we moved into the early years of the Boomer generation, some truly collectable lights came with the label "Made in Occupied Japan." That phrase was on boxes from 1945 to 1952 only, and the brand names were Astra and Fancy Lamps.

The biggest American company in the holiday light business was NOMA, short for National Outfit Manufacturers' Association. The company was founded by Albert Sadacca and his brothers in the 1920s, years after Albert had seen a home go up in flames because a candle fell from the branch of a Christmas tree. That's right—as hinted before, back in the days before electric lights, people actually fastened burning candles to trees. Electric lights, even those early ones that seem so unsafe now, were a big improvement. Still, if that apocryphal story about the burning house is true, it should be no surprise that NOMA came out with another innovation in 1951: teensy safety fuses. What's more, they distributed Santa Lites, all made in Japan, that looked like Disney characters or angels, and in the 1950s, even Howdy Doody.

Sadly, in 1965 NOMA declared bankruptcy, unable to compete with overseas lightmakers who could produce a cheaper product. An Illinois company, Inliten, bought and uses the NOMA name for their holiday lighting line today.

Bubble Lites and More

Here's an American innovation that most Boomers remember: Bubble Lites. They hit stores after World War II, but they were actually invented during the Depression. Carl Otis, an accountant who dabbled in chemistry by night, created and patented them in 1935.

A set of Bubble Lites from the 1950s.

Otis knew that methylene chloride, or dichloromethane, would boil at low temperatures—such as the level that a Christmas tree light would reach when "on." The light bulb itself could be hidden in an ornament-like bubble and sit beneath the tube of methylene chloride. Otis took his idea to NOMA, because they were the biggest company in the industry. NOMA wanted to go into production, but World War II intervened. It wasn't until 1946, a year after the war ended, that families started buying Bubble Lites and putting them on their trees.

Unfortunately, lawsuits with another manufacturer of very similar lights (made by Raylite, who called their bubbling lights Kristal Snow Animated Candles) started almost immediately and dragged on into 1950. Both companies—NOMA and Raylite—accused the other of infringing on patents that the courts invalidated, one after the other. The bottom line for Mr. Otis was that he stopped receiving royalties for his invention. However, well over 25 million had been produced by then. Otis received three cents per light up to that point, so really, he did OK.

If you'd like to read more about the lawsuits and claims, visit the website www.OldChristmasTreeLights.com to read all the technical details you could ever wish for.

Bubble Lites were replaced by other trends by the 1960s. Sales dropped so fast that stores didn't even bother to stock replacement bulbs. In the 1970s, Bubble Lites were revived, riding in on the same nostalgia wave that brought us TV shows like *Happy Days,* movies like *The Last Picture Show,* and Oldies radio stations.

Right about the time Bubble Lites went out of fashion, midget lights came in. Midget light bulbs were only about three-quarters of an inch long. In the 1960s, they were the sets to buy—as long as you didn't have an aluminum tree (no strings of lights on those, remember?). Folks loaded midget lights on the tree, where they looked like twinkling stars. In fact, midget lights made blinking lights popular.

Strands of lights that flashed on and off had been for sale since the 1930s. Heck, since 1882 —remember the lights flashed on the first electrically lit tree that year? But because the lights were big, most folks did not want them blinking on and off in their living rooms. The constant flashes gave people a headache.

Midget lights, however, were small and unobtrusive. We loved them, and they became the most popular tree lights ever sold.

An ongoing problem with all these strands of lights was burned-out bulbs. One dark bulb is not a problem, unless you're obsessively persnickety, but back then one bad bulb meant all the other bulbs following it went dark. That stopped happening in the 1960s when manufacturers starting wiring the strings of 5–10 watt bulbs in parallel, rather than series.

Mini-lights took over in the 1970s and are still used today. They're cheaper, cooler, and use less energy—but ironically, a loose bulb can still darken half the tree. Why? Because mini-lights are wired in series. Each bulb has a shunt mechanism built into it so that power continues to the next bulb, even if one is burned out. But if a bulb gets loose (rather than burning out), the power stops there, resulting in a half-lit tree.

 *Stencils*

Remember window stencils? "It's so easy that a child can do it," said the commercials.

In the early 1950s, Glass Wax, a window cleaner, dried to white when left on the window. Seeing the possibilities, Glass Wax began selling kits with cut-out stencils of Santa's smiling face, holly leaves, the words "Merry Christmas," leaping reindeer, ornaments, snowflake patterns, wreaths, and everything from Nativity scenes to Howdy Doody faces.

The stencil packages sold for a few quarters, but you still had to buy the Glass Wax. This was not an aerosol spray, but rather a liquid in a metal can. While it dried white, you could also mix Glass Wax with red or green food coloring. You held the stencil on the window, and sponged on the Glass Wax mix. Voilà—instant art. In a pinch, you could also use Bon Ami powder mixed with water for a white picture.

Soon other companies jumped in, selling stencils to use with *their* window cleaners. Stanley Home Products put out a glass wax that came in different colors, or better yet—Stanley's Sparkling Snow Flakes. Other companies sold stencils and their own sprays under names like

Frosty Snow, Aero Snow, and Krystal Frost—all of which doubled as spray-on snow for Christmas trees.

Frosty Snow could be used on trees or windows. These cans featured pictures of Howdy Doody characters, dating them to the 1950s.

Chapter Two

Eat, Drink & Be Merry

You're Invited!

Y ou may be too young to remember this, but home cooking changed radically in the 1950s.

True, holiday meals may seem the most traditional of all, but although the food on the table —turkey, cranberry sauce, dressing, and mountains of potatoes—had adorned holiday tables for generations before us, the '50s ushered in changes.

Before that decade, when Mom was in the kitchen, all was right with the world. Dinner was very much like you see on those iconic TV shows: *The Donna Reed Show*, *Father Knows Best*, and *Make Room for Daddy*.

But did those shows reflect reality, even back then? For instance, did you ever see Donna Reed's kids using folding TV trays to hold their dinners while they sat in front of the television set? No, yet that's what was happening all across America. And television neglected another big change: During the Boomer period, new trends in cuisine emerged and had a big impact on how the middle class ate.

Snack and finger foods became popular because they could be eaten in front of the TV without looking. Cookbooks of the day emphasized theme dinners, convenience foods, and short prep times—think tuna casserole with frozen peas and smashed up potato chips. None of these trends appear in cookbooks of the '20s, '30s, or '40s, but in the 1950s, the point of most cooking tips seemed to be to get Mom out of the kitchen as quickly as possible.

Instead of making everything from scratch, companies like Nabisco, General Mills, and Kraft came out with packaged foods that Mom could fix easily and fast: Hamburger Helper, Minute Rice, and Shake 'n' Bake. As consumers, we kids begged for these pre-measured mixes, preferring them to homemade meatloaf or pot roast. Why? Probably because the nice people on TV told us that this was what everyone else was eating. And this advertising affected our holiday celebrations too.

In the 1950s, cereals-as-appetizers were très chic. This page is from a Good Housekeeping / Culinary Arts Institute pamphlet cookbook of 1957.

On Christmas and Thanksgiving, women started cooking at the crack of dawn—or even the night before—as they always had, but now bowls of chips, dips, and appetizers began appearing around the living room before dinner, no doubt a very strange, newfangled way of entertaining guests as far as Grandma and Grandpa were concerned. Frozen vegetables took the place of canned; potatoes, stuffing, and rice came pre-measured in bags and boxes; dessert toppings were frozen in tubs, not whipped up in the kitchen. When you really think about it, our holiday meals were anything but old-fashioned.

And so we present . . . **Boomer holiday foods!**

Appetizers and Snacks

Dippers and Dunks

Dippers and dunks were a new and rather exotic idea in the postwar era: thick sauces for finger foods that we now call dips. They could be made of beans, cheese, or any number of ingredients. One popular variation was Liptauer Spread, made with cottage cheese or cream cheese, onions, capers, anchovies, mustard, and a dash of paprika. Yum.

Influential food writer Helen Evans Brown of California introduced exotic fare like guacamole and other dips in her food columns as early as the 1940s, publishing the recipe for guacamole in her 1952 *West Coast Cookbook*.

Clam dip—made with canned clams, cream cheese, and seasonings—was making the rounds by 1951. *Kraft Television Theater* published the recipe with other perfect-for-TV foods that could be munched on incessantly and absentmindedly while watching their shows. All you needed was a bag of chips or a box of crackers, or even some fresh celery sticks.

Dips and sauces existed before the Boomer era, but earlier recipes were labor intensive. Cooks had to chop up ingredients like hard-boiled eggs, bacon, onions, parsley, or garlic, and measure out lemon juice, wine, and spices. And when we say "chop," remember that there were no food processors or Osterizers back then. It was dull work, so when Lipton came out with a recipe using its dry onion soup mix and sour cream as a dip, everyone jumped on it. Pre-measured flavors and all the cook had to do was stir? Mom never had to miss the start of *I Love Lucy* again!

Lipton's creation was named California Dip, which simply called for adding the soup mix to a pint of sour cream, stirring, and letting it sit for an hour (in or out of the frig) so the onions softened. Ta da! Was there any chip that didn't taste better when dunked in Lipton's dip?

Chex Party Mix

First, a disclaimer: Chex Party Mix was not the first snack mix made with cereal. That honor goes to Kix. In 1950 a recipe appeared in a Betty Crocker cookbook that called for mixing Kix with melted butter and parmesan cheese. But no one remembers grabbing handfuls of cheesy Kix while sitting on the sofa with aunts and uncles who visited only on holidays, do they? For most of us, it was Chex Party Mix in those bowls on the coffee table.

Ralston Purina—owner of Chex cereals, as well as the dog food you first think of when you hear their name—introduced their Party Mix in a 1952 issue of *Life* Magazine. Some websites claim the recipe appeared in June as a summer snack, but the earliest documentation that the company archives contain is September. Soon after, the company printed the recipe on their Chex cereal boxes.

Here's the original recipe as published in *Life* in September 1952 (for those too young to know, a capital T stands for tablespoon and a lower case t means teaspoon):

Melt ½ c. butter in shallow baking pan.

Stir in 1 T. Worcestershire sauce, 1/4 t. salt and 1/8 t. garlic salt.

Add 2 c. Wheat Chex, 2 c. Rice Chex, and 1/2 c. nuts.

Mix well.

Heat 30 minutes in 300° oven, stirring every 10 minutes.

Cool.

Chex Party Mix ad from a 1952 Life Magazine. Courtesy of the General Mills Archives.

Did you notice that Corn Chex were left out? That's because they didn't come along until 1958. For the record, Rice Chex was a Boomer product, debuting in 1950, but the original Wheat Chex came out in the 1930s.

By 1953 the recipe had changed, and it's continued to change every year since. If you want the modern, microwaveable version—with pretzel pieces, less butter, and Corn Chex added—you can find that on the Internet at www.Chex.com/Recipes/. Or you can just pick up a supply, ready-made at your local market.

General Mills bought Ralston-Purina's cereal line, including the Chex cereals, in 1997. General Mills, of course, is represented by Betty Crocker. Blending logos and brands can be as complicated as blending new families. As such, the checkerboard is long gone, though the cereal never changed its name, and the fancy-script "G" appears on all Chex products now.

Cheese Balls

As one cookbook says: "Without blenders, there would be no cheese balls."[3]

And what a void would be left in our lives.

Cheese balls can be made with almost any cheese, even (sigh) Velveeta. In the Boomer Era, the cheese had to be at room temperature, then cubed and mixed with milk—and maybe some onion and spice—all in a blender. After it was blended, it sat in the frig overnight.

The next day, the cheese mix was shaped into a ball or log and rolled in nuts or something crunchy. Then you served it on a plate with crackers.

Pete Schwetty, eat your heart out.

Cheez Whiz

Kraft started Project Cheez Whiz a year and a half before the product debuted in 1953 as the perfect all-purpose cheese spread. Though you may be skeptical, Cheez Whiz is actually made of at least 51% cheese: muenster, gouda, and mozzarella. There's also some mustard and Worcestershire sauce in there, because the original purpose of Project Cheez Whiz was to create a spread for a delicacy called Welsh rarebit.

Rarebit—not rabbit—is basically toasted cheese with a kick, and the kick can come from ale, hot mustard, paprika, or other spices. The cheese-on-toasted-bread dish goes in and out of fashion in the US, but it's a pub favorite in the UK.

In 1951, when Project Cheez Whiz began, the rarebit fad was on an upswing. Kraft quickly realized they were onto something, though, and never marketed it as a rarebit topping. When microwave ovens became standard in kitchens in the 1980s, Cheez Whiz became the preferred topping for nachos.

Aerosol Cheese

Cheese in a can debuted in 1966 thanks to Nabisco. Their product was named Easy Cheese Pasteurized Process Cheese Spread; the company also called it Snack Mate. The big selling point back then was that Snack Mate had a decorator cap so that Mom could make little rosettes and loops on the crackers and serve them like hors d'oeuvres.

Technically, Snack Mate was not an aerosol product. The cheese was propelled out of the can by pressurized nitrogen, kept separate from the cheese spread. The American Can Company designed the can and spray mechanism in such a way that the cheese product didn't even need to be refrigerated … which doesn't make it any more or less healthy. In the 1960s, the novelty of spraying cheese onto a cracker—or straight into your mouth—precluded any thoughts of whether or not it was nutritionally sound. But, hey, it had "Cheese" in the name, it was made in Wisconsin, and it came in Cheddar, Swiss, Pimento, and American cheese flavors. What more could you want? Cheese *is* the first or second ingredient listed on the label.

Eventually, Nabisco merged with Kraft in the late '80s, and the product name was changed to Easy Cheese.

The Big Dinner: All the Fixins

The Greatest Chef You Never Heard of: Dorcas Reilly

Campbell Soup calls Dorcas Reilly the "Mother of Comfort Food." Ms. Reilly, retired and living in New Jersey, probably created thousands of recipes during her 25-year-long career with Campbell Soup, but she is inarguably best known for leading the team that created the Green Bean Bake—or, as it's known today, the Green Bean Casserole.

GREEN BEAN BAKE. In 1-qt. casserole, stir 1 can Campbell's Cream of Mushroom Soup and 1 tsp. soy sauce until smooth; mix in ¾ can (3½-oz. size) French-fried onions. 3 cups cooked French-style green beans, dash pepper. Bake in moderate oven (350°F) 20 min. Top with remaining onions; bake 5 min. more. 6 servings of company-good green beans!

PARTY CHICKEN. In skillet, brown 2 lb. cut-up frying chicken (or two 3-lb. pkgs. Swanson Frozen Chicken Parts, thawed) in ¼ cup shortening with ½ tsp. whole thyme. Stir in can Campbell's Cream of Mushroom Soup, ½ cup water, dash pepper, 10 small white onions. Cover; cook over low heat about 45 min., or till chicken is tender; stir occasionally. 4 servings.

dress 'em up with... *Campbell's* cream of mushroom soup

MUSHROOM MEATBALLS. Mix 1 can Campbell's Cream of Mushroom Soup with ¼ cup water. Combine ½ of soup mixture with 1 lb. ground beef, ¼ cup fine dry bread crumbs, 2 tbsp. minced onion, 1 tbsp. minced parsley, 1 slightly beaten egg. Shape into meatballs (about 1½"); brown in 1 tbsp. shortening in skillet; pour off drippings; add remaining soup mixture. Cover; cook over low heat 15 min.; stir occasionally. Serves 4.

DRESS UP LEFTOVERS. In saucepan, cook 2 tbsp. chopped onion in 1 tbsp. shortening till tender. Blend 1 can Campbell's Cream of Mushroom Soup and ½ cup water; add 1 cup diced cooked beef, ½ cup cooked peas (or any leftover meat and vegetables you have), dash pepper. Heat, stirring now and then. Serve over 2 cups cooked noodles (4 oz. uncooked). 4 souper servings. Look for other recipes on every can of Campbell's Soup.

The year was 1955. Reilly had worked in the Home Economics Department of the Campbell Soup Company for six years. "My initial inspiration for the Green Bean Casserole was really quite simple," Reilly said when asked about her iconic side dish. "I wanted to create a quick and easy recipe around two things most Americans always had on hand in the 1950s: green beans and Campbell's Cream of Mushroom soup."[4]

Here is the recipe as it appears on Campbell's Kitchen website today. The original—written on an 8x11 recipe card—was presented to the National Inventor's Hall of Fame by Ms. Reilly herself in 2002.

Even though the recipe is titled "Classic," clearly some tweaking has been done, pandering to 21st-century fat phobias. In 1955, could anyone have envisioned fat-free or low-sodium soups? You can find variations on the recipe, including light versions, at CampbellsKitchen.com.

Classic Green Bean Casserole

Prep: 10 minutes

Bake: 30 minutes

Makes: 6 servings (about 3/4 cup each)

Cost per recipe: $5.97

Cost per serving: $1.00

1 can (10 3/4 ounces) Campbell's® Condensed Cream of Mushroom Soup
(Regular, 98% Fat Free or Healthy Request®)

1 teaspoon soy sauce

Dash ground black pepper

1/2 cup milk

4 cups cooked cut green beans

1 1/3 cups French's® French Fried Onions

1. Stir the soup, milk, soy sauce, black pepper, beans and 2/3 cup onions in a 1 1/2-quart casserole.
2. Bake at 350°F. for 25 minutes or until the bean mixture is hot and bubbling. Stir the bean mixture. Sprinkle with the remaining onions.
3. Bake for 5 minutes or until the onions are golden brown.

For the cooked green beans: Use 1 bag (16 to 20 ounces) frozen green beans, thawed; 2 packages (9 ounces each) frozen green beans, thawed; 2 cans (14.5 ounces each) green beans, drained; or about 1 1/2 pounds fresh green beans for this recipe.

For Golden Green Bean Casserole: Substitute Campbell's® Condensed Golden Mushroom Soup for the Cream of Mushroom Soup. Omit the soy sauce. Stir in 1/4 cup chopped red pepper with the green beans. For Broccoli Casserole: Substitute 4 cups cooked broccoli florets for the green beans. For Cheese Lovers: Stir in 1/2 cup shredded Cheddar cheese with the soup. Omit the soy sauce. Sprinkle with an additional 1/4 cup Cheddar cheese when adding the remaining onions.

To add a festive touch: Stir in 1/4 cup chopped red pepper with the soup. To add crunch: Add 1/4 cup toasted sliced almonds to the onion topping. For bacon lovers: Add 2 slices bacon, cooked and crumbled, to the bean mixture.

Chef Tip: Try this Italian version with pancetta and rosemary! Cook 4 ounces pancetta, diced, in a skillet over medium heat until almost crisp. Add 1/4 cup chopped onion and 1/2 teaspoon minced fresh rosemary leaves to the skillet and cook until onion is tender. Add the pancetta mixture to the soup mixture in Step 1. In Step 2, sprinkle the remaining French fried onions with 1 tablespoon grated pecorino Romano cheese, then bake as directed in Step 3.

❋　　❋　　❋

Nutritional Values per Serving using Campbell's Cream of Mushroom Soup : Calories 161, Total Fat 9g, Saturated Fat 2g, Cholesterol 4mg, Sodium 530mg, Total Carbohydrate 17g, Dietary Fiber 3g, Protein 3g, Vitamin A 12%DV, Vitamin C 14%DV, Calcium 6%DV, Iron 3%DV

Nutritional Values per Serving using Campbell's 98% Fat-Free Cream of Mushroom Soup : Calories 144, Total Fat 8g, Saturated Fat 2g, Cholesterol 3mg, Sodium 371mg, Total Carbohydrate 17g, Dietary Fiber 3g, Protein 3g, Vitamin A 12%DV, Vitamin C 14%DV, Calcium 7%DV, Iron 3%DV

Nutritional Values per Serving using Healthy Request Cream of Mushroom Soup : Calories 149, Total Fat 8g, Saturated Fat 2g, Cholesterol 4mg, Sodium 342mg, Total Carbohydrate 17g, Dietary Fiber 3g, Protein 3g, Vitamin A 12%DV, Vitamin C 14%DV, Calcium 10%DV, Iron 3%DV

Below is the recipe as it appeared in 1960, already having been revised over five years:

GREEN BEAN BAKE. In 1-qt. casserole, stir 1 can Campbell's Cream of Mushroom Soup and 1 tsp. soy sauce until smooth; mix in ½ can (3½-oz. size) French-fried onions, 3 cups cooked French-style green beans, dash pepper. Bake in moderate oven (350°F) 20 min. Top with remaining onions; bake 5 min. more. 6 servings of company-good green beans!

By the way: The original recipe introduced Americans to Durkee's French Fried Onions, and the French's company says that 50% of all their sales happen just before Thanksgiving, Christmas, and Easter, all thanks to that little recipe. Campbell estimates that 40% of their Cream of Mushroom Soup is used in the casserole. The company thinks that 20–30% of American homes prepare this dish for Thanksgiving—and they advertise heavily to take full advantage of that.

Instant Mashed Potatoes

Since no one likes to peel potatoes, and since some of us suspected that the only reason our parents had kids was to slough that onerous job onto us, the fact that several companies were working to develop instant mashed potatoes in the early Boomer era will not be too surprising.

If you dehydrate potatoes, there are two ways to reconstitute them to make instant mashed potatoes: granules and flakes. Granules were developed right after World War II and used by the military in the Korean War. Potato granules were on the market by the late 1940s, but no one would have served them at the holiday dinner—they had to soak a long time before they began to resemble anything edible, and after 1970 not even the military was buying them. They simply had no taste.

But *mashed potato flakes* were another story. Sliced potatoes were partially cooked to exactly the right temperature, then pressed and quickly dried. The sheets of potatoes were then broken into flakes. The flakes tasted better because the twenty-second drying process used on the potatoes was faster, and it locked in some flavor (not a lot, but some).

A 1960 ad for Betty Crocker Instant Mashed Potatoes— a product that was taken off the market when the tastier Potato Buds came along. Courtesy of the General Mills Archives.

By the mid-1950s, some scientists with the US Department of Agriculture had improved a way of making flakes out of quick-dried potatoes, called the Philadelphia Cook. Retailers like General Mills and Betty Crocker were quick to jump on the bandwagon. The first Betty Crocker instant potatoes came out in 1959. By the 1960s, you didn't even need to add milk to the mix to enjoy "Fresh potato flavor . . . fresh potato texture."

In 1965, General Mills dropped Betty Crocker Instant Mashed Potatoes in favor of a newer product that had tested well in selected markets: Potato Buds . . . like "tiny puffs of real Idaho potatoes." Potato Buds were packaged with the familiar red spoon and the name Betty Crocker at the top of the box, and it remained the most popular brand of instant potatoes for years.

Biscuits

Remember the first time you made a biscuit can explode by either hitting it or pushing a spoon on the black line?

Refrigerated biscuits started out in the early days of the Depression. Mr. Lively B. Willoughby of Kentucky invented them, wrapped them in foil, and packaged them in a cardboard tube. And yes, they were explosive, even back then. The biscuits were marketed by a company called Ballard and Ballard, which Pillsbury Mills bought in the early 1950s—just after Mr. Willoughby's patent for refrigerated biscuits expired.

Unfortunately, there's not much else to say. Nothing particularly new or special happened to canned biscuits in the Boomer Era, though we all remember them fondly. (Unless, of course, your mother made biscuits by hand. In that case, you probably hated to see those cans in the refrigerator.)

Bisquick, by the way, was also developed in the early 1930s, so neither of these products—refrigerated biscuits or biscuit mix—was a Boomer development.

Butterball Turkey

Turkey has always been the traditional holiday entree in most US homes, but in the Boomer Era, ham, prime rib, and lamb also appeared. Turkey and ham, however—specifically, spiral-cut ham—changed during our era.

Butterball turkeys appeared in 1954, a year after Swift and Company began its research to build a better bird—a tasty, succulent, broad-breasted turkey, thanks to selective breeding.

Hence the name Butterball, which they bought from one Leo Peters, who still retains rights to the term "Butterball Farms" for his butter business.

So besides being meatier, what was special about the Butterball turkey? Consumers (meaning Mom and Grandma) no longer had to pull out the pinfeathers (raise your hand if you didn't realize that before 1954, someone had to pull pinfeathers out of the Christmas turkey). How did Butterball accomplish this labor-saving convenience? By using hot-water baths at the processing plant to get all the feathers out. Self-basting turkeys came out in 1954 too.

Two years later (1956), the company began advertising on television. By then they'd figured out a way to remove the tough turkey leg tendons, and were "liquid-freezing" the birds to give them a more appealing color. The little bag that held the giblets and neck came along in 1971 so that home cooks didn't have to go digging for them.

ConAgra ended up owning Swift and Butterball in the 1980s, and ConAgra sold the Butterball business to Carolina Turkey in the 21st century. The company is now called Butterball LLC. It no longer, however, breeds its own turkeys.

Spiral-Cut Ham

If you were fortunate enough to grow up in the Midwest, you may remember this—but most of us discovered spiral-cut hams as adults.

The spiral-cut ham—the ultimate in convenience—was the invention of Mr. Harry Hoenselaar of Michigan. He carved hams for a living and had a dream in 1938—a machine that sliced ham evenly, down to the hambone, that would make the world beat a path to his door.

He did his part, but the world was slow to move.

By the way, he really did have a dream: Hoensalaar went to sleep one night and dreamed of the machine. The next day, he set about building it with a washing machine motor and had a prototype to display at the 1939 World's Fair in New York.

In time, he perfected the machine that would slice hams with precision and beauty, cutting five slices of ham per inch. The ham is set on a spike and secured by another spike at the top; it then rotates while a blade slices through the meat. Hoensalaar was so convinced of the invention's importance that he documented his research with home movies.

Harry Hoenselaar started patenting his new machine in 1944, updating the patent as he fine-tuned the technology, but no one would buy it. The big meat companies that stood to gain were simply not interested, so he went back to his basement and got to work again, this time to invent a new curing, baking, and smoking procedure for hams, as well as the most delicious glaze he could devise. He knew by then he would have to go it alone, and he needed more than a machine that cut meat; he had to make the meat irresistible in every way.

Now, remember how Hoenselaar worked as a meat carver when he had that first dream? Well, he worked for a local firm called the HoneyBaked Ham Company. In 1957, the widow of the owner of HoneyBaked Hams offered the shop to Hoenselaar for $500. He mortgaged his home to come up with the money.

So Hoenselaar opened the new HoneyBaked Ham store in Detroit. It was a success, though no one could have foreseen a nationwide chain back then. Nine years passed before the second store opened in Parma, a suburb of Cleveland, Ohio; and it was Hoenselaar's daughter, Jo Ann Kurz, and her husband who opened it. The family continues to run HoneyBaked Ham today.

Once the patents expired for the spiral cutting machine in 1981, other companies began to imitate the original. The third generation of Hoenselaar ham lovers—four of Harry's grandsons, with the last name of Kurz—run the company business with dedication and 21st century marketing skills. They've even bought out some of their competitors. Hickory Ham and Heavenly Ham are now HoneyBaked Ham stores, which number around 400.

And the company is still growing.

Leftover Turkey and the Birth of the TV Dinner

You think your family had a problem with leftovers? After the 1952 holidays, one frozen turkey supplier had ten refrigerated railroad cars full of unsold frozen turkeys. *Half a million* iced gobblers! They were in Omaha, and the only available storage space was on the East Coast. But was it worth shipping them? Even unthawed, those birds wouldn't last till the next holiday season began.

One employee by the name of Gerry Thomas had the outrageous idea of cooking and packaging the turkey in individual metal trays. His brainstorm came from a chance meeting with another salesman who'd showed him some new serving plates that the airlines would be using for their meals—plates with separate, indented compartments to keep the peas from spilling over the meat. What if the surplus turkey could be packaged in the special plates, he proposed, along with dressing and peas?

Everyone laughed at the poor man, but in the end the Omaha company—Swanson, headed by the Swanson brothers—allowed him to go ahead and create about 6,000 compartmentalized dinners. Thomas suggested they be called TV dinners, and the company sold them for under a buck each. Within the first year, 10 million TV dinners were sold.

In the 1960s, TV dinners for the family were promoted as a treat for both Mom and the family.

Now the caveats:

Some people dispute Gerry Thomas' tale as related above. In its defense, Thomas' credibility has been bolstered by his induction into the Frozen Food Hall of Fame. His version of the story has been promoted by Swanson and their current corporate owners, Pinnacle Foods, as the true tale of how TV dinners came to be.

By the same token, Swanson was not the first company to sell frozen food; they weren't even the first to use three-part containers with separate sections for different foods. A company named Maxson Food Systems had been selling frozen "Strato-Plate" dinners to the airlines and military since 1945. These meals, presented first on Bakelite then on plastic sectioned plates, were designed to be reheated and enjoyed on airplanes, but never sold in grocery stores. This fits with the Gerry Thomas story where a salesman had shown him compartmentalized frozen dinners for use on airplanes, but credit for the aluminum tray is sometimes attributed to Pennsylvania-based FrigiDinner, who said they developed it in 1947.

Although Swanson already made some frozen foods, like pot pies, it was not the first company to make frozen dinners available in grocery stores. Quaker State Food Corporation beat Swanson to the frozen dinner market by nearly a year. *That* company—the brainchild of Pennsylvanians Albert and Mayer Bernstein—started selling three-compartment frozen dinners to Pittsburgh-area bars and eateries in the late 1940s under the brand name One-Eyed Eskimo. When the Bernsteins expanded their business in 1952 and started selling frozen dinners in aluminum trays through grocery stores east of the Mississippi River, they changed their name to Quaker State Food Corp. Two years later, they'd sold 2.5 million dinners.

Swanson's first cartons were designed to look like TV sets.

Sales of turkey meals took off like nothing before—maybe because of the name "TV Dinners," or maybe due to the colorful package that showed the dinner in the center of a woodgrain TV console as if it were the featured show. That box had colors that had never been seen inside a freezer or on a food carton before, and it drew the shopper's attention to succulent details: the melting butter in the center of the peas and potatoes, for example.

By 1954, Swanson had added a fried chicken dinner and the connection to the holidays evaporated. Betty Cronin, the bacteriologist who came up with the successful recipe for that chicken, was one of several detractors to Gerry Thomas' history. She says the Swanson Company was already working hard on developing frozen dinners when she was hired in 1950. Other employees agree that Thomas had little to do with the product and claimed far too much credit. Even Thomas himself admitted that, because he got bored repeating the tale so many times, he started embellishing parts of it.

As for the TV dinner name, Swanson family members say Gilbert Swanson, son of one of the company founders,[5] came up with it while watching *Ted Mack and the Original Amateur Hour*.

Bottom line: through the many corporate ownership changes that began in the 1950s, when the Campbell Soup Company bought Swanson, through 2001 when a new owner, Vlasic (of Vlasic pickle fame) changed its name to Pinnacle Foods, a lot of history and paperwork has been lost. There's just no way to prove any one particular story.

Jog Down Memory Lane:
A smiling clerk, ready to serve freshly cut meat …
and check out those low prices!
Used with permission of MisterToast.com.

 Desserts and Goodies

Cakes and Cake Mixes

The famous Big Red Cookbook of Betty Crocker debuted in 1950, and it included White Christmas Pie, a "pure white heavenly concoction." Later editions featured the Christmas Snow Cake, a layer cake with flaked coconut sprinkled over the white frosting. Right in the middle, using a stencil, Moms could arrange green tinted coconut in the shape of a tree, with chocolate shavings for the trunk and cut-up gumdrops as the ornaments.

That Betty Crocker woman was endlessly inventive.

Speaking of Betty Crocker, you do know that she, like Santa Claus, didn't really exist, right? Sorry to break the news so crassly if you did not.

Betty was invented by the Washburn Crosby Company of Minneapolis, who produced Gold Medal Flour. Washburn Crosby ran a jigsaw puzzle contest with a small prize in 1921 and was overwhelmed by the number of female entrants who not only sent in their puzzles, but included letters with questions about baking.

Like most companies back then, Washburn Crosby had an all-male management staff. They did have some female employees, though. The firm—which merged with other companies to become General Mills a few years later—decided that baking advice should come from a woman, so they created Betty Crocker and her distinctive signature to sign all the responses sent to women throughout the country.

Soon an entire team of women in Minneapolis were signing the Betty Crocker name to gracious, helpful letters that offered advice and recipes. Betty appeared in magazine ads, and by 1924 she was on the radio. Most people thought she was real, right into the Boomer era when she began selling cake mixes for about 35 cents a box.

Cake mixes were around before World War II, but they weren't popular because they spoiled easily, and producing an edible cake from them was a crapshoot. General Mills spent four years trying to make them better, starting in 1943, and in the end—just in time for our holiday celebrations—GM came up with Betty Crocker's "Just add water and mix!" mix.

The first cake with this instruction was Betty Crocker's Ginger Cake Mix, which later became the Gingerbread Cake and Cookie Mix. It was tested on the West Coast, and soon the distinctive red-and-white boxes appeared in grocery stores all over the country, with white, yellow, and spiced cake mixes.

But the cake mixes were not an immediate hit. In fact, the market took a while to build.

The problem was that right after the war, women *wanted* to return to the kitchen. Maybe they had enjoyed their "Rosie the Riveter" factory jobs during the war, but now they wanted to go back to the way things were before.[6] Sugar had been rationed during the war and desserts were a luxury. Once the supply got back to normal, making a cake became the perfect way for the happy homemaker to tell her family she loved them.

Ergo, a labor-saving cake mix wasn't really welcome.

A couple of business psychologists helped General Mills figure out why cake mixes weren't selling. These men—Drs. Burleigh Gardner and Ernest Dichter—suggested that women didn't think they were really making a cake if all they had to add was water. It just didn't feel like cooking.

So Betty Crocker took the powdered egg whites out of the mix and asked women to add fresh eggs to the cake. Their new slogan ("Betty Crocker Cake Mixes bring you that special homemade goodness . . . because <u>you</u> add the eggs yourself") replaced "Just add water and mix!" Sales steadily increased.

In 1948, competitor Pillsbury came out with the first chocolate cake mix. Duncan Hines joined the fun in 1951 with its Three Star Surprise Mix, combining three flavors, and in three weeks captured 48% of the market share. Duncan Hines cake mixes also instructed the cook to add eggs.

Duncan Hines, by the way, is a brand not a food company; it did not make its own cake mixes. Duncan Hines was the name of a famous mid-century foodie—an entrepreneur who rated restaurants throughout the country and published annual editions of his book, *Adventures in Good Eating.* But the man was so closely associated with good food that eventually over a hundred different food items licensed his name to sell their products—including cake mixes. The Duncan Hines cake mixes were actually developed and manufactured by Nebraska Consolidated Mills, who paid Mr. Hines a half cent per box to put his name on their product.

Full-color newspaper ads in major cities announced the new line of Duncan Hines cake mixes. According to a 1952 *Wall Street Journal* article: "Consolidated literally blitzes a town when it moves in. Color ads, so necessary in food promotion, are splashed on billboards and in local papers. Many radio and TV spots are used, as well as redemption coupons."

That was quite a triumph for food chemist Arlee Andre, the real man behind the Duncan Hines cake mixes. He developed the cake mixes for Nebraska Consolidated Mills and had previously been testing flour for cereal.

The cake mixes were sold to Procter and Gamble a few years later, and Arlee Andre went to work for P&G in the 1960s (and Nebraska Consolidated Mills became ConAgra in the '70s, just in case you were wondering). Today, the product is part of the Pinnacle Foods Group.

As for Betty Crocker, here's one more connection to boomers: General Mills bought the toy company Kenner in 1968. Kenner made the Easy-Bake Oven. By 1973, that toy was renamed the Betty Crocker Easy-Bake Oven, and there was a whole line of miniature cake mix boxes to go with it.

Reddi-Whip

An entrepreneurial genius named Bunny Lapin (his real name was Aaron, but *Lapin* is French for rabbit—hence the nickname) slowly developed the first whipped cream in a spray can over several years.

During the war, Lapin, a clothing salesman who had gone to law school, was put in charge of selling his brother-in-law's substitute dairy product, Sta-Wip. It wasn't that great, but World War II had just started and real cream was being rationed. Lapin developed a small aerating dispenser for soda fountains so that Sta-Wip could be used a little at a time before it spoiled.

Independent of Lapin, an industrial chemist in Chicago named Charles A. Goetz figured out how to create milk foam using pressure and nitrous oxide. Another company—Crown Cork and Seal—came up with a seamless, lined aerosol canister. Lapin worked with these new innovations and with help, developed a new valve to keep the nitrous oxide inside the can. By then the war was over, and Lapin could put real whipped cream into his newfangled dispenser. Reddi-Whip hit the markets—made with real milk and cream, as it is today.

By 1951, Lapin's company had made him rich enough to move to California, into a home once owned by movie star Gloria Swanson, where he drove around in one of his several Cadillacs. A chance meeting with Arthur Godfrey's wife led to a spokesperson deal, and soon life-sized cardboard images of Godfrey—a big radio star at the time—were smiling at housewives in supermarkets across the country, telling them to buy Reddi-Whip.

Besides producing Reddi-Whip, Lapin's company was the first to put shaving lotion into an aerosol can. Rather than sell shaving cream, he sold the valves and dispensers to shaving cream companies and made more money. He lost millions too, trying to launch spray products that were ahead of their time—a cinnamon-flavored butter called Touch-n-Spread, a spray milkshake, and even spray-on cleaning supplies.

Shortly before he died in the late 1990s, *Time* Magazine named Bunny Lapin one of the business geniuses of the century.

Cool Whip

Birds Eye, a division of General Foods, introduced Cool Whip in 1967 as the ultimate dessert topping.

Homemade whipped cream, a staple for centuries, was labor intensive (all that beating) and since it was made of cream, it didn't last long. Dream Whip, a mix, also took some work. Reddi-Whip was available, but you had to shake it and push on the nozzle. General Foods must have figured that by the 1960s, people were so pampered that even *that* seemed like a chore.

But Cool Whip? It came frozen in a tub ready to be defrosted and spooned onto pumpkin pie, and it lasted for weeks. You could even defrost and refreeze it as needed. Hallelujah!

The reason it lasted so long was that it contained no cream or milk. That is no longer true in the 21st century: Cool Whip now contains light cream and skim milk. And through mergers and buyouts, Cool Whip is now produced by Kraft. But we digress. Exactly what was in the original Cool Whip, if not milk?

Water, oil, sugar, lots of chemicals that stabilize and emulsify, and air—Cool Whip is mostly air. But it's the semi-solidified plant oils that give Cool Whip its creamy texture. Junior chefs may remember that it was the perfect, smooth ingredient in those quickie mousse, chiffon, or trifle recipes: just mix it with other instant desserts like pudding, Jell-O, and/or frozen fruits.

In 1966 Cool Whip sponsored *The Andy Griffith Show*, and any sponsor of *The Andy Griffith Show* must, by default, become an American icon. Them's the rules.

Christmas Cookies

Many moms and grandmas had a set of metal cookie cutters used only during the holidays. There was a bell, a tree, a wreath, a star, and a Santa profile, among others. Cookie cutters themselves are an American innovation from the Pennsylvania Dutch tinsmiths, but shaped cookies date back to medieval Europe, when monks molded gingerbread to sell at festivals.

It may have been a reaction to the austerity of the Depression and the rationing of sugar during the war, but whatever the reason, baking Christmas cookies exploded in popularity during the Boomer Era. Magazines and newspapers printed recipes for old

Cookies courtesy of David Walbert & family.

favorites like gingerbread men and sugar cookies, and they introduced novelties that became classics, like Pfeffernüsse and Springerle, which are baked and gifted across America today. Everyone enjoys them, no matter what their ancestry.

Ever used Corn Flakes in a cookie recipe? If there's one other thing that defines Christmas cookies for Boomers (besides the sheer popularity of them and the plethora of recipes in magazines), it's the way breakfast cereals were incorporated into the baked goodies. A cherry-topped cookie called "Cherry Winks" won the Second Pillsbury Bake-Off Contest in 1950, becoming an instant favorite. It called for more Corn Flakes than flour. The recipe is still up at Pillsbury.com.

Betty Crocker's Cooky Book of 1963 lists no fewer than eleven recipes that call for breakfast cereal—and that's not counting oatmeal as an ingredient. You could make Cocoa Puff Balls, Wheaties Nut Drops, Kix Toffee, or Cheerio Molasses Patties.

Here are some other Boomer Christmas cookie nuggets. Do you remember:

✦ In most homes, Christmas cookies, even *butter* cookies, were made with margarine, Crisco, or lard—but never butter?

✦ Using little Red Hots as ornaments on cookie-cutter Christmas Trees?

✦ Pouring melted chocolate or butterscotch morsels over small piles of coconut, or—even worse—chow mein noodles?

✦ Putting those little silver pellets—Dragées—on cookies? They've been banned in California, and rumor (or Wikipedia) has it that in the very early 20th century, they actually contained mercury!

The Ubiquitous Fruitcake

Boomer-wise, there is only one anecdote that can be shared about this ancient and aesthetically-challenged dessert: Johnny Carson quipped there was only one, and it just kept circling the globe, re-gifted again and again.

Chapter Three

Forget the Fa La La ... Put on the Chipmunks!

❄   ❄   ❄   ❄   ❄   ❄   ❄   ❄   ❄   ❄

The Most Popular Christmas Song Ever: "White Christmas"

With a little stretching of the rules (which, after all, are not so much rules as guidelines, right?), "White Christmas" becomes a Boomer tune. The song was first recorded by Bing Crosby during World War II, when all the GIs overseas were indeed dreaming of a white Christmas—except the soldiers from California and the desert southwest, of course. The Crosby version—introduced in the 1942 movie *Holiday Inn*—was the number one Christmas song of 1946 and 1947 and stayed on the holiday charts through 1962. Then, after a breather, it hit number one again—in 1969.

"White Christmas" is simply the most popular recording of the previous sixty or seventy years. To date, over 50 million copies have been bought. It was not outsold until Elton John redid "Candle in the Wind" as "Goodbye, England's Rose" after Princess Diana's funeral in 1997.

Records were physical entities back in the '40s and '50s; we called them "platters." "White Christmas" sold so many copies that the record's die stamp, which had gone through seven major pressings in four years, wore out. So in 1947, Crosby and as many of the original musicians as was possible to assemble recorded a new master from which to press records. Another version of the song was laid down for the film *White Christmas* in 1952, and again for a Bing Crosby Christmas Special televised in 1955.

So if you grew up thinking that nobody but Bing Crosby could sing the song, you weren't far off the mark. Even though other stars put "White Christmas" on their albums, Bing Crosby outsold them all. By the way, Crosby's Christmas efforts weren't tied to "White Christmas" alone. The man recorded over 60 different holiday tunes during his long career.

In 1957 Elvis Presley added a chapter to the "White Christmas" song saga when he released his first rock 'n' roll holiday platter. Although four religious songs were included, most of the album was made up of the sort of carols that Bing Crosby usually sang.

Not all the songs were put through a rock 'n' roll grinder; some sounded downright tame. One of the songs that Elvis rev'd up a bit was "White Christmas." Sacrilege! Our parents—and grown-ups in general—were horrified. Elvis managed to anger pretty much everyone except the teenagers who bought his records. Some reports say that Irving Berlin was so incensed over Elvis' version of his song that he orchestrated a boycott by radio stations all over the country, who obliged by refusing to play the piece. A late-night disc jockey in Portland, Oregon, was actually fired *on the air* for broadcasting the Elvis recording against management's orders. Other stations issued statements that described the new album as "degrading" and in "extremely bad taste." Hmph.

On the other hand, many radio stations decried the idea of censoring music and said their listeners would decide what would be played. Advance sales of the album broke records for RCA and Elvis' Christmas Album debuted at number 23 on the pop music charts. A week later it was number three, then it spent five weeks at number one before eventually going gold. So guess who had the last laugh?

And that fired Portland disc jockey? He was back on the air in two weeks, thanks to a mountain of mail from listeners. The on-air firing was (as radio station employees admitted thirty years later) a publicity stunt—one that worked quite well.

More Christmas Hits of the Boomer Years

Here are the top Christmas tunes of our era, from earliest to latest.

1946: "The Christmas Song (Chestnuts Roasting on an Open Fire)"

Nat King Cole

On a sweltering July day in Los Angeles, lyricist Robert Wells jotted down some phrases to cool himself off, like "Jack Frost nipping." The list got started because a relative had brought him some chestnuts, and that led to memories of Christmas on the east coast, where vendors sold roasted chestnuts in winter.

Wells' good friend Mel Tormé dropped by and saw a song in those phrases. It was too hot to do anything else, so the men spent the next 45 minutes at the piano writing "The Christmas Song." Seriously, that's all it took. Three-quarters of an hour = Classic.

And, like any two guys who'd done something marvelous and wanted to escape a hot apartment, Wells and Tormé got in the car and drove around to share the song with singers who would appreciate it. They could have gone anywhere . . . but they happened to go to Nat King Cole's home. The rest is history.

Tormé had a beautiful, velvety voice—in fact, he was called "The Velvet Fog." By 1946 he'd worked with the best: Frank Sinatra, Henry Mancini, Les Baxter. Why didn't he grab this song for himself? Why did he happen to take it to Cole? Perhaps it was fate. But mostly, Tormé was just a nice, giving kind of guy.

And it has to be mentioned that this was 1946—Tormé and Wells were white; Cole was black. No African-American had introduced a major Christmas hit before. But it didn't matter. Dozens and dozens of singers have sung the song since— including Tormé. Some were wonderful. But Nat King Cole's rendition, even 65 years later, trumps them all.

1947: "Here Comes Santa Claus"

Movie and TV star Gene Autry wrote this song after serving as the Grand Marshal in Hollywood's Santa Claus Lane Parade in 1946. As Autry and his famous horse Champion pranced down Hollywood Boulevard (which was renamed Santa Claus Lane for the parade), all the little children jumped up and down, screaming, "Here comes Santa Claus! Here comes Santa Claus!"

He wrote the lyrics that night, and country songwriter Oakley Haldeman composed the music—inspired, no doubt, by the clop-clop of Champion's hooves.

1949: "All I Want for Christmas Is My Two Front Teeth"

What date to put on this? "All I Want for Christmas Is My Two Front Teeth" was written in 1944 but not recorded until 1948, and the recording wasn't released for another year. So we'll settle on 1949.

The writer, Donald Yetter Gardner, was teaching music to a classroom full of second graders during the war and noticed they all had at least one tooth missing. When he asked the children to help write a song about what they wanted for Christmas, they all lisped as they talked. Although none of them asked for their front teeth from Santa, Gardner got the idea in his head and wrote his song in thirty minutes flat.

What is with these songwriters? A mere thirty-minute investment to create a lifelong classic? Wow.

The school—in Smithfield, NY—performed the song in their Christmas pageant that year and in following years. A teacher at a conference heard Gardner sing it and convinced him to publish the piece in 1948. Later that year, bandleader Spike Jones and his City Slickers recorded the version most of us remember.

Yes, that's an adult singing in the Spike Jones recording—the vocalist George Rock, who also played the trumpet. He and other members of the City Slickers experimented with different effects to get just the right whistling sound for the boyish lisp.

It took another year, but the song hit number one on some pop charts in 1949, selling 1.3 million copies in six weeks.

1949: "Rudolph the Red-Nosed Reindeer"

This character started out as a book, not a song, and he originally appeared in the 1930s. Robert May, a copywriter who worked for Montgomery Ward, was tasked with creating a "cheery" animal-themed story for Christmas to bring in customers. He came up with Rollo the Red-Nosed Reindeer. Yup, Rollo. And he wrote a poem about Rollo, to be illustrated and put into a promotional (i.e., *free*) Christmas book.

While May worked on this book, things were anything but cheery in his apartment. His young wife was dying of cancer; the Great Depression was in full swing. Medical bills were enormous, and the Mays were poor. To keep upbeat, May read his verses out loud to his four-year-old daughter, Barbara. She liked it, but not the name Rollo. She suggested Rudolph instead.

After his wife died, Montgomery Ward offered to take the book off May's hands and give him some down time, but he refused. The little story distracted him and Barbara from their grief, so he threw himself into finishing it.

An amazing 2.5 million copies of the illustrated book about Rudolph the Red-Nosed Reindeer were handed out to Montgomery Ward shoppers in 1939 alone. The story went on hiatus during the war, but in 1946 Montgomery Ward reissued the book and passed out another 3.6 million, gratis.

And after that? Montgomery Ward transferred the copyright to May, free and clear. They'd never done anything like that before, but it seems to have been a gesture of fairness and sympathy. May put out a spoken-word record of Rudolph's story, which sold well. Since so many millions of books had already been given away, most publishers shied from printing it, but May finally found a children's book publisher, Harry Elbaum, that sold 100,000 copies over the next two years.

A real-life reindeer named Rudolph was a fixture at many shopping areas in the 1950s and 1960s. Panorama City, California, had one and used his cartoon image on their Christmas photo envelopes.

Robert May, creator of Rudolph
the Red-Nosed Reindeer, and friend.

Gene Autry and the Pinafores.
The ladies were regular guests on radio's
The Gene Autry Show.

Postscript: May eventually remarried, had five more children, and left Montgomery Ward to manage his growing Rudolph-based prosperity. That prosperity did not lead to massive wealth, though. May went back to work for the department store in the late 1950s and retired in 1971.

So what about the song?

In 1947, May's sister married songwriter Johnny Marks, and it was Marks who decided to set the story to music.

Marks was a relative unknown at the time. He invested his money into a music publishing venture so that he could own the rights to the Rudolph poem. He made a few demo records and sent them to Dinah Shore, Bing Crosby, and a half dozen other big stars, including Gene Autry. Only one—Autry—called Marks back.

Autry had a huge Christmas hit in 1947 ("Here Comes Santa Claus," remember?) and was hoping for a repeat. He planned to release a pair of records before Christmas, each one with two songs. He'd already picked three and needed a fourth. "Rudolph the Red-Nosed Reindeer" came along at exactly the right moment.

The singing cowboy didn't like the song—he thought it was silly. But he played the demo at home and his wife loved it. So it became the fourth Christmas song—the one least likely to succeed in Autry's opinion. However, the song he deemed silly caught on and sold 2.5 million records in 1949.

After 4 million copies were sold, Columbia Records presented Gene Autry with a Gold Record—the first artist to be so honored. It's still the second most popular Christmas song ever, after "White Christmas."

1949: "Blue Christmas"

1949 was a good year for Christmas music.

Ernest Tubb, the country music star, gets credit for the first hit recording of this tune in the late 1940s and found himself with a number one Country & Western single in 1949. ("Rudolph the Red-Nosed Reindeer" was also number one. Billboard had so many categories of records—genres, singles, albums, DJ requests, type of radio station, etc.—that a dozen songs could be number one during any given week.)

Two other bands recorded "Blue Christmas" as well, giving the song three separate slots on the Billboard charts. Although they're seldom mentioned, the writers of "Blue Christmas" were Bill Hayes and Jay Johnson, and the first, nearly forgotten recording in 1948 was actually by Doye O'Dell.

Elvis reintroduced "Blue Christmas" on his first Christmas album in 1957. He sang it often, and on one of his television specials called it his favorite Christmas song.

Ernest Tubbs was the first artist to record the song "Blue Christmas" in 1949.

Elvis' first Christmas album featured a red cover with lots of presents.
This is the first reissue of the disc in 1959.

I yust go nuts at Christmas
On that yolly holiday.
I'll go in the red like a knucklehead
'Cause I'll squander all my pay . . .

Yogi Yorgesson, the Swedish alter-ego of comedian Harry Stewart, released this song in 1949 and re-released it on his *Yingle Bells* album of 1954.

During the Depression, Harry was a radio announcer and comedian. That may seem an odd career choice for a man who'd lost a lung to tuberculosis (which he did), but he never let that disability slow him down. According to his biography, starvation seemed a bigger threat in the early 1930s. Harry developed the character of Yogi Yorgesson, the Swedish mystic, who stared into a crystal ball—actually, an upside-down fishbowl.

Harry Stewart created other characters over the years, but Yogi Yorgesson was his most popular, and the biggest recording artist. Sadly, he was killed in a car accident in 1956, but thanks in part to aficionados of Dr. Demento, his crazy Christmas song is still heard.

This song started out as a book, just like Rudolph did. The writer—Jack Rollins—had penned a story called "Peter Cottontail" the year before, and he created the character of Frosty as a follow-up. That same year, Steve Edward Nelson did the music and turned the book into a song.

"Frosty the Snowman" never mentions Christmas, but it became a Christmas hit nonetheless when Gene Autry recorded it. More than a million singles were sold. Since Frosty started out as a story, a cartoon made sense, and in 1954 a three-minute black-and-white animated film was made, which still shows up on afternoon TV at times.

Of course, the cartoon most of us remember is the half-hour Christmas special *Frosty the Snowman,* which Jimmy Durante narrated. Frosty's voice came from comedian Jackie Vernon; Durante got to sing the title song, as well as "Santa Claus Is Comin' to Town," a 1930s hit.

1951- "Silver Bells"

This 1951 song came from a movie: *The Lemon Drop Kid*, starring Bob Hope, who sang it with costar Marilyn Maxwell.

Marilyn Maxwell and Bob Hope introduced "Silver Bells" in the 1951 movie, The Lemon Drop Kid.

Ray Evans and Jay Livingston were the Dynamic Duo of songwriting back then. They'd even won a couple of Oscars: one for the song "Mona Lisa" in the otherwise forgettable movie *Captain Carey USA*, and one for "Buttons and Bows," written for another Bob Hope movie *The Paleface*. (They'd go on to win a third in 1956 for "Que Sera Sera," the song Doris Day sang in *The Man Who Knew Too Much*.)

The men wrote over 400 songs together over the 64 years of their partnership, including the themes from *Mr. Ed* and *Bonanza*.

But in Hollywood, fame can be fleeting. Even though "Mona Lisa" had been a big hit, the contract that Evans and Livingston had with Paramount Pictures was getting close to the expiration date. When the studio ordered them to write a Christmas song for *The Lemon Drop*

Kid, the pair protested and tried to convince their bosses that a non-holiday tune could be a bigger hit. In the end, they finally sat down to hammer out a Christmas song.

They were not enthusiastic. In a radio interview in 2005, the 91-year-old Evans explained: "We figured—stupidly, thank God—that the world had too many Christmas songs already."

The original title of their work was "Tinkle Bells," inspired by a little bell that sat on their desk. That phrase sent Livingston's wife into a fit of giggles when she heard it. The men never realized that "tinkle" had more than one meaning, but once enlightened, they wisely changed the title. A smart move, since "Silver Bells" sold more than 500 million records and was a favorite of JFK.

But it almost got cut from the film. Director Sidney Lanfield hated it, and he filmed it sung by a choir in a very static, boring way. The producer, however, had a different vision. Robert Welch brought in another, uncredited director—Frank Tashlin—to correct weaknesses in the film. Tashlin had Hope and Maxwell sing the song as they walked along the studio's New York City street.

Around the same time, Bing Crosby happened across Livingston and Evans in the Paramount Studios commissary and asked them if they had any new songs for him. They told him about "Silver Bells"; he recorded it, and that's the recording most of us remember.

1951: "It's Beginning to Look a Lot Like Christmas"

Meredith Wilson—a man—was quite a famous composer and former member of the John Philip Sousa Band. He wrote Broadway musicals, including *The Music Man* and *The Unsinkable Molly Brown*. The movies also employed him, and he was twice nominated for Oscars for his scores for *The Great Dictator* and *The Little Foxes*. He wrote songs too, and one of them was "It's Beginning to Look a Lot Like Christmas." Perry Como and the Fontaine Sisters recorded it in 1951, and it edged into the Top 20. Bing Crosby released a recording of it that year as well.

The song was almost forgotten, but in 1963, Meredith Wilson set the 1934 classic movie *Miracle on 34th Street* to music. The play opened on Broadway with the new title *Here's Love*. Don't feel bad if you haven't heard of it; *Here's Love* was hardly box office gold. It's only worth mentioning because it brought the song "It's Beginning to Look a Lot Like Christmas" back into the holiday repertoire.

1952: "I Saw Mommy Kissing Santa Claus"

Thirteen-year-old Jimmy Boyd, who'd been winning talent contests for his vocal skills since he was seven, sang this 1952 hit. The song shot to number one and sold more than two million records during the first ten weeks of its release.

Early on, the Catholic Church condemned the playing of the song on the radio, not liking the implications. After all, the song linked Christmas with sex, even if it was between Mommy and Daddy. According to newspapers, Boyd actually appeared before church leaders to explain the song from his point of view (a child's) and got the ban lifted. If that actually happened, it was a bona-fide miracle.

Jimmy Boyd went on to record other songs and duets in the 1950s and won roles in a couple of sitcoms as well—including an early Betty White vehicle, *Date with the Angels.* He briefly married Yvonne Craig—TV's original Batgirl. In later life, he discovered sailing, and lived quietly on his boat until his death from cancer in 2009.

The writer of "I Saw Mommy Kissing Santa Claus" was an Englishman named Tommie Connor. He had one previous hit that was even bigger than this one: the English lyrics of "Lilli Marlene." *That* song became one of the most popular of World War II, even though it started out in Germany, and was about the only song to be a hit with both Allied and Axis troops.

1953: "Santa Baby"

What can we say? This was a naughty song, sung by the sultry Eartha Kitt—the original Catwoman of the 1960s, and everyone loved it. But it may have been too sexy for your home. Some of us didn't really know the song until Madonna released her version decades later.

1954: "Caroling, Caroling"

Surprised to see this on the list? It seems like a much older song, but "Caroling Caroling" was written a little before 1954.

A musician named Alfred Burt composed and sent out a Christmas tune each year, the way some people send out Christmas cards. Burt used lyrics by his father, and after his dad's death he worked with a friend, Wihla Hutson. One of his earlier works, "Some Children See Him," is still sung.

Burt finally began to get some recognition in 1952, but tragedy struck before he could build on it. He was diagnosed with cancer and died in February 1954, at only 33 years old. Burt spent much of his last year putting together an album of his carols, which came out after his death. One of those, written in 1953 for the album, was "Caroling Caroling."

Since then, his works have been sung by Simon and Garfunkel, Kenny Loggins, and others—but it was Nat King Cole's version of "Caroling, Caroling" in 1960 that is probably the most well known.

1955: "Nuttin' for Christmas"

Little Barry Gordon sang this song and it's fair to say he did an incredible job. The song shot to number six on the Billboard record charts of late 1955 and is still popular. At six years old, Gordon was the youngest person ever to reach such a spot on Billboard, and the record eventually went gold.

Whatever happened to Gordon? Quite a lot, actually. As a popular child actor, he made appearances on many shows, from *Leave It to Beaver* to *The Jack Benny Program.* As he grew up, he appeared on Broadway and in the movies as a very successful character actor. He even played a Ferengi on *Star Trek: Deep Space Nine* and lent his vocal talents to animated shows like *The Smurfs* and the original *Teenage Mutant Ninja Turtles* (he was Donatello).

But wait—there's more! Gordon also earned a law degree and was the longest-serving president of the Screen Actors Guild. In addition to that, he's run for political office and hosted his own radio show (on both an old-fashioned station and today, on the Internet).

1957: "Jingle Bell Rock"

Bobby Helms recorded this song and released it just days before Christmas. He'd already had big hits with "Fraulein" and "My Special Angel," but "Jingle Bell Rock" seemed to have staying power. Helms' version climbed the charts again during the holidays in 1958, 1961, and 1962. The rockabilly song has also been recorded by Chubby Checker with Bobby Rydell in 1961, Brenda Lee in 1964, Bill Haley and the Comets in 1968 (though that record wasn't released for decades), the Beatles, the Chipmunks—just about everyone from Ashanti to Tatsuro Yamashita.

1958: "Chipmunk Song"

Ever hear of Ross Bagdasarian? Probably not, but that was the real name of David Seville—whom we all remember as the godfather/guardian of our three favorite chipmunks: Alvin, Simon, and Theodore. And the "Chipmunk Song" is how they all got started.

David Seville, Father of Alvin, Simon, and Theodore.

Under his real name, he penned a hit for Rosemary Clooney: "Come On-A My House." After that, Bagdasarian became David Seville. Why that name? Bagdasarian had been stationed in Seville, Spain, during World War II.

In the 1950s, Seville's fortunes rose and fell until the day he was down to his last two hundred dollars. That's when he wrote the nonsense song "Witch Doctor." Liberty Records released that tune and it put him back on top.

What does that have to do with the Chipmunks? Everything. "Witch Doctor" called for some wild vocals—remember the "OO-EE-OO-Ah-Ah, Ting Tang Walla Walla Bing Bang" part? Seville played with the tape speed to get that voice right. His kids loved the song and it went on to sell millions of copies, not only saving Liberty Records from insolvency, but also paving the way for Seville's next hit.

As his son wrote years later on the website www.thechipmunks.com:

Pop loved the voice of the Witch Doctor but wanted to marry that voice with personalities. However, he hadn't decided if they should be singing reindeer, potato bugs, or God knows what else. While he was driving his car in Yosemite, a tiny chipmunk dashed in front of his four-thousand-pound car. The chipmunk stood on its hind legs, daring my Dad to pass. Pop loved the audacity of that chipmunk. He knew he had found his star.

Chipmunks it was. Alvin, Simon, and Theodore were named for the three execs of Liberty Records. Their Christmas song was finished in early November, but a problem cropped up: no Los Angeles radio stations would play the record before December because of its Christmas theme. It was just too early for holiday music. Liberty Records was in financial straits again and needed immediate cash, so they took the record to Minneapolis, where stations didn't have such strict rules.

The early chipmunks looked nothing like their 1960s cartoon selves.

The effect was immediate. A DJ played the record, and the station's switchboard lit up with callers demanding to hear it again or find out where they could buy it. Listeners called other stations, asking for the "Chipmunk Song." It sold five million copies in its first year and won two Grammys to boot.

"The Chipmunk Song" wasn't just available in record stores. Flower shops, gift stores, cigar shops—all had stacks of the record by their cash registers and rang up "The Chipmunk Song" all day. Think Starbucks and their nifty CD collections. Same idea—only "The Chipmunk Song" holds the distinction of being the first recording to be sold outside of record stores.

1960: "Rockin' Around the Christmas Tree"

Remember Johnny Marks, the guy who wrote the music to "Rudolph the Red-Nosed Reindeer?" Well, this one's his too. By 1958, when he penned "Rockin' Around the Christmas Tree," he was pretty well known and didn't have to send homemade demos to big stars to get attention. A sixteen-year-old Brenda Lee turned this song into the holiday hit of 1960.

Lee had actually recorded the song the previous year, but it was the reissue in 1960 that soared to the top of the charts—probably because Lee had just enjoyed a huge hit with "I'm Sorry" that fall. The song had been recorded on a warm autumn day, but there were Christmas decorations in the recording studio to get everyone in the mood.

Brenda Lee never expected that song to become a classic, she wrote in a 2002 autobiography, but she's proud that it did. "People tell me they've raised their children with that song and that it wouldn't be Christmas for them without it."

"I got the surprise of my life," she said, "when I went to see *Home Alone* in 1990 and heard myself singing on its soundtrack."[7]

Sleeve for the 1960 single; Brenda Lee was a young teen.

1962: "Do You Hear What I Hear?"

This song has a beautiful love story behind it.

Noël Regney was a classically trained composer who was forced into the Nazi army. He later escaped, joined the resistance in his native France, and was wounded in the arm during an ambush of Nazi soldiers. His name was actually Schlinger, and if you drop the Schl and spell it backwards, you have something pretty close to Regney.

After the war, Regney worked as a musical director for the Lido nightclub of Paris, then toured with Lucienne Boyer, a famed singer. He emigrated to America in the early '50s. One day, Regney wandered into a New York hotel dining room where a beautiful woman played piano. He spoke, she responded, and though his English wasn't great, they were married within a month.

Regney's new wife, Gloria Shayne, was not just a pianist but a songwriter as well: James Darren's hit "Goodbye Cruel World" was her work. Regney's biggest success was writing the English lyrics to "Dominique," sung by the famous Singing Nun, Soeur Sourire in 1963.

Gloria and Noël wrote several songs together, such as "What's the Use of Crying?" an Eddie Fisher hit. Usually when they collaborated, Gloria did the lyrics and Noël the music, but for "Do You Hear What I Hear?" they reversed roles.

During the Cuban Missile Crisis, Noël wrote a poem about the peace of the First Christmas because he was deeply affected by the constant threat of war—first from the Nazis, then the Cold War. His words were both a prayer and a plea for peace. He asked his wife to write the music so that it would sound more pop than classical.

Once finished, the couple took "Do You Hear What I Hear?" to a publisher, who contacted Harry Simeone, whose singing group had recorded "The Little Drummer Boy" a few years earlier. The Harry Simeone Chorale released the new single just after Thanksgiving in 1962, and the 250,000 copies pressed sold out in a week. The next year, Bing Crosby sang it onto the charts again. Since then, almost every song stylist and balladeer has taken a turn singing it, some with great success. Robert Goulet's version was a favorite of the songwriters.

Unlike their music, the love story between Noël and Gloria was not eternal, and they divorced in the 1970s. Both remarried, however, and enjoyed long lives before they passed away.

1964: "Holly Jolly Christmas"

Burl Ives made the tune famous when he sang it on the TV special *Rudolph the Red-Nosed Reindeer* and followed up by releasing a single for the 1965 Christmas season. On the flip side was another song from the animated show, "Silver and Gold." He also released an album that year: *Have a Holly Jolly Christmas.*

Burl Ives in 1955, photographed by Carl Van Vechten.

There is some irony in this—both songs in the TV show were meant to be sung by the character Yukon Cornelius, voiced by Larry D. Mann. Once the producers signed Burl Ives to play the narrating Snowman, they switched things around. Ives was a well-known actor, but he was more famous as a folk singer, with kid-friendly hits like "Lavender Blue" and "Blue-Tail Fly."

"Holly Jolly Christmas" and all the other songs in the show were written by Johnny Marks—the man who'd written the song "Rudolph the Red-Nosed Reindeer" and who had married the sister of Rudolph's creator, Robert May.

More irony: Marks and May were both Jewish yet their claims to fame rest largely on Christmas songs and stories. Marks was a prolific songwriter, but most of his hits were nonreligious holiday tunes.

1966: "We Need a Little Christmas"

One of the few Christmas songs to come from a Broadway musical, "We Need a Little Christmas" was written for *Mame* (you may remember the movie version that starred Lucille Ball). As Mame, Lucy sang this song right after the stock market crash, when everyone needed to lift their spirits.

Composer Jerry Herman said that this song almost wrote itself because it said so much about the indomitable character of Auntie Mame. Herman was nominated for a Tony for *Mame.* Though he lost out to *Sweet Charity* that year, his previous musical *Hello Dolly* had swept the Tonys in 1964, and twenty years later, *La Cage Aux Folles* would bring him another Tony.

Angela Lansbury, the star of *Mame,* sang the 1966 version, and like all great songs it's been redone many times—most recently, by the cast of *Glee.*

A Christmas Album for Certain Adults

Think the height of holiday hilarity was reached by Yogi Yorgesson or the Chipmunks, or that songs never got any racier than "Santa Baby"? Think again.

Nightclub performer Kay Martin owned the Kay Martin Lodge in Reno. Her group Kay Martin and Her Body Guards—Jess Hotchkiss and Bill Elliot—entertained the 21-and-older crowd in Hawaii, Florida, Vegas, and Reno from the early '50s to the early '60s.

All her LPs were risqué and their covers X-rated—usually featuring a nude woman, with a slightly cleaned-up cover version also available. Occasionally, Kay herself—a former model—was on the cover.

Kay Matin and Her Body Guards released a Christmas album in 1962. As if the cover didn't make it clear enough, a sampling of the song titles let listeners know what they were in for:

✦ "Hang Your Balls on the Christmas Tree" (When your balls are on the Christmas tree, you'll be as tickled as can be)

✦ "Santa's Doing the Horizontal Twist" (He was a crazy twister, that fat old friend of mine . . . He came down my chimney!)

✦ "Girls Should Be Obscene and Not Heard"

✦ "He Loves to Bang those Bells"

And so on. Lyrics of the album's title song "I know What He Wants for Christmas . . . I Just Don't Know How to Wrap It" go:

"I need one hand to wrap it,
Another hand to clutch it,
It wiggles and it squirms
It even tickles when I touch it . . ."

If you want more, check out YouTube . . . or your parents' closet.

Chapter Four

YULETIDE ENTERTAINMENT

Entertainment in the Boomer Era was quite different from any previous period, and television was the reason. Technically, engineers and inventors were tinkering with and occasionally broadcasting TV shows as far back as the 1930s. The massive world war overshadowed any excitement over those developments, though, so it wasn't until the late 1940s that most of us got a glimpse of the new technology.

By 1948, only a few tens of thousands of sets were in homes across America; one encyclopedia says 35,000. In 1951—just three years later—that number was 8 million, and in 1960, 52 million. Put another way, by 1955 half the homes in the country had a television. No other invention, not even radio, had been adopted so quickly. And until the mid-1960s, those TVs carried black-and-white shows only.

Much of the entertainment listed in this section was created for television—it became the quickest way to capture an audience, and once caught, to sell them Neat Stuff.

TV Christmas Specials

The first televised Christmas special—*One Hour in Wonderland*—appeared on December 25, 1950. Yup, it was from Disney, and yup, it came out about seven months before the animated movie, *Alice in Wonderland.* The idea (copied many times over the years) was that Walt Disney threw a holiday party in his home. We were all invited to enjoy Christmas with his family and his special guests—namely, Edgar Bergen and puppets Charlie McCarthy and Mortimer Snerd. And of course, we as guests got to watch previews of the upcoming movie.

Movie stars began to dabble in the newish medium. Bob Hope put out his first Christmas special in 1954; Sonja Henie presented *Holiday on Ice* in 1956—in color. You might also remember *The Bing Crosby Christmas Show* in 1962. One of the best—rebroadcast more often than the others—was Judy Garland's 1963 Christmas show. She also invited us into her home, where Mel Tormé himself sang the song he'd written, the one that begins "Chestnuts roasting on an open fire ..."

Most television series featured their own Christmas-themed episodes—so many of them, in fact, that Wikipedia has a list of all United States Television Christmas Episodes. Shows are listed in alphabetical order and sorted by dramas, sitcoms, and children's shows. Every series—from *227* and *Adam 12* to *The X-Files*—with a Christmas episode is listed. Here are some highlights:

President Eisenhower's color TV is still on display at his home in Gettysburg, PA.

✦ In 1952, *Ozzie and Harriet* had two different Christmas episodes—one before, and one after the holiday. In the second episode, the Nelson family encounters a single mom whose kids didn't get much for Christmas, prompting the Nelson clan to help out.

✦ *The Honeymooners* had a Christmas party in 1953. Alice (Audrey Meadows) sent Ralph (Jackie Gleason) out for potato salad, and while he was gone a bunch of characters came to the party—all played by Gleason.

✦ *Alfred Hitchcock Presents* in 1955 featured a Christmas story in which an ex-con playing Santa is redeemed by helping a young child.

✦ In 1969—the *Brady Bunch's* first year on the air—Carol (Florence Henderson) developed laryngitis just before her big solo at Christmas services. Alice (Ann B. Davis) ended up teaching the kids the "true meaning of Christmas."

Someday maybe we'll figure out the true meaning of "the true meaning of Christmas" because in most Christmas shows, someone always got to explain it. Their speech usually included platitudes about love and coziness and giving rather than receiving, but it all gets a little fuzzy when the featured stars try to pin it down. The one special that nailed "the true meaning" for many was *A Charlie Brown Christmas*, with Linus' recitation of the gospel—and that got into the show only because of the cartoonist's extreme stubbornness. More about that shortly.

As for truly animated Christmas specials (as opposed to blatant movie promos), the first made-for-TV animated cartoon special was *Mr. Magoo's Christmas Carol,* which aired on December 18, 1962 and is still shown today. Featuring the voice of Jim Backus—also Thurston Howell III on *Gilligan's Island*—this special had the myopic Mr. Magoo playing Scrooge on stage. Jack Cassidy voiced Bob Cratchit, and the show was filled with music. The catchy "We're Despicable," sung by cartoon lowlifes as they stripped Scrooge's room of his curtains and possessions, might still play in your head whenever someone mentions *A Christmas Carol.*

Mr. Magoo's Christmas Carol was followed by many other specials. Who can forget *Frosty the Snowman*—with an animated Jimmy Durante? Or the voices of Fred Astaire and Mickey Rooney in *Santa Claus is Comin' to Town?* Or the many versions of *A Christmas Carol*—one with Alastair Sims voicing Scrooge, while Sir Michael Redgrave narrated. Those, of course, are trick questions as the specials are difficult to forget—mostly because we have to watch them every year with our own kids and grandkids.

The most popular and most often broadcast Christmas specials came in the mid-1960s: *Rudolph the Red-Nosed Reindeer, A Charlie Brown Christmas,* and *Dr. Seuss' How the Grinch Stole Christmas.*

Rudolph the Red-Nosed Reindeer

This 1964 special was the first from Arthur Rankin, Jr. and Jules Bass, who perfected an appealing, stop-action style of puppetry they called "animagic." They used it again in *Santa Claus Is Comin' to Town* and other popular specials. In fact, with the success of *Rudolph the Red-Nosed Reindeer*, their first animagic special, the pair became so popular that they had more offers than they could accept. Everyone wanted Rankin and Bass to produce a holiday special or a story based on a song.

Rudolph the Red-Nosed Reindeer happened largely because of coincidences. Both Rankin and Bass lived in Manhattan, and Rankin's home was in Greenwich Village, near that of Johnny Marks, who wrote and owned the rights to the song "Rudolph the Red-Nosed Reindeer."

At this point, Rankin and Bass had created several stop-motion commercials and shorts for General Electric, and they were looking for a larger project. Marks was protective of Rudolph's story and it took some convincing, but he finally agreed to let the tale be animated. General Electric was on board early—it turned out that the GE executive in charge of the television production had worked for Montgomery Ward in Chicago back in the 1930s, when copywriter Robert May wrote the original Rudolph story. He had fond memories of that time. When all these elements came together, Rankin and Bass started work.

They created characters from scratch to match the song, and Johnny Marks wrote more songs to suit the story as it developed. A couple of his ditties —"Holly Jolly Christmas" and "It's the Most Wonderful Time of the Year"—became holiday classics in their own right, though they started life as extra music for Rudolph and his friends.

When the music and storyline were completed, Rankin and Bass assembled a cast and recorded the soundtrack—dialogue and music—in much the same way a radio show was recorded. No animation had been done at this point.

In fact, since the 1930s and Walt Disney's *Snow White and the Seven Dwarfs,* animated films and longer shows were always produced this way: the music and soundtracks were recorded first, and the animation was then drawn or modeled to match the sound.

Burl Ives and songwriter Johnny Marks for the debut of the Rudolph TV special.

Billie Mae Richards, a 40-year-old woman, was Rudolph, Stan Francis played Santa, and Paul Soles was Hermie the Elf. All of them came together with Larry D. Mann, who voiced Yukon Cornelius, and the musicians and directors. They did all the music and dialogue, and in that original recording, Yukon Cornelius sang "Holly Jolly Christmas."

Only after all that work did the creators realize that Sam the Snowman wasn't right.

For us, the story of *Rudolph the Red-Nosed Reindeer* is cosmically linked to the voice of Burl Ives, who narrated it and introduced "Holly Jolly Christmas" to the viewing public. But Ives was not part of the original plan for the show.

In fact, Sam the Snowman did not sing any songs in the original script. GE wanted a bigger star to sell the show—something unique in those days. Most cartoon voice actors were not famous, and stars did not do this type of work.

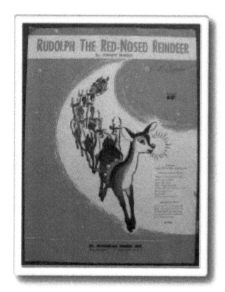

Printed in 1964, this sheet music paid homage to an earlier image of Rudolph.

The producers looked around and realized that Burl Ives, a popular folksinger, would be magical; he was the missing element. They wooed him and Ives became part of the show. He was smart—or at least, his agent was—and signed a contract that, thanks to the show's popularity, guaranteed him royalties till the end of his life.

But the soundtrack was already recorded. Rankin and Bass had Burl Ives redo all of Sam's lines, going into a recording studio by himself and speaking the lines that would be inserted. In the early 1960s, this was innovative. Today, it's simply the way most cartoon soundtracks are made.

As for the animagic itself, the stop-motion technique had been developed in pre-WWII Europe and later in America by Hungarian George Pal, who called his creations "Puppetoons." Pal created wooden puppets, but instead of hinged legs and arms, each moving limb was replaced constantly—with limbs moving a fraction of an inch in each frame. This was exquisitely detailed animation and had never been done on TV before.

(George Pal, by the way, went on to fame and fortune. Remember *Tubby the Tuba*? That was his last Puppetoon, made in 1947. He moved on to feature films and directed some of our favorite movies: *Houdini*, starring Tony Curtis; *The Time Machine* with Rod Taylor, Yvette Mimieux, and Alan Young; and *The Wonderful World of the Brothers Grimm*. Oh, and *Tom Thumb*, a mix of live action and animation.)

Back to *Rudolph the Red-Nosed Reindeer.* The special required twenty-two sets that took a year to complete, each one built as the story was hammered out and the cast assembled. Each puppet character cost about $5,000 to craft (in 1964 dollars) and had dozens of detachable mouths and eyes to mimic the various expressions and lip movements.

The show debuted on Sunday December 6, 1964, at 5:30 pm on NBC. Remember that in 1963, GE paid for a showing of the speech in 1963 and in the following year. Apparently the GE execs thought they needed new material to convince people to tune into a show that was technically a rerun, so a new song "Fame and Fortune" was added, along with new animation to make it fit. Most repeats of the show exclude this song. NBC aired the special every holiday season through 1971, then CBS took over.

By 1964, when this TV special was made, Rudolph books appeared in over twenty-four languages, and more than 500 licensed Rudolph products—cuckoo clocks, purses, lamps, plates, pencil boxes, you name it—were available. The Rankin and Bass show did not create more—unless you count GE's Christmastime advertising, which used Rudolph, Sam, and Hermie in magazines to sell electric blankets and waffle irons. The soundtrack from the show was given away free too. But decades passed before anyone produced toy figures of the show's characters.

Today, of course, our kids and grandkids know the songs and characters as well as we do. *Rudolph the Red-Nosed Reindeer* is the longest consecutively aired animated special of all time. There were later Rudolph specials, including one that paired him up with Frosty, but the original remains a favorite nearly fifty years later.

Rankin and Bass went on to produce *Rudolph's Shiny New Year, Frosty the Snowman, The Little Drummer Boy* and a few Easter specials, as well as theatrical releases, such as the 1977 version of *The Hobbit.* Not all of these were animagic; *Frosty the Snowman,* for one example, was a conventionally drawn cartoon.

A Charlie Brown Christmas

The ultimate Christmas classic debuted in 1965, but it wasn't the first time that Charlie Brown, Linus, Lucy, Snoopy, and the rest of the gang appeared on TV.

Charles Schulz had licensed his characters to sell a car—the Ford Falcon—as early as 1959. Those commercials made Schulz rich and were a pleasant experience in other ways—mainly because he had final approval of all scripts, storyboards, and even the voices of his Peanuts gang.

Still, even though he was thrilled with the way the ads turned out, he said no to other offers for TV and movies.

Then a director named Lee Mendelson gained Schulz' trust by producing a filmed interview with him for a *Peanuts* documentary. The film included a two-minute animated sequence, and for that, Mendelson brought in Bill Melendez, the animator from those Ford commercials. Schulz liked the results.

Unfortunately, however, the completed documentary sat unloved and unappreciated on a shelf; no network would buy it. But the show was screened for potential sponsors over the next few months, and one of those screenings inspired an adman to call Mendelson. The adman asked if Mendelson would be interested in producing a *Peanuts* Christmas Special for sponsor Coca-Cola.

Of course he would! Mendelson called Schulz right away to give him the good news, then the not-so-good news: Coca-Cola wanted an outline of the show within five days. Schulz didn't balk. He invited Mendelson to his house, and they got to work.

The outline sold so Mendelson called animator Bill Melendez, and *A Charlie Brown Christmas* came to life. Schulz had complete control over the script, and the director was on board with most of his ideas. A school play, an unloved tree, lots of outdoor scenes, and an anti-commercial theme were fine, but Schulz also insisted on a nativity scene. Mendelson agreed, but he was shocked when he learned that Schulz planned to have Linus recite from the Gospel of Luke for over a minute. He tried arguing against that and lost. Schulz did not negotiate when he knew he was right.

As for the music … whose brainstorm was it to have Dr. Funk—Vince Guaraldi—score the show? Not Charles Schulz; he disliked jazz. Producer Mendelson had asked Guaraldi—a big fan of *Peanuts*—to write a couple of minutes of music for the earlier documentary. That work, called "Linus and Lucy's Theme" became the piano piece everyone thinks of when they remember the Charlie Brown specials.

The song "Christmas Time Is Here" was also written by Guaraldi, but everyone felt it needed some lyrics. As the show's deadline approached, Mendelson scribbled some lines on the back of an envelope, and boom: another instant classic.

Charles Schulz was fine with every element except for one: he fought the producer and director over having a laugh track. He didn't want one. When Mendelson and Melendez argued for it, Schulz got up and walked out. As we all remember, Schulz won that fight. Thank goodness.

As for those great voices, most belonged to actual children, not adult actors, which was a real innovation in 1965. Snoopy was voiced by animator Bill Melendez, who spoke some lines into a recorder and sped up the tape. Melendez became Snoopy's voice for the next 37 years, and Mendelson called his character "a veritable canine Harpo Marx."

The first Charlie Brown, an eight-and-half-year-old actor named Peter Robbins, had experience in sitcoms and commercials. He continued to play Charlie through five specials and a movie, and his godmother—an agent—found the little boy who voiced Linus, Christopher Shea.

"We did the whole show in a few hours," Robbins said years later when Mendelson interviewed him about the project. But when he arrived for work at Fantasy Records in San Francisco, Robbins remembered the scene as "chaotic, with a bunch of kids, six to nine years old, running all over the place and too excited to calm down."[8]

Playing Charlie Brown's little sister, Sally, was Cathy Steinberg, who was barely six years old and hadn't yet learned to read. Melendez (the animator) fed her one line at a time to record, and Christopher Shea (Linus) was not much older—his lines had to be read to him too. Melendez had a running joke with Schulz and the other adults that Linus and Sally would have Mexican accents because of Melendez' help.

A Charlie Brown Christmas did not have any adults in it—the "waa-waa" voice of the teacher came along later in other specials. What made the waa-waa sound? A trombone. The teacher—believe it or not—had scripted lines, and the trombone player imitated the inflections of a human voice.

Though it seemed like all the elements came together well, the first screening of *A Charlie Brown Christmas* did not go well. The two CBS VPs who watched found the show flat and slow. The one critic invited to this early showing got up and left without a comment, or even a smile.

"I'm afraid we won't be ordering any more," the VPs told Mendelson. "Maybe it's better suited to the comic page."

Since the network had already paid for and advertised the show, it aired the special at 7:30 PM on Thursday, December 9, 1965, pre-empting *The Munsters*. Besides Coca-Cola, McDonald's and Nabisco had paid for commercials during the show. Earlier in the week, *TV Guide* came out with a glowing review of the cartoon from the critic who had seemed so unimpressed at the screening.

Still, the creators were gloomy and didn't expect the show to do well.

Guess what? Those VPs were wrong. We loved the show. Our parents loved the show. *A Charlie Brown Christmas* became an instant classic, won an Emmy and a Peabody, and is still the longest-running cartoon special ever.

As for that first *Peanuts* documentary, the one that brought Sparky Schulz, Lee Mendelson, Bill Melendez, and Vince Guaraldi together for the first time: it eventually got aired in 1970. And it won an Emmy too.

How the Grinch Stole Christmas

What is Christmas without the Grinch? Well, since 1957 anyway, the year the book was first published. But before we get to the TV special, did you know that the book itself was an immediate bestseller?

Dr. Seuss (Ted Geisel) drawing the Grinch for his new book in 1957.

The author, Dr. Seuss (Ted Geisel) was already a proven success, so the publisher printed 50,000 copies—a new high for a children's book. Macy's had its first $2 million dollar day on December 10, 1957, thanks to sales of that book—and that $2 million record was for *any* department store, not just Macy's.

Dr. Seuss—like Charles Schulz—resisted the idea of animating his characters. But once *A Charlie Brown Christmas* was so well received, an old friend from the army asked the author to let him adapt one of the Dr. Seuss books as a Christmas special. That old friend, Chuck Jones, was the genius behind hundreds of Looney Toons and Merrie Melody cartoons and one of the top producers of animation during its golden years.

The friendship between the men was very real. During World War II, Jones and Seuss—who of course went by the name Geisel then—collaborated to produce a series of educational cartoons for the army about Private Snafu. Snafu—as his name suggests—did everything wrong and suffered the consequences. Geisel was one of three writers on the cartoons, while Jones directed them.

By 1966, Jones headed up the animation department for MGM. He wanted to work with his old buddy again. Sounds like a no brainer, right? Not quite—Dr. Seuss said no.

Fortunately Mrs. Seuss—Helen Geisel—convinced her husband to reconsider.

Jones and Seuss worked closely together on the special, but others were amazingly unexcited about putting the Grinch on television. Jones had a hard time convincing any big company to sponsor the show. The usual kids' advertisers—Nestle, Kellogg, and the rest—were just not interested. He finally got the Foundation for Commercial Banks on board.

In the book, if you remember it, the Grinch himself is as white as copy paper, and he does not look much more ferocious than, say, the Cat in the Hat. As the show came together, though, the Grinch got more and more evil looking. His frown turned farther down, and his eyes and body became green. Because Jones insisted on more backgrounds and animation frames than most cartoons, it ended up being an extraordinarily expensive show to make.

Only three actors lent their voices to *How the Grinch Stole Christmas,* one of them being Boris Karloff—who, already in his late 70s, narrated the piece and played the Grinch as well. He also voiced several of the Whos, quite a linguistic feat since Karloff suffered from emphysema and painful arthritis.

One day Dr. Seuss brought a friend, who happened to be a cardiologist, to listen to one of the recording sessions. The doctor told Seuss that Karloff was so ill he doubted the man would survive much longer. Karloff, however, went on to make four more movies before his death in 1969.

Although he didn't get a screen credit on the original show, Thurl Ravenscroft sang the song "You're a Mean One, Mr. Grinch." Know where else you've heard that marvelous bass voice? He played the cartoon Paul Bunyon, sang back up vocals in *Cinderella* and *Lady and the Tramp* and other films, and his voice is played daily at Disneyland itself on several rides. For instance, on the Haunted Mansion ride, he's one of three Grim Grinning Ghosts, and at the Enchanted Tiki Room, he plays Fritz, the German parrot.

But Thurl Ravenscroft's biggest claim to fame (aside from having one of the coolest names in the world) is his fifty years as Tony the Tiger. Yup, he's the voice that says "They're grrrrreat!"

Lastly, Cindy Lou Who was played by June Foray, a prolific and well-known voice actor who started on the radio in the 1930s and is still working in 2013. She was Lucifer the Cat in *Cinderella* (co-star Thurl Ravenscroft played a mouse) and played Rocky the Flying Squirrel (as well as Natasha, the evil secret agent) on television. One of the most famous cartoon voices ever, a lot of her work was done without credit—including, initially, *How the Grinch Stole Christmas.*

CBS bought the rights to two showings of *How the Grinch Stole Christmas,* one in 1966 and one in 1967, for $315,000. Jones said he expected the show to be telecast for at least ten years and knew he and Dr. Seuss would be richly paid for the time they invested—and of course, he was right. CBS showed the 30-minute special every year until 1987, when Turner Broadcasting bought MGM's catalogue (MGM was officially the producer). From then on, *How the Grinch Stole Christmas* has been on TNT, the Cartoon Network, and other Turner-owned stations each year.

Other Christmas Happenings

Tracking Santa's Flight

In 1955, a Colorado Springs newspaper ran an ad for Sears Roebuck & Co. The ad showed a big face shot of Santa Claus and the words: "Hey Kiddies! Call me direct on my telephone." The telephone number was printed—twice—with a few more lines of invitation, all signed by Santa.

Unfortunately, the phone number had a typo in it, and believe it or not, that typo connected kids to the Operational Hotline of the Continental Air Defense Command. Colonel Harry Shoup got the first call, from a little girl in Colorado Springs who asked, "Are you one of Santa's helpers?"

Another officer might have hung up, but Colonel Shoup had three daughters. He told the little girl he *was* Santa and had a very nice conversation with her. More calls followed. Once he figured out why kids were phoning him, the colonel pretended to be one of Santa's helpers. His job was to keep the skies safe for Santa's trip, he told them—and in fact, he could see Santa's sleigh on the radar right in front of him.

The media caught wind of the story. And kids kept calling.

By Christmas of 1958, the agency was called NORAD—North American Aerospace Defense Command, and "Santa tracking" was part of the mission. Christmas Eve broadcasts on television were interrupted to report an unidentified object. Remember, this is when we all learned to "duck and cover" in school, so UFOs could be scary. But it was Santa! What a relief!

Each year, volunteers were brought in to man the phone lines, answering calls that began coming in from all over the world. From the beginning, corporate sponsors—not tax dollars—paid for the service, and both Canadian and US forces and agencies helped publicize it.

In 1964, NORAD released an LP that radio stations could use, with "a series of spots citing the progress of Santa as he makes his annual journey down through the space tracking and radar facilities of the North American Air Defense Command." The LP had a couple of ads too that played in advance of Christmas Eve, as well as lots of Christmas music played by the big band "NORAD Commanders."

NORAD's Santa Tracking Operation has gotten more and more elaborate and high tech over the years. Besides fielding tens of thousands of phone calls, the 21st-century NORAD volunteers answer emails and post tweets and Facebook updates. Beginning December 1st, you can check it out at www.NORADSanta.com.

Parades

Boomers may be the last generation to truly enjoy parades, even if it seems dorky to admit it now. Parades are a spectator sport with long gaps between waving celebrities and forward movement, but then the same can be said of golf.

Macy's Thanksgiving Day Parade kicks off the holiday season for most of us, a tradition that started in 1924—although at the time, it wasn't really seen as a tradition so much as a sales promotion. Back in the pre-television days, stores depended on their colorful window displays to bring in customers. Store managers were always looking for a new angle or innovation to make *their* windows more attractive than the competitors'.

By the Roaring Twenties, other stores in other cities had tried circus acts and parades as a way of drawing customers to their door, with some success. Macy's decided to hop on that bandwagon too. They hired a famed puppeteer named Tony Sarg to orchestrate a parade and bring the public to their famous windows, which were filled with animated displays. Everyone loved the parade and it generated tons of publicity, so Macy's announced the show would become an annual event. Because it was local, however, it was loved by New Yorkers, but not really noticed by the rest of the country . . . until TV.

From the 1920s to the 1950s, Macy's windows and the displays therein were as important as the parade and its balloons—but once the parade was televised, the windows became secondary. In 1959, the three major networks (CBS, NBC, and ABC) decided to cover the parade live, sponsored by Lionel Trains and the Ideal Toy Company. For us and the generation that followed, watching Macy's Thanksgiving Day Parade became part of the holiday tradition.

Out on the West Coast, also in the 1920s, another parade started in Hollywood, California. Local merchants and the Chamber of Commerce put up decorations and strung lights over Hollywood Boulevard, changing the street's name to Santa Claus Lane. It too was a big success, so starting in 1928, Hollywood went all out.

They christened the event the Santa Claus Lane Parade. A hundred fir trees were dug up and hauled from what is now a National Forest near Big Bear Lake in the San Bernardino Mountains. Once in Hollywood, safe in huge planters, the firs were decorated with strings of incandescent lights. These lined Santa Claus Lane, and the trees were later transplanted near the Hollywood Bowl, a natural amphitheater in the nearby hills.

During that 1928 Christmas season, Santa Claus and his reindeer rode down the street accompanied by Jeanette Loff—the first starlet in a long line of beauties and celebrities.

For a few years, Santa, the reindeer (real reindeer, mind you, tended all year by the County Parks Department), and a starlet strode up and down Santa Claus Lane nightly in December. In 1932 the procession became a one-time parade. Floats replaced the reindeer, the American Legion provided a drum and bugle corps, and huge, shiny metal trees lined the streets.

The Santa Claus Lane Parade went on hiatus during World War II, and those 16-foot tall metal trees were sacrificed to the war effort as scrap metal.

In 1946 the parade was back with Grand Marshal Gene Autry riding his horse Champion. All the children bobbed up and down in excitement when they saw him, so right after the parade, Autry was inspired to write the hit song "Here Comes Santa Claus." After all, what's the next line? "Right down Santa Claus Lane!"

In 1978, the procession changed its name to the Hollywood Christmas Parade. It was almost scrapped in 2007 due to low turnout, but under the new name Hollywood Santa Parade, it continues today.

In the 1940s, 1950s, and 1960s, parades were everywhere. Coastline and lakeside towns promoted boat parades, with sails decorated like trees and Santa in his sleigh—towed on a barge or waving from a crow's nest. Towns large and small put on religious parades with floats displaying nativity scenes, accompanied by shepherds leading donkeys and lambs down Main Street. Other cities had Toyland Parades with marching toy soldiers in the band or processions celebrating the holiday in all the countries of the world, with singing groups dressed in national costumes, clogging along the street in wooden shoes or lamé Aladdin-style slippers. Most parades called on the local high school to supply baton-twirling, flag-whirling teenagers dressed in short skirts, with skin-colored tights protecting them against the cold as they marched before the school band. Come on, you remember—maybe you were even in one!

The Nutcracker Ballet

Did you drag your kids—or grandkids—to see *The Nutcracker* last year? Most major cities and dance companies stage *The Nutcracker* ballet each Christmas, and though you might not associate the ballet with the post-war era, the show is absolutely a Boomer phenomenon.

How? Because although Russian composer Pyotir Ilyich Tchaikovsky wrote *The Nutcracker* ballet in the 1890s, it wasn't a hit for the first sixty years.

There's an urban legend that the composer hated the piece and that it flopped in Moscow, but that's not true. Tchaikovsky had trouble with the music but ended up proud of it, and the reviews were sort of mixed. One critic called it "a pantomime absurd in conception and execution, which could please only the most uncultured spectators," but another found it "astonishingly rich in inspiration."[9]

Tchaikovsky's *Nutcracker* used children in the cast, but that actually worked against it. Russians in the 1890s did not think in terms of entertaining children and saw little magic in the show. In fact, ballet soloists resented sharing the stage with kids.

In the early 20th century, Tchaikovsky's music—but not the whole show—enjoyed some popularity. Bits of *The Nutcracker* score were included in performances across Europe. Ballet legend Nijinsky danced to the Sugar Plum Fairy theme, and Anna Pavlova used the score as well

—but neither actually appeared in a production of *The Nutcracker*. They merely pulled out their favorite musical segments to use as background for their own dancing.

Disney's 1940 movie *Fantasia* used *The Nutcracker* music too. Remember the dancing mushrooms and fish, flowers, and fairies? For most Americans, that was our introduction to *The Nutcracker*. Touring companies brought the full ballet to North America in the 1940s . . . which brings us up to the Boomer Era. George Balanchine staged a new and Christmas-y *The Nutcracker* in 1954 in New York. When that production got raves, it could officially, finally be called a hit.

Who was this Balanchine? Born Georgi Melitonovitch Balanchivadze in Russia, Balanchine is considered one of the greatest dancers and choreographers of the 20th century. He fled the Soviet Union while in his 20s and eventually settled in the US, where he founded his own ballet school, the American Ballet Company, and later the New York City Ballet. *The Nutcracker* was his first full-length show for the New York City Ballet.

The Snowflake Waltz from the 1954 Nutcracker, performed by the NYC Ballet, the year of its untelevised debut.

Unlike earlier productions, Balanchine made children the stars of his ballet. He blended the old story with all the Christmas paraphernalia that Americans love: a tall, bright tree; reindeer;

rambunctious children in Victorian clothes, with ribbons, capes, and fur muffs; and lots of presents. The heartwarming spectacle of a big, happy, extended family in a warm, decorated home created just the right picture for Americans.

Balanchine's *Nutcracker* became an immediate holiday smash and was presented every Christmas season. In 1957, CBS aired a live performance. A year later, the TV special (again live) included narration by June Lockhart—Timmy's Mom on *Lassie*—who sat on a sofa with a big book, explaining the story to children.

Magazines like *Look* and *Life* featured pictures of New York's *Nutcracker* each year. The *Ed Sullivan Show* and other TV variety shows asked soloists to perform dances as the Christmas season got underway. The country caught on, touring companies formed, local ballets began making costumes and sets, and *The Nutcracker* became a part of our traditional holiday season.

White Christmas, the Movie

As previously mentioned in Chapter Three, "White Christmas" became a surprise hit after the wartime movie *Holiday Inn* opened with it. Although the black-and-white film featured more than a dozen tunes written by Irving Berlin, many with patriotic themes, "White Christmas" struck the exact chord that lonely servicemen and their families needed to hear.

A dozen years later, the song served to launch a bright, colorful musical filmed in VistaVision (for a crystal-clear appearance on wide screens), Technicolor, and Cinemascope. But believe it or not, the critics of 1954 were not crazy about the film. As often happens, that didn't matter much. Audiences loved it, and watching the movie became a holiday tradition in many homes.

Though neither *Holiday Inn* nor *White Christmas* has much of a plot, the myriad of musical numbers stitched together pushes all the right emotional buttons: patriotism and nostalgia for *Holiday Inn*, unabashed romance, fun, and spectacle for *White Christmas*.

In every way, *White Christmas* is big, and it seems rather sad that most people today know it only in a shrunk-down TV—or worse, iPhone—version.

Part Two

All Those Wonderful Toys

Toys—a big part of the best Christmas ever!

oys—dolls, balls, games and the like—have been around for millennia, but toys as Christmas gifts are a more recent tradition. A Christmas season full of toy displays, commercials, and media blitzes—well, that just didn't exist before the Boomer Era.

The way was paved for this explosion by a wartime phenomenon. Through magazine ads and other outlets, the US Post Office announced during World War II that if families wanted their beloved soldiers—who were serving thousands of miles away—to receive presents on Christmas, they'd better mail them early. How early?

In 1943, December 10th was the deadline. By 1944, it was December 1st. This urgency led stores to set up Christmas displays before the month of December even began. The idea was to encourage families to do their shopping and mailing early, but it actually moved the Christmas season back to around Thanksgiving.

After World War II, the American toy industry took off. Boomers were the first generation targeted by toy marketers, and these marketers never looked back. From around 1912 to the 1950s, the US population rose by about 45 percent—but consider that in 1912, toy sales accounted for $30 million a year, and by the 1950s, they topped $1.25 billion—an increase of about 4000%!

The first toy-making firm to regularly advertise on television—a fairly new medium—was the Mattel Company, which started as a garage business in 1945. These companies—and the dozens that joined them—advertised all year, of course, not just at Christmas, and Mattel kept getting bigger and bigger, proving that there were plenty of toy customers out there.

One reason for the increase in toy sales was a boom in population, accompanied by a rise in prosperity. Look at the fifties: men made the money, women made the dinner, and kids made believe—with Howdy Doody hand puppets when they weren't glued to the TV set.

We—or at least, our parents—were the perfect customers for eager marketers with enticing toy campaigns.

Chapter Five

Ye Olde Standbys

T hough many fabulous inventions in the toy world were born during the Boomer Era, some of our favorites were from bygone days. You'll undoubtedly remember some of the classic toys in this section; maybe you were prescient enough to hold onto them through the years. In that case, you may want to plan a visit to an *Antiques Roadshow* taping and learn just how much your collectible toy is worth.

 *Tinkertoys*

Do you remember the low, thumpy, echo-y sounds you could make when you emptied a Tinkertoys cylinder? If you were fortunate enough to own a set, betcha didn't know that they were invented by a man who cut tombstones for a living. Yes, you heard right.

Charles Pajeau saw some children playing with pencils and spools and got the idea for a building set—not standard blocks, but sticks, dowels, and spools. He toiled in a rented garage creating the set, but when he finally brought Tinkertoys to the market, they flopped.

Pajeau, however, was not out of ideas; what's more, he was not working alone. He'd met Robert Pettit on a commuter train—a businessman from Evanston who sat on the Chicago Board of Trade and soon became vice president of Pajeau's Toy Tinkers Company. The partners called their new toy The Thousand Wonder Builder.

Before Christmas of 1914, Toy Tinkers hired very short people to dress up like Santa's elves and assemble Tinkertoys in the windows of Grand Central Station and Marshall Field's in Chicago. That was it—the toy started selling at sixty cents a set, and that first year alone, it sold a million sets.

By the Boomer Era, over two million sets were selling every year. Up till that time, the toys were plain wood—except for red spools, added in 1932—but in 1953 red sticks were included. Kids liked them, so in 1955 Tinkertoys came with blue, green, and yellow sticks as well.

Playskool took over the company in 1985, and today the toys—same shape and idea—are made of plastic by the K'NEX company in the USA.

Tinkertoy container, 1950s.

Lincoln Logs

Another World War I-era toy, Lincoln Logs were invented by John L. Wright, the 24-year-old son of the famous architect Frank Lloyd Wright. The younger Wright went to Tokyo as the chief assistant to his father in 1916 for the building of the Imperial Palace Hotel. Frank Lloyd Wright used a lot of timber in the hotel, which became one of his most celebrated buildings—it survived an 8.3 earthquake in the 1920s, one of the few buildings in Tokyo left standing.

As Wright designed the most earthquake-resistant foundation for the Imperial Palace Hotel —one in which interlocking beams would float the building on top of alluvial mud flats—his son developed wooden Lincoln Logs using that same principle. When he returned home after being fired by Dad,[10] he began making and selling them under his own brand, Red Square Toy Company. He patented them in 1920.

In 1943, Playskool bought the company, and by most people's reckoning, John L. Wright sold it too soon: Lincoln Logs' most successful years were ahead. But since Wright's papers were destroyed in a fire and he himself died in 1980, no one knows what prompted him to sell—or for that matter, why he'd named his original business Red Square Toy Company.

Playskool began advertising the toy on television in 1953 on a show named *Pioneer Playhouse.* The tie-in to the Western craze—sparked by TV shows like *Davy Crockett, Hopalong Cassidy, The Lone Ranger,* and dozens of others—was perfect, as Lincoln logs could be used to construct forts, corrals, log cabins, wagons, or ranch buildings.

Lincoln Logs were sold to Milton Bradley in 1968, then Hasbro acquired them when they bought Milton Bradley in 1984. Hasbro currently licenses Pennsylvania-based K'NEX to manufacture Lincoln Logs.

 *Erector Sets*

They may seem modern, but metal Erector sets were invented before World War I by a most unlikely toymaker.

A. C. Gilbert taught himself magic tricks during his 19th century childhood and used that skill to earn money while studying medicine at Yale (the A.C. stood for Alfred Carlton—names he never used—just in case you're curious). Gilbert also set world records in the long jump, pole vault, and pull-ups, and won a gold medal in pole vaulting at the 1908 Olympics. Clearly, Gilbert was an all-American overachiever, but he was just getting started.

Although he earned his medical degree, Gilbert never practiced medicine. While still in college, he and a partner began selling magic equipment for amateur magicians. After college, the partners set up Mysto Manufacturing, making magic kits for professionals and beginners. The business did well, and it was during the many sales trips between his home in New Haven and his store in New York that Gilbert got the idea for the Erector Set.

"I looked out the window and saw steel girder after steel girder being erected to carry the power lines," Gilbert said. This was in 1911, and electricity was just coming to some areas. "I went right home and got some cardboard to cut out girders."

Gilbert knew that boys loved to build things—why not let them build with miniature girders? He had his factory fabricate them and add nuts and bolts to the set. The final stroke of genius that made it all hang together was a lip along the edge of each piece, enabling a builder to make a square girder with four pieces, attached by two bolts.

Even though his partner wasn't interested, Gilbert knew this was a great idea. His own enthusiasm inspired others, and his father loaned him $5,000 to start production of the Mysto Erector Structural Steel Builder.

Erector Sets were the first toy advertised in national magazines. Gilbert spent $12,000 in 1913 for ads in *American Boy, Good Housekeeping, Popular Mechanics, Saturday Evening Post, Cosmopolitan,* and other mostly forgotten magazines. The slogan? "Hello, boys! Make lots of toys!"

A. C. Gilbert, age 71, plays with a young friend.

Gilbert and his father bought out Mysto's other partners and renamed the firm the A. C. Gilbert Company in 1915. In two decades, 30 million Erector Sets were sold.

For awhile, A. C. Gilbert was known as "The Man Who Saved Christmas." Here's how that happened:

In 1917, America entered World War I. The military powers-that-be wanted to suspend toy sales during the holiday season—their idea was that patriotic Americans would use the money to buy war bonds (yes, the leaders of our nation really believed that). The US Council of National Defense, which included the Secretaries of the Navy, Interior, Commerce, and War, brought up the idea and were prepared to enforce it.

Gilbert and a few other representatives of US toymakers finagled a 15-minute appointment to address the US Council of National Defense at the end of a long day of debate. He brought at least forty toys, including the erector set, into the heavily guarded Navy Building in Washington DC for the meeting. As Gilbert talked about how important toys and Christmas were to American families, he set toys before each of the high-ranking men on the Council. Somehow, the men just couldn't keep their hands off. The meeting went on for an extra three hours—much of it spent on the floor, where the esteemed gentlemen played with their toys.

The idea of banning toy sales was dropped, the secretaries got to keep the toys, and the national media nicknamed Gilbert "The Man Who Saved Christmas."

Another bit of patriotic trivia: During the second World War, architects and engineers used Erector Sets to help them design portable bridges—bridges that became a reality, carried in 10-foot sections by Allied soldiers throughout Europe. Soldiers assembled the portable bridges to replace those that were destroyed while the Nazis held them.

Gilbert's company grew, adding chemistry sets, microscopes, and more to their catalog. But they continued to sell magic kits as well, right up to Gilbert's retirement in 1954. Ever the innovator, the A. C. Gilbert Company was one of the first to offer coffee breaks to employees.

Before World War II, Erector Sets came in wooden boxes. In the Boomer Era, though, most were packaged in a bright red metal case. The Amusement Park Set debuted in 1950, with instructions on building a merry-go-round.

After he died in 1961, Gilbert's heirs sold their interest in the company, and it went bankrupt six years later. A company named Gabriel Toys bought the brand and continued to market Erector Sets into the 1980s. Today, Meccano—a company whose history is even older than A. C. Gilbert's, though they went through ownership changes, liquidations, and restarts too—makes the sets. They're marketed under the Meccano name all over the world, but in the United States they're still sold as Erector Sets.

Radio Flyer

The company that eventually became Radio Flyer was started by Antonio Pasin, one of the thousands of immigrants who passed through Ellis Island before the first World War. Only a teenager then, Pasin—born in Italy and trained by his father to make cabinets—settled in the Chicago area and quickly found work.

By his twenties, he started his first business: Liberty Coaster Wagon Company. He and his employees made wooden wagons, scooters, and tricycles, switching to stamped steel by 1927 to keep up with the demand. Even the best carvers, working with the best tools, could not turn out as many wooden wagons as machines and steel could. Pasin loved the new technology, and he called his new steel wagon the Radio Flyer.

The author with her 1955 Rex Wagon, made by Radio Flyer.

Even through the Depression, Pasin's company produced 1,500 wagons a day. He rechristened the firm Radio Steel and Manufacturing, and his suppliers called him "Little Ford" because of the way he mimicked Henry Ford's assembly line success.

During World War II, production changed to service the war effort. Radio Steel (the corporate name didn't change to Radio Flyer until 1987) made Blitz Cans for Uncle Sam. Blitz Cans, developed by Germany in the 1930s, were rectangular steel containers that held five gallons of fuel or other liquids. They could be stacked on planes for transport overseas, then mounted on jeeps or tanks to move around. After the war, the company was right back on track, turning out wagons for all the Boomer toddlers.

The classic Radio Flyer wagon #18, in production for over 80 years now, was the top-selling model—and still is today. In 1955, though, the company came out with some new models (as they'd done in other decades):

- The "Rex" line of wagons, a lower-cost version of the Radio Flyer wagon. The Rex 100 was maroon and had ball bearing wheels; the Rex 90 was red with semi-pneumatic wheels. The Rex 80—also red—was about ten inches shorter than the others.
- Television tie-ins that included a yellow Davy Crockett model and a bright blue Mickey Mouse Club version of the coaster wagon.
- The Radio Rancher Convertible, with removable sides.

Through the decades since, the company has come out with new products like bikes and cars for kiddies, and they've ventured into plastic, but the mainstay has always been the shiny red wagon. And guess what? No one's bought Radio Flyer, the company. Today's corporation is run by Antonio Pasin's grandson, Robert, who took over the reins from his dad as Chief Wagon Officer in 1996.

 ## Toy Trains

For many Boomers, Christmas meant unpacking, cleaning, and assembling an elaborate train set and all its accessories. This could be a father-son bonding ritual—or rivalry—depending on how attached your dad was to the toys.

And while toy trains have a rich history that has been documented in books, magazines, and on the web, we'll focus our attention on two companies: Lionel and American Flyer.

Lionel Trains

Inventor Joshua Lionel Cowen started making electrical gizmos (he called them novelties) and founded his Lionel Manufacturing Company with the new century in 1900. His first train piece was the Electric Express, a wooden gondola car with a miniature electric motor hidden beneath the floor.

Cowen meant for that little car, which ran on a brass track set, to carry other toys around a store's window display, attracting attention. After all, in 1900—before TV or even radio commercials—that was the purpose of big display windows in shops: to attract the attention of people walking by.

It worked. People stopped, stunned and riveted by the sight of a tiny train car moving around by itself. Even in exciting New York City, few had ever seen anything like it. The idea of using the car to promote other toys or merchandise backfired, however. No one cared about the cargo—they all wanted to buy the little moving train and track! So the Lionel Manufacturing Company began making toy trains.

And the rest is history.

Robert Von Gerichten still puts up his 1950s train set in his Orange, California, home.

A subtle puff of smoke comes from the uppermost engine.
From the collection of Joe Schneid of Louisville, KY.

The firm grew through good times and bad. During both World Wars, Lionel abandoned its toy trains and assembled small equipment for the armed forces, such as compasses and fuze setters for bombs.

The year after the war—1946—Lionel bought 16 pages of ad space in *Liberty Magazine* and showcased their entire Christmas catalog. *Liberty* even put trains on the cover. The magazine's sales went up, but the real winner was Lionel, who kicked off their best decade ever with those ads.

Over the next few years, the lineup of new toys included trains with Magne-Traction, remote-controlled couplers, engines that belched smoke when a pellet was dropped into the smokestack, the top-selling F3 diesel locomotive, animated switch towers, water towers, coal loaders, sawmills, and even milk cars from which a tiny plastic milkman automatically delivered cans of milk onto station platforms.

In 1950, Joe DiMaggio hosted a Saturday TV show for NBC called *The Lionel Clubhouse*. Before the end of the fifties, Lionel introduced a rocket-launching train car and missile-launching platforms, as well as the "Lady Lionel"—a feminine train set with a pink engine, lilac hopper, yellow box cars, and a light blue caboose. The Lady Lionel line bombed, but it's now so rare that collectors covet the pastel trains and pay big bucks for them.

Ever been in a restaurant where toy trains ran on tracks, either overhead or near the counters—sometimes even carrying food? That was another post-war Lionel gimmick, and everyone loved it.

In their best year—1953—Lionel sales were nearly $33 million, but by the end of the 1950s that figure had fallen by more than half.

Joshua Lionel Cowen retired in 1958; a year later, the aging founder sold his stock in the company to a nephew, surprising many. After all, Cowen's own son Lawrence—whose boyhood picture had been on Lionel boxes and who had worked beside his father for decades at the company—was supposed to be in charge. He had inherited the company the year before when his father retired. Why the stock transfer to someone else? No one knows.

Whatever the reason for the sale, it hurt the company deeply.

Lionel bought out its competitor American Flyer in the 1960s, but both product lines continued on a downhill grade. Naming rights were sold to a General Mills subsidiary called Fundimensions, who then made Lionel trains and revived many classic models. The company's fortunes, however, went up and down. In 1981 and again in 1994, Lionel filed for bankruptcy protection and reorganized itself. There were multiple owners, including songwriter and musician Neil Young.

Lionel trains are still produced by Lionel LLC, a corporation based in Michigan. Although they consider themselves the real deal and are proud of Lionel's history, to most collectors the Lionel company ended back in 1958 when the original owner retired.

American Flyer

A. C. Gilbert—the entrepreneur extraordinaire who invented Erector Sets—bought the American Flyer Trains company in 1938. The previous owner, W. O. Coleman Jr., had made tinplate trains like many other companies, not worrying about scale or accuracy. Gilbert wanted true, die-cast replicas to run on his tracks, so he changed American Flyer drastically. He even used railroad blueprints as the guides for his new die-cast molds, making trains of 1/64th scale.

Production was halted during World War II when Gilbert's companies switched to crafting military items: flares, mines, electric motors for trim tabs on fight planes, and range indicators for anti-aircraft guns.

After the war (our time!) American Flyer Trains introduced their new S-gauge track with faster, tighter curves. American Flyer's accurately scaled loco-motives could hit those sharp turns, outpacing all

The American Flyer trains pass above the Plasticville Jail, livestock, and the water tower.

other brands of trains. Still, the company nabbed only a third of the toy train market, and Lionel trains took the lion's share.

In fact, after toy trains peaked in the 1950s—and after the death of A. C. Gilbert—Lionel took even more: they bought American Flyer lock, stock, and S-gauge in 1967. The American Flyer name disappeared, and Lionel, while still in business, suffered the slings and arrows of bankruptcies, ownership changes, and declining consumer interest over the decades.

Raggedy Ann and Andy

Enough about gears and trains and boy stuff . . .

How did one of the oldest dolls we know come to be? Several versions of the story exist. Perhaps artist and comic-strip illustrator Johnny Gruelle found an old rag doll in the attic of his parent's home, kept it, and years later designed stories around it; or maybe, as the more popular tale goes, it was Johnny's daughter Marcella who found the doll in the attic. She took it to her Papa, who broke away from his work to lovingly draw a face on the tattered, faded rag doll.

Homemade dolls by Georgia Hill, circa 1950.

In any event, Gruelle received a design patent on the rag doll in 1915, three years before he actually published his *Raggedy Ann Stories.* The success of the book was bittersweet, however, because for the previous three years, Gruelle had been mourning the loss of little Marcella. At barely thirteen, she had died after receiving a questionable vaccine at her school. Her favorite toy, that rag doll, remained in Gruelle's study for years after her death.

Before Christmas in 1918, publisher P. F. Volland released both the book and a line of handmade Raggedy Ann dolls. The first prototypes of the doll were made by the Gruelle family, and Marcella's brother claimed that they did indeed sew candy hearts into each doll. The few early Volland dolls—based on those prototypes—are rare, but the Gruelle family's handcrafted dolls are priceless.

Raggedy Andy came along in 1920, and Gruelle created the comic strip, as well as the books, that chronicled their adventures. A fierce court battle over rights to the doll erupted during the Depression when another company challenged Gruelle, making their own Raggedy Ann dolls. The battle dragged on till 1938.

Though he eventually won in court, Gruelle's health was ruined. After his death in 1938, his family signed new licensing agreements, published the last of Johnny Gruelle's books (his son Worth continued to illustrate more stories) and sold film rights for the first Raggedy Ann and Andy cartoons. Myrtle Gruelle, Johnny's widow, ran the wholesome empire until 1960. Then, after consulting with family, she transferred the licenses and rights to Raggedy Ann to the Bobbs-Merrill Company.

Believe it or not, Raggedy Ann is the oldest continuously licensed toy character. Up to eight companies have made Raggedy Ann dolls over the decades, including Georgene Novelties and Knickerbocker Toys in the Boomer Era. McCall's began printing patterns for handmade Raggedy Ann dolls in 1940, and doting grandmothers and aunts have made thousands of them since.

Madame Alexander Dolls and Cissy

The daughter of Russian immigrants, Beatrice Alexander grew up in Brooklyn over her father's shop—a doll hospital—and founded her Alexander Doll Company in the Roaring 20s. With her husband Phillip Behrman, she guided her company through the Depression and war years, making dolls of the Dionne Quintuplets and movie stars like Shirley Temple and Margaret O'Brien. And, of course, there were always baby dolls.

Madame Alexander was the first to license and create dolls based on movie and literary characters, like *Alice in Wonderland* and *Gone with the Wind.* She invented the sleep eyes that close when the dolls are laid down for naps, and she was the first to make dolls of hard plastic. What's more, four years before Barbie was born, she was the first to introduce a full-figured fashion doll who wore tailored designer clothes: Cissy.

Madame Alexander dolls were a bit pricey, but if you got one in 1950, chances are it was Nina Ballerina or the 14-inch-tall Cinderella (either in rags or a ball gown). Cinderella actually had the same face as Margaret, from the Little Women collection.

Two mint condition Madame Alexander dolls from the 1950s, one with eyes open and one with them shut, from the collection of Lucille Hays.

There were also baby dolls (which drank and wet after 1954), as well as dolls portraying Queen Elizabeth, Mary Martin, and Sonja Henie (who all looked like toddlers, not adults), and beautifully costumed Portrait dolls (worth a mint if you hung onto them). But the biggest hit was the 20-inch Cissy doll.

Cissy had arched feet for her high heels, and some of her shoes even had ankle straps. Her shapely legs, waist, and bust were at odds with her rather pouty and childlike face, which often hid behind the net veil of her fashionable hats. Cissy wore clothes of satin, taffeta, tulle, and other fine fabrics, sometimes trimmed in lace or with rhinestone buttons. Besides the hats, Cissy had tiaras, gloves, costume jewelry, belts, you name it. Prices for the doll started around $18. Today? Hundreds and hundreds.

Madame Alexander lived into her 95th year, passing away in 1990, but her company still prospers. The latest offerings? How about Glinda and Elphaba from *Wicked,* or a leggy Rockette?

 *Betsy Wetsy*

This incontinent little darling actually came out during the Depression. B. F. Michtom, son of Ideal's founders, noticed how jealous the three-year-old child of friends became when the friends brought home a new baby. As a result, he came up with the idea of a doll that needed to be fed and changed like an infant.

By 1954 Betsy was a big seller. She drank from a bottle, cried real tears, and wet herself. Betsy came in different sizes, between 12 to 22 inches long, and could be bought for under $5. A layette—or baby wardrobe—was also available.

And for the poor girls named Betsy who grew up during the era? Let's be honest: they likely never escaped being called the funniest doll name ever.

 *Nancy Ann*

A Depression-era company that hit its stride during the early Boomer years, Nancy Ann dolls were named for their creator, Nancy Ann Abbott—although she had been born Rowena Haskins. She came south—from Northern California to Hollywood—to work in the movies, and may have gotten some bit parts. Mostly, though, she designed and made clothes for other actresses. Eventually, she moved to the San Francisco area.

During the Depression, she started her doll company with $125—which was actually quite a lot for a home business back then—and worked over 16 hours a day to make it prosper. In 1937, she took on a business partner, Les Rowland, who handled the promotion and finances of Nancy Ann Dressed Dolls.

For the first years, Abbott used small doll figures from Japan—less than four inches tall—

Nancy Ann's Orange Blossom Bride doll, with a muslin crinoline slip under the dress and an elaborate net veil.

that she called Hush-A-Bye Baby dolls. She later switched to a five-inch doll, opening her own factory in California to create the bisque figures for her Storybook line. There, artists painted the faces of dolls named after nursery rhyme and fairy tale characters.

Through the war years, demand was high. Nancy Ann dolls were shipped to Hawaii and to Naval hospitals where servicemen bought them to send home to their families or sweethearts. Nancy Ann became a million-dollar-a-year business, and after the war produced more dolls each year than any other company.

There were up to 125 Nancy Ann Storybook Doll characters during the early years of the war, but that number was cut in half by wartime shortages of materials. In 1948, the dolls became plastic. In the 1950s, some had "sleeping" eyes, and larger lines were introduced: the eight-inch Muffie, and the eighteen-inch Style Show dolls.

Nancy Ann produced princesses, around-the-world figures, days-of-the-week and months-of-the-year dolls, characters based on songs and operettas, and even sports dolls. Many survived in mint condition because they were made for show, not play. Today they are all highly collectible, but identifying them is complicated and a task for experts.

The company slowed down as the two partners' health failed. Nancy Ann Abbott died in 1964, and Nancy Ann Storybook Dolls declared bankruptcy in 1965. It was sold to Albert Bourla and his stockholders, who made plastic dolls for a while, then the company liquidated its inventory.

Thirty years later—1998—Bourla successfully brought Storybook Dolls back as a limited-edition collectible. Buyers were assured that no more than 7,500 of each type of doll costume would be made, and they had to purchase two dolls at a time. Those buyers got a discount if they signed up to buy the entire collection. The venture was successful enough that Bourla was able to sell his company to two sisters, Claudette Buehler and Delene Budd, who had collected Nancy Ann Storybook Dolls for years.

With top designers on board, the new Nancy Ann Storybook Dolls, made of porcelain and slightly larger than the originals at six-and-a-quarter inches, are available from www.nancyannstorybookdolls.com.

 *Crayola*

The first crayolas were sold in 1903, at a nickel for a box of eight. Here's the backstory:

Edwin Binney's dad owned a charcoal-making company in the Civil War days. C. Harold Smith was a cousin to Edwin. Papa Binney brought both young men into his Peekskill Chemical Company in the 1880s and retired, so the boys began expanding the product line with things like black coloring for lamp oil.

They also came up with dustless chalk, combining the black coloring with wax. *That* product was not for sale initially—they made it to mark up their own inventory easily, eliminating dust and smears in the warehouse. But dustless chalk was the foundation for Crayola crayons.

Salesmen from Binney & Smith—the company took on the new name in 1900—noticed a need for cheap coloring chalks or crayons in schools, and the firm responded, mixing their dustless chalk with new colors. Alice Binney thought up the name Crayola, combining the French word for chalk (craie) and adding "ola" from oleaginous. (Clearly, she'd been spending a lot of time around chemists.)

You could never accuse Binney & Smith of overexposing their crayons—forty-five years went by before they packed Crayolas in a big box of 48 colors, stacking the rows in stadium-style seating. Not until 1958 did the now-standard 64-color packs get introduced, with a sharpener in the back of the box.

Remember when there was a flesh crayon? As of 1962, it became peach. Why? The name change was preemptive, prompted by the Civil Rights movement and growing aware-ness that calling *one* color "flesh" was short-sighted and ignorant at best. This was not the first time Crayola changed a color to be what we today call "politically correct"—the first time was four years earlier, when the company dropped the name Prussian Blue after only nine years of use. Prussia was an area of Germany then behind the Iron Curtain, and teachers, concerned that calling a color Prussian sent the wrong message to students, wrote and requested the change. Later came fluorescent colors in 1972, but other changes were slow in coming until the 1990s.

Binney & Smith became a publicly traded company in 1961. They bought Silly Putty in 1977 and were themselves bought in 1984 by Hallmark, who is still their corporate overlord—a nice, ecologically responsible corporate overlord. Today, Crayola's corporate headquarters in Forks Township, PA, runs on the electricity produced by 30,000 solar panels of the Crayola Solar Farm, and they turn out millions of crayons per day.

It wasn't until 2007 that Binney & Smith officially changed its name to Crayola (you don't want to rush these things). Well over a hundred billion Crayola Crayons have been sold. And if you have children or ever wandered into a toy store, you know that Crayola has expanded into pencils, markers, and elaborate themed art and activity sets over the last couple of decades. And in the new century, the Toy of the Year (per *Child* magazine) was the Crayola Crayon Maker —a little device that takes broken, worn bits of crayons, melts them down, and produces new ones.

Hmph. (Can you see my arms crossed?) How many of you had to make do with a cookie tin or plastic container of old, paperless crayons that were barely big enough to hold? Kids today have it soooo good.

 *Monopoly*

According to popular myth, Monopoly was invented during the Great Depression. Jobless Charles Darrow drew on his memories of an Atlantic City holiday to sketch out a board game on a piece of linoleum. Friends liked it, so he approached Parker Brothers. Would they be interested in a real estate game that took hours to play? Actually, no. Parker Brothers didn't think anyone would want to sit and play such a game all afternoon.

So Darrow cut a pay-as-you-go deal with a printer and sold hundreds of games on his own. Yep, you guessed it: Parker Brothers changed their mind. Today, sales of Monopoly total in the hundreds of millions . . . but despite this happy, capitalistic ending, Monopoly's history is a lot more complicated.

All this happened long before the Boomer Era, so you can skip the next few paragraphs if you want—but it's an interesting story, so why not stick around?

First, Darrow did not invent the game, though he did stumble across it during the Depression. *Who, then, is the inventor*, you ask?

Lizzie Magie, a clever woman from Illinois, patented her own board game in 1904: The Landlord's Game, which gained its biggest following in Eastern college towns. Just like Monopoly, players threw dice to move around a square board, where most squares bore the name of a property that could be bought—or that could cost them rent. There were "Chance" spaces, a "Luxury" tax spot, four railroads, two utilities, and a jail—and when you passed the starting square, you collected wages.

In the 1920s, Magie—who had married and was now Elizabeth Magie Phillips—took the game to Parker Brothers herself but was turned down; The Landlord's Game was fun, but it was also critical of tax laws that allowed landlords to amass unearned wealth just because their land increased in value. It was a game that mocked greed rather than celebrated it.

Many versions of the game, old and new, circulated up and down the Midwest and the East, with people making up their own variations on the rules. A group of Quakers in New Jersey played a typical version—setting fixed values on the board's properties, which they named after places in Atlantic City—and they played the game often.

Darrow—the man credited with creating Monopoly—had a small family to support during the Depression, and he'd been unemployed for three years. He was handy, good at repairing almost anything, and owned a jigsaw. He used this tool to make jigsaw puzzles, until the day a fellow showed him the Atlantic City version of The Landlord's Game. Darrow tweaked it into the game we know today, copyrighting his version.

At first, Darrow spent about a dollar and a full day to make a game set, using his jigsaw to craft hotels and houses. His first game board was round, and he used stencils for the railroad spaces and such, selling each game for two dollars. After he farmed out certain tasks, he got production up to six games a day.

When both Parker Brothers and Milton Bradley declined to buy the game from him, Darrow borrowed money to have thousands of game boards, cards, and tokens made up, and got the game into Philadelphia stores like Wanamakers and Gimbels. Success caught Parker Brothers' attention, and in 1935, *they* came to *him*.

By some accounts, Monopoly saved Parker Brothers—a 19th century company—from going belly up as so many other firms did during the Depression. It certainly made Darrow a millionaire. As for Lizzie Magie Phillips, who was approaching her seventies by then, Parker Brothers wanted no trouble. They bought out her latest patent in return for a small sum of cash and a deal to produce three other games she designed (none of the three was successful).

And that's that. The game we played on long afternoons in the '40s, '50s, and '60s was the same—there weren't many developments other than minor design changes to the box.

 *View-Master*

They may seem iconically post-World War II, but View-Masters were introduced a decade earlier—at the New York World's Fair—all because of a lucky meeting at The Lodge at Oregon Caves.

Piano tuner William Gruber, recently married and—as always—struggling to make a living, was on his way to tune a piano. His hobby was photography, and he was especially fascinated by 3D photography. Since he was passing Oregon Caves National Monument in the Siskiyou Mountains, he made a detour, determined to get some stereoscopic images. He had a custom setup—he'd strapped two Kodak cameras together to take pictures.

Also at Oregon Caves that day was Harold Graves, the president of Sawyer's Photographic Services, a Portland firm that made picture postcards. Graves came to take pictures of the deer, and when he saw Gruber's strange camera set-up, he approached him with questions. Gruber explained his novel idea that the twin photos, taken with 16-millimeter film, could be printed as transparencies and mounted on a reel, then viewed together so that the pictures showed depth. That's exactly the principle used in the View-Master—which didn't yet exist outside of Gruber's head.

Graves brought Gruber into his company and the two went to work. Within months they had a product to display at the 1939 World's Fair in New York—a viewer with a hinged bottom that opened like a compact for the reel. The reels didn't look that much different from those produced later in the 1950s and beyond: two cardboard circles with the small transparent pictures sandwiched between them—all assembled by hand. The distance between pictures was based on the distance between our own two eyes.

A Model-G View-Master from the early 1960s, with three sets of
Christmas pictures—including one of a very Bambi-esque Rudolph!

These early View-Masters were not marketed as toys, however; they were for adults. The cardboard reels contained seven pairs of stereographic Kodachrome pictures, showing forests and pretty scenery.

The viewers were made of Tenite plastic till 1944—then Bakelite through 1966—but a plastic model was turned out in 1959 as well, and that's the one that became most popular. Much later, a View-Master shaped like Mickey Mouse introduced a new line of character View-Masters, and soon there were Power Rangers and Tweety Bird models.

What we Boomers remember about View-Masters are the brilliant pictures of Disney characters and, from the late 1950s, Disney TV shows and Disneyland itself. Disney had licensed the True-Vue Company to market its pictures, but View-Master bought out that rival and took over the license in 1951.

The company hired artists to make clay models of the characters for the children's pictures —and even for the Disney photos. These clay models were posed in small, carefully arranged settings. So in addition to their reels of pictures of circuses, Hawaii, Egypt, TV cowboys, and fairy tales—we could see, for about $2 for six reels—Mickey and Minnie and all their friends.

Sawyer's Inc. made View-Masters until 1966 when the company was acquired by GAF (General Aniline & Film Corp.) Over the decades it's owned or been owned by Ideal, Tyco, and finally Mattel—which consigned View-Master to its Fisher-Price line and moved production to Mexico, where the toy and picture reels are still stamped out.

Over a billion and a half reels have been sold; if you think you remember seeing Mr. Spock, Abraham Lincoln, Roy Rogers, or Lucille Ball through a View-Master, you're probably right.

 # Wrist Watches

OK, so watches are nothing particularly new. And the first Mickey Mouse watch came out in 1933, so they were old hat by the 1950s. But the fun part was that all the popular comic characters had their own. Although production died out during the war—since novelty watches were deemed nonessential items—those wristwatches came back with a vengeance in the Boomer Era.

Getting a wristwatch as a Christmas present was almost a rite of passage for Boomers. You were nearly grown up; your parents thought of you as mature. Hopalong Cassidy, Roy Rogers, Tom Corbett, Space Cadet, and Mickey himself were prized by boys from the early 1950s; Roy Rogers, King of the Cowboys, was featured with his horse, Trigger, as early as 1951. Girls got Cinderella—sold in a glass slipper—or Snow White, Dale Evans, or Minnie Mouse.

If only we still had some of those watches today . . . still in their cases, in pristine condition, imagine what they would be worth. But if we still had the watches in their cases, we never would have enjoyed wearing them, winding them, and playing with them, would we?

Chapter Six

The Small Stuff

Aside from the occasional orange or walnut nestled in the toe, here are some of the all-time classics found in Christmas stockings.

Silly Putty

Where did this weird goo come from? Wartime research. Silly Putty was invented in 1943 when General Electric investigated ways to make synthetic rubber using silicone. And just why did they need synthetic rubber?

Since the beginning of World War II, Japan controlled most rubber-producing countries, and rubber was needed for things like tires, gaskets, and boots.

Nutty putty, as the GE engineers called this new combination of silicone oil and boric acid, did *not* work as synthetic hard rubber; it was merely an interesting byproduct of the research. In fact, the scientist in charge, chemical engineer James Wright, threw the blob on the floor in frustration. When it shot right back up at him, he said, "Golly, look at it bounce!"

(At least, that's what the *Saturday Evening Post* reported. Remember that publication?)

For six years, nutty putty balls circulated at labs and offices all over the world. Wright patented the stuff as Bouncing Putty, and GE sent samples to top scientists and inventors, but no one could find a use for the goo—that is, until an engineer from GE brought it to a party. That probably happened a lot; nutty putty had become somewhat of a company joke (Bouncing Putty even had a nickname: Gupp). But toy store owner Ruth Fallgatter happened to be at *this* party and she was intrigued. She showed it to ad man Peter Hodgson, who was producing a toy catalog for her store.

Hodgson wrote up Bouncing Putty as a grown-up toy and it sold quite well. But Wright—the inventor—wasn't interested in manufacturing the stuff and neither was Ruth Fallgatter, so Peter Hodgson signed an agreement with GE. He bought $147 worth of Gupp, thought up the Silly Putty name, and procured surplus egg-shipping cartons on the cheap from a poultry association. It was just before Easter, so he packaged Silly Putty in plastic eggs.

The result? Yawns.

Well, not entirely: Doubleday Bookstores ordered a few Silly Putty eggs, and they sold well in New York City as a novelty item. But the toy didn't take off until a writer for *The New Yorker* bought one, loved it, and wrote it up in his magazine. Three days after the magazine hit the streets, Hodgson had orders for a quarter million Silly Putty eggs.

Success! Well, not quite.

The Korean War reared its ugly head, and Hodgson could not get the silicone product that *was* Silly Putty. He nearly went out of business, but thankfully, the war was brief. Within a year, Hodgson—whose personal finances were probably giving him ulcers—was shipping tons of Silly Putty . . . to adults.

That's right—all through this stage, no one realized that children liked Silly Putty. Hodgson's marketing was aimed at grown-ups until the mid-1950s, when he wised up.

Margaret Paradise, an associate in The Block Shop, looks over special
displays for Easter, Christmas, and Valentine's Day.

*Margaret Paradise of The Block Shop with Silly Putty
displays for different holidays.*

By 1957, the one-dollar toy appeared in commercials on the *Howdy Doody Show* and *Captain Kangaroo*. That proved so successful that Hodgson changed the packaging, presenting the egg in a rectangular cardboard frame that looked like a television console.

Peter Hodgson kept his company focused; he made nothing but Silly Putty until he died in 1976, leaving a $140 million fortune. A year later, Peter Hodgson Jr., who had worked beside his father for years, sold Silly Putty to Binney & Smith, now Crayola LLC. They've produced it ever since.

Fun fact: NASA packed Silly Putty on Apollo 8 because it retained its stickiness, even in zero gravity. The astronauts used it to hold their tools in place.

Silly Putty hasn't changed much in sixty years, but here are three ways 21st-century Silly Putty differs from the original:

- Early Boomers might remember how sticky it was—their parents sure do. Left on the sofa or carpet, Silly Putty was nearly impossible to remove. In 1960, the formula was changed and a non-sticky Silly Putty has been sold ever since.

- Newsprint no longer clings to it because newsprint isn't made from petroleum products, so Silly Putty doesn't lift images from the comics as easily as it used to.

- Starting in the 1990s, Silly Putty has been offered in different colors, even glow-in-the-dark shades.

 *Slinky*

In 1943, civilian engineer Richard James worked in Cramp's Shipyard of Philadelphia. He boarded new US Navy battleships and went on trial cruises, monitoring the performance of delicate marine torsion meters. The vibrations caused by heavy seas and wartime gunfire interfered with these meters. Other engineers had come up with the idea of suspending them from coil springs, and James experimented with different types and sizes of springs, hoping to find a way to set the instruments so they'd work no matter how bad the weather.

One day he knocked a spring off the shelf. The spring "walked" end over end from its shelf onto a pile of books and then to the floor. James was intrigued and took it home to his wife and toddler, Tommy, who sent the spring down the stairs . . . over and over again.

It didn't take much for James to realize that it made a nifty toy, so over the next year or so, he experimented and made the toy on a machine that coiled 78 feet of flattened wire into 98 coils. Wife Betty, who helped wrap and package the springs, saw marketing potential and thumbed through a dictionary to come up with the name Slinky.

James had faith in the toy, enough that he quit the air-conditioning repair job he got in the summer of '45 and borrowed some money to have 400 Slinkys made. The Jameses also got a patent on their new toy. But how to show what it could do? Nothing like the Slinky had ever been marketed before, and folks really had to see it in action to realize how much fun it could be.

In late November James got a chance to demo the toy at the Philadelphia Gimbels. A crowd grew as James put a Slinky at the top of a slanted board and let it go. The shoppers loved it! Within minutes, customers stood six deep to buy the 100 Slinkys stacked behind the counter. James called his wife and asked her to bring the rest of his stock—some boxed, some not. Within 90 minutes of the demo, Gimbels sold 400 Slinkys.

Mr. and Mrs. James borrowed more money, went into production, and sold 22,000 Slinkys by Christmas. After that, they had no problem getting the financing to open their own factory, followed by another. Magazines like *Readers Digest* printed articles—not ads, but articles—about the toy, and James Industries sold 100 million Slinkys in its first ten years.

James initially wanted to add color, but in 1945 that proved impossible. The first Slinkys were blue-black, the color of the high-grade Swedish steel he bought. He switched to American-made steel within a year, and for a brief time in the late 1940s, James got his wish—Slinkys were advertised as coming in red, blue, or green.

The company continued to grow, and Richard James changed. His many girlfriends initially strained the marriage, but after his wild phase he found religion and strained the marriage in a different way. Instead of going out partying, he went out evangelizing and witnessing, telling crowds of potential converts what a rat he had been. Betty sat in the audience at some of those meetings, cringing with embarrassment at his confessions.

A reproduction of the 1945 Slinky box, for sale on Amazon.com.

Richard stopped advertising the Slinky, apparently because ads were worldly and sinful. Things came to a head when he decided to include religious tracts with the toy. Horrified, companies and sales reps threatened to cancel their orders. Betty told the factory not to pack the tracts, and when Richard told them to start again, Betty said: "Stop!"

At that point, Richard decided he no longer cared.

In 1959, after having given much of their money away, Richard followed his religious calling to Bolivia and left Betty to either run James Industries or shut it down. He stayed in South America and died there in 1974.[11]

Betty—who had learned her business skills by working alongside her husband for a dozen or so years—brought James Industries back from the brink of bankruptcy.

How bad were things at their lowest? The company once had 125 employees; now there were four. The lack of advertising had wreaked havoc on sales, and Betty would need to throw herself into the company to save it—but she had six children to raise. The youngest was only two when James left.

She moved her family to Hollidaysburg, PA, where she had family to help watch the kids. For a year she lived with them Thursday through Sunday; the rest of the week, Betty was at the factory, over five hours away. As soon as she could, she relocated the business, sold the old factory, and started paying off long past due bills.

Advertising resumed, and inventory and sales rose. Shortly after, in 1962, the song we all remember came along:

> *What walks downstairs, alone or in pairs,*
> *And makes a slinkety sound?*
> *A spring, a spring, a marvelous thing!*
> *Everyone knows it's Slinky.*
> *It's Slinky! It's Slinky!*
> *For fun it's a wonderful toy.*
> *It's Slinky! It's Slinky!*
> *It's fun for a girl and a boy.*

Those lyrics were written by Homer Fesperman and Charles Weagley and is today the longest-running jingle in advertising history.

The Slinky's original price was a dollar. Betty James fought to keep the price low through the 1990s, noting that with 16 grandchildren, she appreciated that a family could go into debt buying expensive toys. Twenty-some years later (today), Slinkys cost between $5 and $7.

Betty remained CEO until 1998 when, after discussing the move with her children (one son, Tom, was VP and Sales Manager), she sold James Industries to Poof Products. That business is now Poof-Slinky. One of the conditions of the sale was that the expanded Slinky plant and headquarters would remain in Hollidaysburg.

From the beginning, college and high school professors saw the learning potential in Slinkys and used them to illustrate wavelengths and movements, sound transmission, and other concepts to students. During the Vietnam War, radio operators tossed Slinkys over tall branches to serve as antennas for their equipment.

Over 300 million Slinkys have been sold—including a few to NASA, who took them up on the Space Shuttle for some zero-gravity experimentation. And the United States Post Office issued a stamp commemorating the Slinky in 1999—how many toys can say that?

Today, a gold-plated Slinky in a polished wood case makes a fine executive gift.

So here's to the Slinky—no assembly or batteries required, and the only modification to the original design has been to crimp the wire ends for safety. Of course, today you can buy them in light-up neon colors or even gold-plated—but you can also get the original.

The Slinky Dog

The Slinky pooch debuted in 1952 and has enjoyed renewed popularity thanks to a featured role in Pixar's *Toy Story* franchise.

The pull-toy Slinky Dog was actually designed by a lady named Helen Malsed. She created the Slinky Train too, but she never worked for James Industries. She simply liked to design toys, and she sent Betty James a couple of drawings with a letter.

Mrs. Malsed never visited the factory—she lived in Seattle—but she collected $60,000-$70,000 dollars a year for her Slinky designs and other toys that she thought up. Not bad, huh?

And in 1995, Betty James and all sixteen of her grandchildren went to the movies together—to see *Toy Story*.

Matchbox and Hot Wheels

Matchbox is a genuine Boomer company from across the pond.

Two old friends, both British World War II veterans, started a die-cast company—die-casting being a way of making small parts by pouring liquid metal into a mold, or die. The fellows combined their two first names, **Les**lie and Rod**ney**, and called their company Lesney. The last name of both men was Smith, but they weren't related.

The men pooled their military pay to rent a bombed-out pub in London where they turned out small parts for industrial use. They brought in another partner, Jack Odell, who owned die-casting machines but needed a place to put them (such machines weren't allowed in residential neighborhoods). Odell not only brought in larger orders from companies like General Electric, but he developed improvements in the die-cast method that gave Lesney an edge over other die-cast companies.

A first-issue Models of Yesteryear Matchbox toy.

They began making toys to get them through the slowest part of the year: mid-winter. Their first toys were larger than matchbox size, but those never came out in big numbers because of a shortage of a major ingredient—zinc—caused by the Korean Conflict. Lesney switched to tin, and the toys were popular enough that the company made them for a year or so. About that time, Rodney Smith—the "ney" in Lesney—bowed out.

By 1953, zinc was plentiful. That was also the year that young Elizabeth was crowned queen, so Lesney created a 15-inch long replica of the new queen's coronation coach and horses. The toy sold well, but the lightning struck when Lesney created a four-and-a-half inch version. Over a million tiny coaches with eight horses were made and sold.

After that, Lesney produced tiny vehicles that could fit in a matchbox, because partner Jack Odell's daughter wanted to take a toy to school—and only toys that could fit into a matchbox were allowed. Even the coronation coach was too big, so Jack made her a tiny brass steam roller. All the other children wanted one, and the men realized there was a huge market for small, cheap toys.

Lesney's first Matchbox models were the steam roller, a cement mixer, a dump truck, and a tractor—or, as the Brits named them, the Road Roller, Cement Mixer, Dumper Truck, and Tractor—all packaged in matchboxes.

Success! Those early trucks crossed over to America, and by 1955, the company had to find new, larger digs. They rolled out their "Models of Yesteryear" series of classic vehicles, and soon collectors as well as children were buying the toys. By Christmas of 1957, newspapers were advertising over forty models of "Matchless Matchbox" toys at 49 cents each.

By the way, Lesney was not the first British company to turn out small metal cars and trains —that would be Dowst Manufacturing, who made Model T's as early as 1914. But because of Jack Odell's improvements, Lesney sold quality toys at lower prices than the other companies in that arena, so they sold more … and more … and more. Lesney soon reached their "magic" number of 75 unique cars in the line each year, which they maintained for decades.

Lesney went public in 1960 and began an American branch in 1964. They put Fred Bronner in charge, a man who had been Lesney's distributer in the US since 1954 and knew the company well. By 1966, 40% of the 100 million Matchbox toys were sold in America, and the numbers continued to rise.

Hot Wheels came along in 1968, when Matchbox cars were already being collected and traded. Besides using hot, almost psychedelic colors, Mattel's Hot Wheels added an axle and rotating wheels, so they could really move … *fast.*

Mattel committed $10 million to promoting the new line of tiny cars, and Matchbox sales plummeted. To compete, Lesney came out with its SuperFast line in 1969—cars built for speed, in bright colors. Matchbox rebounded.

During that same year, Mattel ran afoul of the FCC when it developed a Hot Wheels TV show. The FCC determined the show was a "program-length commercial" and killed it. Not until 1983 did Mattel succeed in this arena—with the *He-Man and the Masters of the Universe* TV show and action figures. By then, many industries were backing off regulations (encouraged by the Reagan administration), and cable TV had introduced so many stations that the old rules about children's programming and commercials got changed or dropped.

Over the next few years, Hot Wheels introduced race tracks with loops, hairpin curves, launchers, and other fun features. Like most toy tracks, the racetrack came in components so it could be broken down and redesigned again and again.

Lesney created racing tracks in the 1970s, mainly to compete with upstart Hot Wheels. Mattel upped the game with supercharger (battery-run) power boosters and spring-loaded launchers. When Mattel moved production to China to further reduce costs, Lesney could no longer compete.

The Lesney Company declared bankruptcy in 1982, and many of the original dies were bought by Universal Toys—then, over the next fifteen years, by Tyco and eventually Mattel.

Yes, since 1997, Matchbox and Hot Wheels vehicles have been made by the same company. Always a fan favorite, Hot Wheels became a NASCAR sponsor in the 1990s, and a licensee of Formula One race teams in 1999.

SuperBall

Remember the slogan: "Bounces six times higher than a rubber ball!"? Well, what you may not know is that Chemist Norman Stingley created the SuperBall by accident in his lab in Whittier.

Stingley worked for Bettis Rubber Company, and one day he put a synthetic rubber compound under 3500 pounds of pressure per square inch. The ball that was created bounced—really, *really* bounced!

The company asked Stingley to find a practical use for his new polymer, called Zectron. Stingley was unsuccessful in fulfilling that request, but he thought it would make a neat ball.

The problem, however, was that a ball made of Zectron—with 92 percent rebound—tended to break apart easily, and neither Bettis Rubber nor Stingley knew what to do about that.

With his employer's blessing, Stingley took the purple ball across town to Wham-O and met with co-owner Spud Melin. What sold the toymaker on the ball was how it returned when it bounced against the underside of a table—Melin loved that.

Stingley worked with Wham-O's product engineers for a few months, making the toy more durable. Once it hit the market, the SuperBall took off like—well, like a SuperBall. Between six and seven million were sold by Christmas 1965 at 98 cents each. There were mini-SuperBalls too. Twenty million were sold in its first decade, and at peak production, Wham-O was turning out 170,000 SuperBalls a day. Stingley reportedly got a penny royalty for each.

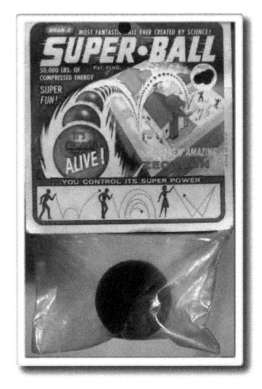

One of the many c. 1965 SuperBalls sold by SuperBalls.com, along with other retro Wham-O toys.

By 1966—the very next year—other companies were making knockoffs of inferior material (Stingley patented Zectron, which was largely polybutadiene with a dash of sulphur as a vulcanizing agent). Those knockoffs are still sold today in what we used to call gumball machines.

The following year, the SuperBall was responsible for naming the Super Bowl. The concept of a World Championship Football Game to be played in January was set and the contract signed, and Lamar Hunt—owner of the Kansas City Chiefs—inspired by his daughter's SuperBall, suggested calling the championship game the Super Bowl. The rest is history. In fact, there's a commemorative SuperBall on display in the Pro Football Hall of Fame in Canton, Ohio.

One more anecdote: Kids in the Orange County town of Fullerton, CA, hit the SuperBall jackpot in 1989 when thousands of SuperBalls appeared near the railroad tracks, spilling over into streets, gutters, and lawns. What's more, all the SuperBalls had the date 1965 molded onto them. People stood knee deep in a sea of loose SuperBalls, filling bags, boxes, pockets, pickup truck beds, and anything else they could with the unexpected bounty. For decades, OC residents got starry-eyed and nostalgic when they recalled "the day the SuperBall factory exploded."

No factory exploded, of course. The old, long-abandoned warehouse of the Fullerton Manufacturing Company had been demolished, uncovering the toys that had been stored there more than twenty years before. Fullerton Manufacturing was probably one of many companies that made the balls for Wham-O, storing them in heavy-duty paper bags, the kind that hold fertilizer. When those bags were torn open, the neighborhood was flooded with SuperBalls.

The property owner made no attempt to retrieve the balls, and according to rumor even encouraged kids to come and help themselves. Apparently (rumor again) Zectron might have been considered hazardous waste and no one wanted to ask questions that may have resulted in a costly SuperBall disposal operation.

Local schools had to ban the balls after windows and lights started breaking, and soon the legend of "the exploding SuperBall factory" was born. One enterprising young man scooped up enough SuperBalls in 1989 to set up his own website, selling the toys to aficionados committed to holding a piece of their childhood (and breaking a lamp) once more. You can see them for yourself at Superballs.com.

Other Stocking Stuffers

The following treasures, additional stocking stuffers from the late '40s, '50s, and early '60s, also sent kids into paroxysms of excitement on Christmas morning.

Toy Soldiers & Army Men

Modern toy soldiers were made of lead, or a glue and sawdust composite, until the Boomer Era. Plastics were far cheaper to mold and the little figures didn't have to be painted—they could just be bundled in bags and sold for under a buck. Marx Toy Company sold many styles and marketed tanks, jeeps, or terrain pieces with them. Most of the good guys were molded in army green and were one piece with a helmet or weapon. You could stage battles with enemy Nazis who were gray or Japanese soldiers fashioned in yellow.

Other popular types of plastic toy figures were cowboys and Indians, spacemen, Civil War soldiers in blue and gray, pirates, and knights. Incidentally, you'll be happy to know that the lead variety of toy soldier was banned in 1966.

Only eight of hundreds from this collection survived the '60s to pose for these combat photos in 2013.

Photos courtesy of Robert Von Gerichten.

Wannatoy

The WannatoyCoupe came out with molded plastic, bubble-topped coupes in 1946, at 25 cents each. Cast to look like futuristic Hudsons, they came in green, red, blue, or orange, with a clear or tinted top. Millions sold in 1946, and today they sell on Ebay for a couple of dollars each.

Magic Rocks

In 1944, Jim and Arthur Ingoldsby were in a store trying to sell their plant vitamins, but the shoppers ignored them. Why? Because someone else was demonstrating their "Magic Underwater Garden," made of mostly white crystals that absorbed water to grow into peaks and hills about two inches high. The Ingoldsby brothers bought some.

The crystals, they found, were basically Epsom salt mixed with sodium silicate. The brothers tweaked the crystals for months, trying different substances to add permanent color to the crystals. After many failures—most dyes simply faded away in the water—they figured out how to add not one, not two, but *eight* different bright colors that didn't fade. In 1945, the Ingoldsby brothers took their product—Magic Isle Undersea Gardens—to the marketplace.

Everyone loved it. When demonstrated for audiences, the product sold out. Stores stocked it. There was just one problem: the name. Magic Isle Undersea Garden sounded clumsy and was way too long. The brothers experimented with different names until finally the crystals became Magic Rocks, the name most of us remember.

And just how long did it take to come up with that name? *Thirteen years.* Yup, it wasn't until 1958 that the right moniker stuck. Why so long? It may be that the Ingoldsby brothers just didn't have an ear for words that rolled off the tongue. After all, if you grew up with a name like Ingoldsby, Magic Isle Undersea Garden might sound absolutely melodic.

At any rate, the brothers turned over the marketing and distribution end of their business to another firm in Chicago in 1960, but they kept the secret formula that made all those pretty colors locked up in a safe, so that in case of their ultimate demise, the world would not lose the secret of Magic Rocks.

Pez

The name is shorthand for Pfefferminz, the German word for peppermint, and the candy alone was first marketed in Vienna in 1927. Edward Haas III was an executive with a food company— not a candy maker—but he developed a cheap way to make compressed mints in a boxy shape so they could be wrapped by machines. The candies were breath mints, and they went into little tins. Twenty years later, Haas designed a dispenser that looked like a cigarette lighter.

Pez made it to the USA in 1952, but Americans didn't like the intense taste, so Pez became a fruit-flavored candy, aimed at children. Since the target market was now kids, the cigarette lighter look was reworked. No one knows who came up with the idea of putting a big cartoon head on top, but the first models had Mickey Mouse and Popeye on them. A full-body Santa enclosed another early dispenser, and any of these antiques can be worth thousands of dollars.

As Tim Walsh wrote in his coffee table book, *Timeless Toys*: "Pez is the *Rolling Stone* cover of the cartoon world." A character that's made it to the top of a Pez dispenser has literally made it to the top, and it can be legitimately called a cultural icon.

Besides finding your favorite cartoon character Pez dispenser in your stocking, you might have gotten a Pez Space Gun. These were sold from the mid-'50s to mid-'60s, then replaced by the Pez Candy Shooter, shaped like a .32 caliber pistol. Oh, joy—we got to put a gun in our mouths and pull the trigger, shooting candy down our throats.

Trivia: As of 2011, fans guess that 1500 different types of dispensers have been created. Since the company is privately owned, the actual records are not available, but *Time* Magazine reports that three billion Pez candies are consumed in the US each year.

Troll Dolls

Troll dolls became a fad in the US by 1964, but they were introduced in Denmark first. A Danish baker named Thomas Dam, out of work and reduced to shoveling snow for money, carved a toy for his son Niels. His friends all wanted one, so he carved more. Niels said the toy's face—which

later became a troll face—resembled a local butcher who tried to collect a debt from Dam. (All this happened in the small town of Gjøl, by the way, where Dam's company is still headquartered.)

Dam began selling his hand-carved funny figures door to door, and he made much more money than he could by shoveling snow—and had a lot more fun too. Soon he got commissions for larger carvings to be used as store displays or monsters in haunted houses. In creating those models, Dam learned about sculpting clay —rather than wood—into figures, then fashioning a mold for the rubber statue. As a result, he was able to turn out more toys quickly.

Dam Trolls from the mid-'60s who survived the decades by hiding in a Ken doll case.

His first trolls—made as a Christmas window display—used mattress springs for the troll bodies, with rubber hands and faces. Clothes hid the springs, but a wooden mechanism in the window kept the trolls bouncing. Everyone wanted to buy them.

In 1956, he sold all the springy trolls he could make. A year later, Dam replaced the springs with stuffed bodies. By 1959 the Dam Things Establishment (are you reading this out loud?)

factory arose, and a couple of years later it was turning out Good Luck Trolls made of plastic molds. Their hair was carded wool in white, black, or bright orange, and their eyes were glass.

Trolls first got popular in the US on college campuses among female students. Some claimed they brought good luck, so a little troll became the must-have gift for a friend facing final exams. But trolls quickly spread beyond colleges.

Betty Miller, a pilot who retraced Amelia Earhart's final journey, carried a 12-inch troll doll onto her plane instead of a copilot. Lady Bird Johnson, the president's wife, even had one. Next to Barbie, troll dolls were the biggest-selling dolls of the 1960s. And for such a hot-selling toy, it can be remarkably valuable today—into the hundreds of dollars for rare models.

A million Good Luck Trolls were sold under the official US brand, Uneeda Wishnik, but not all trolls were authentic. Imitations flooded the marketplace, and millions more non-Dam dolls gobbled up US dollars. Dam had not protected his copyright in America to the satisfaction of US courts, and in 1965 troll dolls were declared to be in the public domain. Future trade agreements set standards that would protect copyrights on such toys, but it took the Dam family until 2003 to get US courts to enforce his copyright.

You've heard that lightning never strikes twice? Wrong! The trolls got hot again around 1990 when sales reached the billions of dollars. Again, there were imitators, but the official Dam Trolls were sold as Norfin Trolls, and in 2000 as Totally Trolls. In 2005, Hasbro won the right to manufacture the new Trollz dolls to accompany a new TV show featuring Trollz—all licensed by Dam.

Chapter Seven

Toy Companies

You Can Tell It's Mattel—It's Swell!

The Mattel name represented a partnership between Harold "Matt" Matson and Elliott Handler. If you don't remember Matson, it's because he left Mattel in the late 1940s, shortly after the company took off, due to his unhappiness with the stress of success. He is remembered only as the first syllable of the Mattel name.

The second syllable, El for Elliot, might have been Iz, as in *Mattiz*. Before marrying and moving to California, Elliot Handler went by the name Izzy. Imagine the catch-phrase, "You can tell it's Mattiz, it's . . . ?" Hmmm . . . "a whiz?"

But the real driving force behind Mattel was Ruth Mosko Handler, who didn't even get a syllable in the name because women didn't own or name companies in the 1940s.

Ruth Mosko—nee Moskowitz—the 10th child of Polish immigrants, came to California as a teenager because her family wanted to separate her from a boyfriend. Their plan backfired, however. Ruth loved California, and she got a job at Paramount Pictures in the secretarial pool. Eventually she convinced her boyfriend, Izzy Handler, to get married and follow her west—*and* change his first name.

That was in 1938—the year they started a business. It took a while, but their first big sale was an order for die-cast models of DC-3s requested by the Douglas Aircraft company for distribution to their employees as Christmas gifts. Ruth made the sale; Elliot and Matt oversaw the newly hired workforce that made the models.

By 1945 Matt Matson, a skilled woodworker, had become their business partner. Elliot and Matt were gluing together picture frames in the Handlers' garage, using electric saws and equipment from Sears bought on the installment plan. They were forced to make the frames of wood rather than plastic (which they preferred) due to war-caused shortages. To use up the leftover wooden scraps, Elliott crafted doll furniture which, it turned out, sold better than the picture frames. The company—which by now had devised the name that would become a household word—changed its emphasis to toys.

With Ruth as their marketer, the company grew quickly. Mattel's Uke-A-Doodle, a toy ukulele, came out in 1947 and became a dependable seller. A plastic piano and a musical Jack-in-the-Box followed. Millions were sold, and Mattel grew into a large company though Matson bowed out.

By 1955, Mattel was ready for an innovative step: national TV advertising. The company signed up to be the sole sponsor of a 15-minute segment of a new show from Disney, *The Mickey Mouse Club*. The contract was for a year of advertising and cost Mattel $500,000—almost all of its net worth. No toy company had done anything like that before.

The risk paid off immediately, turning a lackluster toy—the Burp Gun—into a sensation. In three years, Mattel's annual sales grew to $14 million. The toy world was rocked: toy ads, previously aimed at parents and shown before Christmas, now became a year-round phenomena—and the target audience was children.

A couple of years after that, Mattel's biggest hit came out—but Barbie has her own section in this book. We'll just mention here that Elliot Handler once said to his wife: "Ruth, no mother is going to buy her daughter a doll with breasts."

We're guessing that he won very few arguments after that.

Mattel pioneered market research in the toy industry, generating reports that guided them toward greater success each year. The company went public in 1960 and was listed on the New York and Pacific stock exchanges, and by 1965, it was part of the Fortune 500, with $100 million in sales. By 1968, that figure doubled.

The Handlers "retired" in 1975, but not by choice. Although Ruth Handler suffered serious health issues, fighting off breast cancer in 1970, the last thing she and Elliot wanted to do was give up their role in Mattel. So why did they?

There's actually a salacious story behind it. A Securities and Exchange Commission (SEC) investigation began three years earlier, when Mattel—in order to keep its stock price up —"pre-sold" toys to suppliers before the end of the fiscal year to inflate its profits. Now, if all those millions of dollars in pre-sold orders had actually been shipped, it would have been fine. Unfortunately, a good percentage of the orders were canceled once the profits got reported to shareholders—making them *fake* profits.

Elliott and Ruth Handler in 1959 with a rocket and a Barbie.

Mattel was sued by its own stockholders and settled that lawsuit for $30 million—the largest such settlement ever at that time. When the SEC investigation concluded years later, the company had to pay heavy fines. Ruth barely avoided prison and both Handlers were forced to resign.

Time, however, heals many wounds—the Handlers became the first living people inducted into the Toy Industry Hall of Fame. Ruth Handler lived to be 85 years old; Elliott died in 2011 at the age of 95. Their son Kenneth died in the 1990s of a brain tumor, but Barbie's namesake, Barbara Handler Segal, attended the dedication of Mattel's Handler Team Design Center in El Segundo, California, in June 2012.

That's the nice version of Mattel history, the story you find on company websites and in Ruth Handler's autobiography, published in 1994. There is another, less wholesome version of the Mattel tale, however—one that credits folks other than the Handlers with Mattel's greatest success.

Like who? you ask. Well, like one Jack Ryan. No, not the CIA agent from Tom Clancy's novels. This Jack Ryan was short, flamboyant, and—according to some—a bipolar sex addict. He was also brilliant.

The Handlers recruited Ryan from Raytheon, an aerospace firm, in the 1950s and put him to work to help make their still-on-the-drawing-board Barbie doll a reality.

Ryan went on to develop—and in some cases patent—other toys and top-selling features. For example, the twist-and-turn movements of Barbie, the talking mechanisms for Mattel's dolls —including Barbie and Chatty Cathy—and the V-RROOM tricycle and toys.

Always a quirky character, Ryan bought himself a Hollywood mansion and turned it into a fantasy playground staffed with UCLA students. At one point he briefly married Hollywood celeb Zsa Zsa Gabor—he was husband number six of nine, if you're counting. Marriage did not deter Ryan from enjoying the Swinging Sixties lifestyle, however. According to *Toy Monster*, a lurid corporate biography of Mattel by Jerry Oppenheimer, Ryan staffed his Research & Development Department at Mattel with tall, beautiful, big-breasted women and slept with many of them. Oppenheimer also paints a picture of wild partying and pill-popping in the department—none of which endeared him to the Handlers, who did not share his swinging tastes. Animosity developed.

Did the Handlers, out of spite, "break" Ryan's patents by changing the designs so they would no longer have to pay him royalties? That's one claim, and Ryan did win a court case against Mattel to collect said royalties. That case dragged on for years, took a deadly toll on Ryan's health, and satisfied no one.

Author Oppenheimer also claimed that Mattel fostered a cut-throat, backstabbing executive culture, before and after the Handlers' departure. True? Some folks buy it, some don't, saying the book was poorly researched, fueled by stories from disgruntled ex-employees. Where's the truth? Maybe you had to be there.

After the Handlers left, Mattel's recovery was rocky; the company's fortunes were up and down through the early 1980s. Mattel was saved—meaning the company was restructured and refinanced—through the efforts of investors like Michael Milken (remember junk bonds?) and Richard Riordan, a future mayor of Los Angeles.

At one point, Mattel declined the opportunity to license action figures from a soon-to-be-released film, *Star Wars*. Rival Kenner ended up producing the small figures, which turned into a bottomless gold mine. In fact, you may remember that the insane initial demand caught Kenner unprepared, so they resorted to selling "Early Bird Certificate Packages." You got no toys in hand but could send away for the *Star Wars* set after Christmas.

Indirectly missing the boat on the *Star Wars* action figures sent Mattel looking for the Next Big Thing in action toys, which led to the development of another multimillion-dollar seller: the muscle-bound He-Man and the Masters of the Universe collection. That debuted in 1982 and grossed nearly three-quarters of a million dollars in sales the next year. The He-Man TV show first aired in September 1983, which provided a major boost.

The He-Man phenomenon didn't last long, though, and Mattel continued its roller coaster ride. But unlike so many of its rivals—some of whom Mattel absorbed—the Handlers' company is still thriving in the 21st century. Many of its biggest successes were post-Baby Boomer era, like He-Man and the Masters of the Universe action figures.

Some of the other ups include:

✦ An alliance with Disney that lets Mattel produce Mickey Mouse, *Toy Story*, and Disney Princess toys.

✦ Another alliance with *Sesame Street*—resulting in the Tickle Me Elmo phenomena. Tickle Me Elmo is actually made by Fisher-Price, a company Mattel bought in 1993. That giggling doll sold to the tune of $100 million the first year, and $200 million the second.

✦ As part of Mattel since 1993, Fisher-Price Toys now produces all the infant and preschool toys put out by Mattel: Barney the dinosaur, Blue's Clues products, and Disney and *Sesame Street* tie-ins.

✦ Mattel acquired View-Master when it bought Tyco in 1997.

✦ They own the American Girl franchise.

✦ It produces most Harry Potter toys and Nickelodeon products.

What about the downs? Mattel was caught in the middle of the recent lead paint debacle, forced to recall millions of toys made in China because they contained lead-based paint. The tainted toys included Disney's *Cars*, some *Sesame Street* and *Dora the Explorer* items—even Barbie playsets. The same month—August 2007—Mattel recalled another 18 million toys because of magnets that could be swallowed by children.

Then there's the Bratz lawsuit. Bratz designer Carter Bryant left his job at Mattel and took his designs for the sexy dolls with him to MGA (Marvin Glass Associates). The legal question: Had he actually worked on the dolls at Mattel, and if so, didn't they own the rights to Bratz?

After years of litigation, a jury agreed with Mattel and awarded them $100 million in damages. Two years later, a federal jury reversed the decision, stating Mattel had stolen designs from MGA and owed that company $88.5 million, for starters. Another judge then awarded MGA $309.9 million in damages and court costs. That judge even refused Mattel's request for a new trial.

And it ain't over yet, because MGA is also pursuing an antitrust lawsuit against Mattel. Kind of reminds you of *Clash of the Titans*, huh? Or at least, like some of those battles between He-Man and Skeletor.

Boy oh Boy, It's a Hasbro Toy!

Sounds a lot better than "Boy oh Boy, It's a Hassenfeld Brothers Toy!" doesn't it?

In 1922, Henry and Hillel Hassenfeld, immigrant brothers from Poland, made their living by selling cloth remnants. They began using the fabric scraps to make hat liners and pencil box covers, which were in high demand back then. By the time the brothers incorporated, they had eight employees—all relatives, all making pencil boxes. Younger brother Herman was a fireman, so they hired him to be the factory foreman.

Pencil boxes were hot items back then; Woolworths alone bought plenty. By the time the Depression hit in 1930, Hassenfeld Brothers had 200 employees—most of whom were *not* relatives. Sales topped half a million a year.

During World War II, the company expanded from school supplies to toy nurse and doctor kits. Right after the war, Hassenfeld Brothers bought the Empire Pencil Company. Hillel, who had no children, took over the pencil-making branch of the company, which at the time was the more lucrative concern.

Henry ran the pencil case/toy division, such as it was, and his son Merrill worked beside him. It was Merrill who decided to turn the pencil boxes into toy doctor and nurse kits during the war. He also created warden and guard kits. When Merrill noticed that his little daughter was constantly venturing into Mom's make-up drawer, he started a toy cosmetics line.

So, by the Boomer Era, Hasbro—as it was then called—was clearly in the toy business. Officially licensed Disney characters decorated the pencil boxes they continued to make, and in 1951, lightning struck when a man named George Lerner called on Merrill. He had a box of eyes, ears, and other appendages that could be stuck into vegetables . . . and Mr. Potato Head was born. It was the first toy ever sold on local TV, on a little East Coast show hosted by a fellow named Captain Kangaroo.

In 1960, Henry died and Merrill officially took over. Another one of Henry's sons, Harold, became head of Empire Pencil. As it's been since the beginning, the toy company is headquartered in Rhode Island, the pencil company in Tennessee.

As FundingUniverse.com described Hasbro: "Truly successful toy companies do not just make toys; they manufacture popular culture." Hasbro's most famous toys like Mr. Potato Head, GI Joe, and Flubber surely fit that definition.

But not every toy was a hit. Do you remember Hasbro's Flubber? Probably not.

Flubber, a mix of rubber and mineral oils, was inspired by the movie *The Absent-Minded Professor* and timed to come out with the follow-up flick *Son of Flubber*, early in 1963. The product sold well—until children started developing a rash after playing with it. Hasbro had to recall Flubber and then figure out how to get rid of it. It wouldn't burn in the city dump, and when it was lugged out to sea and sunk (legally, with permits), it rose to float all over Narragansett Bay. Hasbro had to pay for the cleanup, and the company then gathered the errant Flubber pieces together, eventually burying them under a new plant and parking lot. After 25 years, popular lore has it, the goo had raised floors and asphalt several inches.

The Flubber fiasco was the stuff legends are made of. It cost Hasbro $5 million, and the company actually had to borrow the money to launch the toy that would save it: GI Joe.

The rest is history.

Well, it's all history, actually. This whole chapter.

The GI Joe saga and how it saved Hasbro is told later, so we'll continue the company's story here.

Officially, the toy half of Hassenfeld Brothers became Hasbro in 1968. By that time a third generation of Hassenfelds—Stephen and Alan, Merrill's sons—were being groomed to take over the company. Stephen was already president when his 61-year-old father, who was respected throughout the industry, died in 1979.

Stephen became CEO of Hasbro Toys, which was still tied to the Empire Pencil Company, run by Uncle Harold. Empire made money steadily; the toy business was up and down. In fact, throughout the late '60s and early '70s, Merrill had borrowed on his personal wealth to make payroll.

In short, Stephen Hassenfeld did not inherit a thriving enterprise. Hasbro took a $5.2 million loss the year before Merrill died because GI Joes had lost their appeal, and newer toys like the *Charlie's Angels* dolls just didn't take off. Mattel—the industry leader—was eight times larger than Hasbro, and Hasbro's non-toy ventures (like Galloping Gourmet kitchen wares) fizzled too.

Family loyalty could not hold the Hassenfeld ventures together. The relatives split their company into two, with Merrill's sons running the toy business and Harold holding onto Empire Pencils, which at that time was still a much bigger concern. People started calling the company "Has-been."

So what kind of CEO did Stephen Hassenfeld turn out to be? Within five years, he had trounced Mattel and turned Hasbro into the biggest toy company ever, with $1.2 billion in sales.

Under Stephen, sales doubled for several years; he steered his company away from the video game market, which turned out to be a smart move. Video games tanked in the mid-1980s (though they were revived in the next decade and have stayed popular since). Instead of video games, Stephen led Hasbro to acquire the Milton Bradley game company for $380 million, a price most pundits thought way too high, then introduced blockbusters like My Little Pony and Transformers.

Unfortunately, Stephen died at the age of 47. At the time and for many years after, his death was said to be from a heart attack, but it was later revealed that the underlying cause was AIDS. His younger brother Alan took over and guided the company into the 21st century before retiring. Under Alan—the last Hassenfeld to head Hasbro—the company diversified, spinning off video games and TV shows of its most popular toys. In the '90s, Hasbro acquired Tonka Toys, which by then included Kenner and Parker Brothers games, and—through Kenner—*Star Wars* toys.

But Alan was a very "hands-off" CEO who hated to fire people; in comparison to his big brother, he was not a strong leader. Alfred Verrecchia, who'd been with Hasbro for 38 years and had run many departments, took over in 2003. The current CEO is Brian Goldner, who is largely responsible for bringing *Transformers* to the big screen.

The company has been headquartered in Rhode Island since the 1920s, but it now has a movie studio in Los Angeles and outlets all over the world. In addition to the other companies already mentioned, Hasbro now owns and manufactures Raggedy Ann, games like Life and Candy Land (which it acquired through Milton Bradley), Clue (Hasbro bought Waddington Games, a UK company), Lincoln Logs (through its acquisition of Playskool), Scrabble, Monopoly,

Pictionary, Nerf, Spirograph, Furby, Laser Tag, Dungeons and Dragons, and for awhile, they even made Cabbage Patch Dolls.

Ideal Toy Company

You may want to download some ragtime music on your iPod for this story.

When the president of the United States goes anywhere, the media tags along, even a full century ago when President Theodore Roosevelt went hunting in Smedes, Mississippi. After

three days with no luck at all, Roosevelt's aides cornered an old bear and tied it to a tree for him to shoot. To his credit, the president refused to target a captive bear—although the bear was injured and had to be killed anyway. The newspapers ran the story, and a cartoonist drew pictures of Teddy and the bear—an animal that appeared cute and babyish.

A 1903 Ideal teddy owned by the Smithsonian.

Morris and Rose Michtom were living above their Brooklyn candy store when they saw the cartoon in the paper and thought the little bear would make a sweet display, so Rose cut up some velvet and crafted a little bear that sat up, using shoe buttons for the eyes. The Michtoms put it in their store window with a sign that said "Teddy's Bear."

Not one, not two, but thirteen people asked to buy the bear that day, and they were willing to pay $1.50 for it. Morris, an immigrant who'd fled Russia's anti-Jewish pogroms as a teenager, sent the original bear to the White House as a gift and asked the president's permission to use his name. He got it. Meanwhile Morris and Rose busily sewed and stuffed bears in the living room upstairs and sold them in the store downstairs.

The toy was an instant hit. Michtom engaged a wholesaler named Butler Brothers and founded the Ideal Novelty and Toy Company. When President Roosevelt ran for a second term, he used the Teddy Bear as his mascot.

During its eighty years, Ideal produced a multitude of toys that were wildly successful—dolls like Betsy Wetsy, Tiny Tears, and the Shirley Temple doll; and other toys, such as Gaylord the dog, Magic 8 Ball, Mouse Trap, and Mr. Machine.

To celebrate the company's 50th anniversary, Ideal introduced a Smokey the Bear doll. By this time, Ideal had hit on the money-saving measure of convincing other firms to pay for advertising their toys (like Dupont, who produced the hair for some dolls). Ideal used the same strategy for Smokey the Bear. The iconic figure had been introduced by the US Forest Service in 1945, so Ideal got the government to pay for some of the toy ads. Because of that tie-in, kids could send away for a Junior Forest Ranger card. In three years, over half a million cards were issued.

Benjamin Michtom, the second generation to run the toy company, hit on the idea of reissuing the Shirley Temple doll in the 1950s, followed by

Clifford Berryman's original cartoon that led to the creation of the Teddy Bear. November 16, 1902, in the Washington Post.

other celebrity and comic book character dolls. He built Ideal into the nation's largest doll manufacturer in the 1950s, but that was before Mattel came out with Barbie.

But Ideal had its failures too. In 1958, Ben Michtom became convinced that a Baby Jesus doll would be a big hit. The nine-inch tall Christ Child was, instead, a disaster. No one wanted their kids dragging around a representation of Jesus—it seemed downright disrespectful. Ideal had to buy the doll back from retailers and quietly dispose of it.

Ben died in 1980, but Ideal stayed in his family under the leadership of Lionel Weintraub, at least for a couple of years. In 1982, Ideal was sold to CBS Toys for $58 million. Five years later, CBS Toys sold Ideal to View-Master, which renamed itself View-Master Ideal. Tyco bought that company, then Mattel merged with Tyco in 1997.

As for that original Teddy Bear, after being loved by Teddy's children and grandchildren, it now resides in the Smithsonian.

Wham-O: A History

Rich Knerr and Spud Melin (real name Arthur), the guys who started Wham-O and invented the Hula Hoop, were destined for entrepreneurial success . . . or juvenile hall. Even as children, they both showed signs of marketing ability: Knerr used to make rubber-band guns out of fruit-crate wood and clothespins, then sell them to neighborhood kids; Melin once rigged a clothesline with 50 hooks, attached the line to a rowboat, and went fishing. He then iced and sold his catch —fresh halibut and bass—up and down the street from a wagon.

As teens during World War II, they met and formed a quick bond; they once got arrested for throwing rotten oranges at each other in Pasadena, home of the Rose Parade. Both went to USC (Knerr graduated) and then went into business together: importing goods, reselling cars (still a rare commodity in those first years after the war), and finally raising, training, and selling falcons.

How do you train falcons? Well, Spud Melin actually had some experience in that. During a two-year stint in the Air Force, he'd raised hawks and used a slingshot to knock down blackbirds to feed to them. Now, the two entrepreneurs used slingshots to shoot meatballs up like rockets, hoping the falcons would dive at them. People offered them good money for the slingshots, not the birds, so Knerr and Melin shifted gears.

"We purchased a Sears band saw for seven dollars down and seven dollars a month and started our business in my parents' garage in Pasadena," said Knerr.

Rich Knerr cut the slingshots of Southern ash and Spud Melin sanded them. Both men went door to door, but sales were low until they paid an old college friend to draw up an ad. The payment was three beers; the ad ran in *Popular Mechanics*, and it brought in orders.

For the ad, Melin and Knerr had to think of a name for their venture. Wham-O is the sound that a slingshot missile makes when it hits the target. Thus, Wham-O was born in 1948.

Paying the ad designer in beer was standard procedure for Knerr and Melin. When they set up their garage assembly line, they paid their old college buddies in beer to help them sand and paint.

Advertising in more magazines like *Field & Stream,* Wham-O, the sporting goods manufacturer, did quite well. Sales of $100,000 a year allowed Wham-O to move from the garage to an abandoned grocery store, and then to its own building in San Gabriel, California. Slingshots originally sold for 75 cents each but the price quickly doubled, and the company also sold hunting knives, tomahawks, boomerangs, dueling swords, blowguns, and crossbows—all by mail order at first. Later, sporting goods stores set up accounts to buy from them.

Wham-O had been in business for a few years when Knerr and Melin saw a guy playing with a Pluto Platter on the Santa Monica beach and asked about it. The Pluto Platter had been bought at the Los Angeles County Fair, which was still going on. Knerr and Melin headed over to the fair to find and meet Fred Morrison.

While Wham-O tinkered with what eventually became the Frisbee, they found another toy that took off: the Hula Hoop. The worldwide fad left the Wham-O folks reeling. They actually didn't make much money on it, but they sure learned a lot, and they put that marketing know-how into practice to grow their company.

Spud Melin, Wham-O VP, appeared on What's My Line in September, 1958.

One thing they learned was not to invest in high-tech machinery to make individual products; instead, they farmed out the manufacturing. Their San Gabriel facility grew into a 171,000 square foot complex with a rail spur that brought trains right up to the loading docks, and they never had to move. The decision to let others do the manufacturing also freed up Wham-O to take more risks on products they loved. And they did.

The warehouse became known as the Fun House, for good reason. Frisbees, Hula Hoops, Slip 'n' Slides (nine million sold between 1961 and 1992—but not for Christmas!), Silly String, SuperBalls, SuperElasticBubblePlastic, and all the other toys, practical jokes, and stories contributed to an atmosphere where anything could happen. Employees loved working there and brought their own kids in to help test the toys.

Spud Melin and Rich Knerr were both VPs—there was no president of Wham-O. The two men got along great: Rich was more of a salesman while Spud came up with ideas. Spud had more business and organization know-how too, though Rich was the one with the college degree.

Rich said of Spud, "He was crazy. I had the greatest partner in the world."

Fast forward to 1982. Knerr and Melin, then in their late 60s, retired—still best friends and expert Frisbee players. After flirting with Hasbro, they sold their company to a higher bidder: The Kransco Group, which made toys and sporting goods. The two former owners stayed on as consultants for five years while the San Gabriel plant continued to handle administration and distribution.

Under Kransco, Wham-O hit gold one more time with the Hacky-Sack in the 1980s. But that was it—Kransco even lost its edge with the Frisbee, as other companies designed superior discs for tournaments and play.

In 1994, Mattel bought Kransco and sold the Wham-O name and trademark to a private group of manufacturers three years later. In 2006 that firm was bought by Cornerstone Overseas Investments, a company that moved their corporate headquarters to Emeryville, CA. On the plus side, the new owners relaunched Wham-O's most successful toys, like the SuperBall, and made a big investment in water sports and toys. Both Melin and Knerr passed in the first decade of the 21st century.

In 2009, Kyle Aguilar talked to the owners in China about possibly manufacturing better Frisbees for them. During that phone call, Aguilar learned that the company might be up for sale, and he pounced. A longtime fan of Wham-O, he put together a group of investors along with his own Aguilar Group and bought the company in 2010.

Many of Wham-O's big sellers like Frisbees, Hula Hoops, and SuperBalls—which each have its own section in this book—have become icons of the Boomer Era, but they never could have existed without Knerr and Melin's crazy combination of fun and marketing genius. Here are some other Wham-O hits you may remember:

◇ The Wham-O Tank of 1959 was an 8-foot-long roll of cardboard. That's it! You got in the roll and crawled, as if you were the wheels of a tank. Were you in a tank, or a hamster's exercise wheel?

◇ Remember doing wheelies on your bike in the '60s? The Wheelie Bar, fastened on the lower half of your rear wheel, had two tiny wheels on it to stabilize you as you reared back. The package featured a Rat Fink drawing by Big Daddy Roth.

◇ Water toys! Although they were seldom under the Christmas tree, Wham-O's biggest hits included the Water Wiggle with its goofy smile and the Slip 'n' Slide, introduced in 1961 and still selling in the millions today.

Leaving the 1960s (and the Boomer toy era) behind, Wham-O debuted Silly String in 1969, and in the 1970s, the Magic Window, with two colors of sand that formed and reformed landscapes, as well as SuperElasticBubblePlastic.

As for today, Wham-O is still with us. Catherine Zeta Jones (wearing stiletto heels) taught Ellen DeGeneres how to Hula Hoop in 2013, and the current Wham-O owners have recently brought out a new offering that Rich and Spud would recognize and love—the Arctic Force Snowball Crossbow.

 Tonka Trucks

The very first Tonka toy actually carried the name Streater. That's because in 1947, a new metal stamping company bought a manufacturing plant from Streater Industries. The plant—originally a three-story brick schoolhouse—was in Mound, Minnesota, and the new company that bought it was named Mound Metalcraft.

The plant came with dies and tools, including the dies for a toy Streater had made the year before: the Streater Steam Shovel. This toy was made of pressed steel and had been shown at the New York Toy Fair, but buyers weren't interested. Streater decided to drop its toy line and concentrate on more lucrative divisions; that's why it sold the plant in Mound.

And who bought the plant? A company of three: Avery Crounse, a businessman and engineer; Lynn Baker, who'd sold Crounse a car in the 1920s and formed a decades-long friendship; and Al Tesch, a mechanical genius Crounse had worked with before.

The new owners made tie racks, shovels, and hoes, but they were also interested in goods that could generate sales during the slow time of year—winter. What better than toys? So they made a few Streater Steam Shovels. Tesch tinkered with the design, changed its colors, simplified the movable shovel—and boom! The new toy went into production.

Mound Metalcraft also created a toy crane, using the same die for its cab. For the crane, they chose the colors yellow (for the cab and the clam) and black—colors that would soon become their signature.

They paid a freelance artist $30 for a logo, and the name "Tonka" came from nearby Lake Minnetonka, which just happens to mean "great" in the Sioux language.

The little company grew, taking their Tonka Toys to the 1947 New York Toy Fair. By their second year, Tonka sold 79,600 toys.

The old school house was expanded more than once, and neighboring properties were purchased. Tonka added nine more toys to each year's lineup, including a dump truck. Tie racks and gardening tools were distant memories; Mound Metalcraft, using the brand name Tonka, was a toy company.

Remember the Allied Van from Tonka? That came out in 1951, and it was designed by Charles Groschen, who worked part-time for Tonka and full-time for another company in Mound. The toy was an amazingly accurate miniature version—in appearance at least—of a real Allied moving van. In order to market the van, Tonka signed an agreement with Allied that lasted for thirty years.

Allied was the first, but not the last company to allow Tonka to replicate its trucks. Carnation Milk, Ace Hardware, United Van Lines, Hormel, Star-Kist Tuna, and Marshall Field were among many others.

Tonka started packing little catalogs with its toys in 1952, and even those old catalogs have become valuable collectables these days. In 1955, Tonka moved into a bigger, newer facility and then added 50,000 square feet to that. And—finally—the name Mound Metalcraft was dropped, and the company officially became Tonka Toys.

The company had competition, of course. Enterprises like Nylint and Buddy L had been around longer and made sturdy toy trucks as well, so Tonka threw itself into making better, stronger toys. Those first Tonka cranes and trucks were not durable or very realistic, and Tonka developed new technologies to combine its tooling operations for each toy, streamlining and specializing production.

Tonka designers also developed a special way of spray-painting the toys, using paint that had a positive charge so that it adhered better to the metal. Then they worked with Dupont to develop a "wet on wet" painting process for the next coats, followed by baking in an oven to thoroughly dry the paint. Conveyor belts carried the toys through the oven and out, allowing them to cool down before delivery to the assembly line.

(below) Some lovingly used Tonka toys.

(above) A classic 1960s truck from Tonka.

Such innovations allowed Tonka to fine-tune the designs and make the toys more realistic, typically using an 18:1 scale. For example, Tonka's Road Grader, made from 1951 through 1989, was modeled on an actual road grader from the Cox Brothers Construction Company in Spring Park, Minnesota. Their first fire truck was likewise modeled after a Minneapolis aerial ladder truck. It had two 19-inch aluminum ladders and a cone-shaped flasher—but no siren. One of these trucks was sent to President Eisenhower's grandson, David.

Tonka also produced a fire truck that came with a hydrant—one that screwed onto a garden hose and pumped water through the fire truck's 40-inch hoses. Named the Outstanding Toy of 1956, the Tonka Fire Department's Suburban Pumper had a removable ladder, and the hoses could be wound on a reel or hooked to the ladder. It sold for under $9.

That same year (1956), Tonka debuted toy sets that couldn't be purchased separately, with features like a fire chief's badge, metal road signs and barriers, and tricked-out vehicles with flashing lights.

By 1961, when they turned out their 15 millionth toy, Tonka had earned their reputation for durability and quality. By then the company had gone public, and soon sales exceeded $10 million. 1961 was also the year that the last original owner turned over the company to Russell Wenkstern, who had been running things for the past eight or nine years.

To backtrack a bit, two of the original three owners had sold their interest in Tonka in the early 1950s and moved on, leaving Lynn Baker in charge. He'd had a heart attack in the early years of the company and handed a great deal of the work over to others.

Wenkstern had once worked for Streater Industries and joined Mound Metalcraft in 1952. Much of Baker's workload fell on Wenkstern, who shaped Tonka into a powerhouse among toy companies—the largest manufacturer of vehicles in the world. Under his steady hand, sales went from $400,000 a year to $80 million in the late 1970s when he retired.

The company started making Jeep replicas in 1962 and sold them for under $3. That made the Jeep line a year-round hot seller, not just a Christmastime gift. A very popular version of the Jeep was the girl's model: pink, with a fringed top. The idea for it came from a sales manager who'd spent his 1961 vacation in Acapulco and saw fringe-topped Jeeps driving tourists around. The girlie Jeep was a hit—over half a million were sold in its first year alone.

Tonka's biggest seller was the Mighty Tonka Dump Truck, which hit stores in 1964. CEO Wenkstern helped to design this toy, which was actually based on a truck used in open-pit mining in South Africa. The Mighty Dump (no sniggering—that was its nickname) was big enough for toddlers to sit in, as many of us proved.

Besides selling $15 million worth of Mighty Dumps over the next 35 years, Tonka made sure we all knew it was one of the toughest toys ever—remember that commercial where the elephant put all its weight on the dump truck? That spot won a Clio Award in 1975.

Not all Tonka Toys were hits, however. A 1970s attempt to compete with Mattel's Hot Wheels—the Tonka Totes—was retired after three years due to low sales. Today, they're rare and collectable.

Nothing lasts forever, but the employees of Mound, Minnesota, were shocked when Tonka announced it would be closing its offices and plants there and moving all operations to El Paso,

Texas, and Juarez, Mexico. That was in 1983—nearly forty years after Mound Metalcraft had opened.

The company prospered after the move, bringing out such 1980s hits as GoBots and Pound Puppies. Before the decade was out, Tonka bought Kenner-Parker Toys, but in 1991, Tonka Toys was bought itself—by Hasbro.

That buyout didn't mark the end of the line, though. Tonka Toys is an international brand, still manufactured and sold all over the world. And—according to a June 2012 press release—Sony Pictures and Happy Madison Productions are working with Hasbro to bring a Tonka Truck animated movie to the big screen.

As a last note: Ever heard of Winifred in central Montana? The Winifred Museum houses over 3,000 Tonka Toys, some in their original packaging, which is probably the largest collection in the world.

Legos

The toy companies mentioned in this chapter so far have been American and produced a variety of toys. We'll finish up with a company from Denmark that has concentrated on one toy, and one toy alone since the 1960s—and that single focus has been so successful that a chain of theme parks all over the world celebrates it.

Once upon a time (1932), Danish carpenter Ole Kirk Christiansen lived so far out in the Jutland boondocks that he couldn't support his four sons with carpentry, not with a worldwide Depression hitting everyone. To make matters worse, his wife died, and he worried that he'd lose the workshop he'd run for 16 years. Ole said later that he'd told himself: "You must choose between your carpentry and the toys," and then, everything started to make sense.

He began carving wooden toys—yoyos, animals on wheels, planes, trains, and automobiles, as well as blocks—and selling them door to door. In a couple of years, Ole ran a contest, offering a bottle of wine to the person who picked the best name for his company. Ole won the wine himself, suggesting Lego from the Danish words "Leg godt," meaning "play well." In Denmark, it's pronounced "LEE-go."

The Lego warehouse became a family business for Ole and his four sons. One son—the third, Godtfred—dropped out of school to work with his father and ended up developing Legos, the legendary interlocking plastic blocks.

Godtfred listened when merchants said they wanted toys that were unique and that appealed to a child's mind and imagination. The family made blocks already, so Godtfred focused on developing a type that would lock together and not fall apart, and that could be used to build almost anything. The idea of hollow blocks with studs on top was not completely new; a British company called Kiddicraft made those in the 1940s, calling them Self-Locking Building Bricks. When Ole and Godtfred went to England to buy their first plastic injection molding machine, a salesman showed them some Kiddicraft bricks and other examples of what the equipment could do.

The new machine was used to make baby rattles and toy cars, but Godtfred didn't forget the Kiddicraft idea. He kept tinkering, and early sets of what we call Lego blocks had slits on the side to hold windows. The company called them Lego Mursten (meaning bricks). They were hollow and bright, but they didn't have the interlocking studs on them yet.

By 1954, the Legos we know and love hit the marketplace. Success was not immediate, but at the next International Toy Fair, father and son Christiansen tried out a new idea: all the Lego toy sets revolved around building a town with a unified look and theme. Tiny people, cars, and trees were included. This new System of Play, as Godtfred named it, caught on and Lego sales took off.

By the way, both companies (Lego and Kiddicraft) patented their designs, and neither ever took legal action against the other. Lego, however, ended up acquiring Kiddicraft many years later in 1981.

The Kristiansen family—the spelling changed with Godtfred—tweaked the design of the blocks, patenting the final version in 1958, ironically the year that the company's founder, Ole, died. That means that Legos made in the 21st century will fit with those in a 1958 set. Lego molds must produce blocks accurate to one-thousandth of an inch to work properly, and out of every million Legos that are produced, only an average of twenty-six are rejected by quality control.

Thanks to Godtfred's business acumen and innovation, Legos became such a huge success in Denmark that within a few years, the family discontinued all its other toy lines to focus strictly on Legos. It was Godtfred's idea early on to bypass the usual toy distribution wholesalers and set up his own network. It paid off—there are some years when Legos alone account for 1% of Denmark's exports.

Samsonite licensed Legos for manufacture and distribution in the US in 1961, but the company is owned by the Kristiansen family to this day and still headquartered in Billund. However, Godtfred's son Kjeld turned the reins over to an outside manager in 2004, after huge losses to the computer game market nearly ruined the company. That manager—Jorgen Vig Knudstorp—turned things around and put Lego back on top. While nothing will dethrone the primacy of Lego bricks and kits, a newer product line called Mindstorms guides the budding engineers of the 21st century to a new level: boys and girls can now assemble and program robots, using modern concepts like cloud-sourcing to push the technology further.

(left) A few of the original wooden toys carved by Ole Kirk Christiansen in the 1930s. Photographed at Legoland Windsor Creation Center by Carlos Luis M. C. da Cruz.

(right) An early 1949 version of the Lego brick on left, and a 1958 brick on right.

The first Legoland opened in 1968 in Billund, where 90% of Legos are still made. The population has jumped from 1300 in 1967 to over 6,000 today. Not so large, but it's the millions of tourists who visit Legoland each year who are responsible not only for Billund having the country's second-largest airport, but also for sparking the establishment there of the SAS Airline's headquarters.

As of 2013, according to *Smithsonian Magazine*, enough Legos have been produced to supply every man, woman, and child on planet Earth with 80 Lego bricks each—about 600 billion in all.

Chapter Eight

Make Believe Toys

Isn't every toy technically a make-believe toy? After all, kids don't really play with molded plastic figures; they pretend that those figures are babies, soldiers, nurses, superstars, dangerous spies, or superheroes, right?

Think about it: when you rode your bike down a hill as a kid, did you really think of yourself as a 10-year-old sitting on metal framework mounted on wheels, or was the voice in your head shouting: "Here goes daredevil/gold medalist/world record-holder Streak McGraw, showing the rookies how it's done!"

Yep, I thought so.

So allowing that make believe permeates every sort of toy, this chapter highlights the items that really don't fit anywhere else. These toys aren't games or dolls or stocking stuffers—their only purpose is as a prop for playacting.

Costumes

By 1955, Halloween costumes were nothing new. But when the Sears catalog called those clothes "Playtogs from the Land of Make-Believe," they weren't focused on Halloween—they wanted to ornament our everyday imagination.

Most of the playtogs outfitted children for the Wild West. *Hopalong Cassidy* was the first TV western on the networks in June, 1949, followed by *The Lone Ranger* (previously a radio show) just a few months later. *The Cisco Kid* and *The Roy Rogers Show* debuted in the early 1950s, and there were dozens more. Official Hopalong Cassidy gun and holster sets were top Christmas presents, along with the Lone Ranger's mask. There were even Hopalong Cassidy and other western hero bicycles, complete with saddlebags. If you already had a bike, you could ask your folks to buy you the saddlebags separately—they cost around $7 in an era when the bike itself was under $40.

Those accessories were great, but it was the cowboy and cowgirl *costumes* that made the Old West real. Outfits were modeled after those worn by Hopalong Cassidy, Roy Rogers, and even Dale Evans . . . after a fashion. The most important part of the Lone Ranger costume was the mask, but there were also gauntlets and cuffs, chaps-like pants, the official flannel shirt, boots, spurs, belt, hat, and holsters—all with silk-screened, appliquéd, or embroidered logos. Later ensembles emulated Wyatt Earp, Annie Oakley, Maverick, Zorro, Marshall Dillon, and even a few feather-topped generic Indians.

Walt Disney's Wonderful World of Color rolled out its first episode of "Davy Crockett" on December 15, 1954. Since merchandise tie-ins were not as sophisticated as they are today, no store stocked Crockett's costumes, guns, or coonskin caps that year—but in 1955

Kids could pretend they were Jay Silverheels as Tonto with this Pla-Master Play Suit. Courtesy MomandPopToys.com

Disney and its retail customers were ready. Over $100 million in Crockett items sold by the end of the 1955 holiday season. Coonskin caps were so popular that the price for raccoon fur (yes, they skinned real raccoons for our enjoyment) went from 25 cents to $8 a pound.

The author's brother has held onto his genuine Western Cowboy lamp for over fifty years.

Although costumes are the topic of this section, we must digress for a moment. When it came to western TV star merchandise, marketers sold anything they could think of. Case in point: ten million recordings of the Davy Crockett theme were sold in '55, along with countless games, play sets, flashlights, thermos bottles, guitars, watches, toothbrushes, books, bedspreads, lamps, and more. *Davy Crockett* was the first hour-long TV Western shown during prime time, and it proved the appetite for all things western was bigger than anyone had guessed.

Cowboy outfits weren't the only costumes being sold, however. Tom Corbett, Space Cadet, had his adherents, wearing his uniform and shooting his space gun. As the decade wore on, cavalry uniforms like those worn by Rusty Rinty (remember him from *Rin Tin Tin?*) or modern day Marines in camouflage were popular with boys.

And what about girls? They got to dress up as nurses, drum majorettes, ballerinas, flappers, Gibson girls, and brides. For awhile, "Mommy and Me" outfits—lookalike dresses for both mothers and daughters, or for little girls and their dolls—were the rage. You could sashay around in the same gingham skirt and pinafore as your baby, or go shopping or to tea with Mom.

Toy stores also sold fake fur stoles, tiaras, "fancy pants" grown up lingerie, and high heels for little girls to play pretend in (the shoes, ads claimed, were "safely constructed for growing feet"). And in spite of decades of breaking with old stereotypes, here's the hard truth: Stroll through any big toy store today—or at any point in the last fifty years—and you'll find the same sparkly tiaras and high heels for little girls.

Two-year-old Susan Strother
got a coonskin cap
for Christmas.

Cowgirl Cheryl and Gentleman
George were ready for action.

Accessories outsold the clothing, maybe because accessories didn't need to be laundered. Coonskin hats and cowhide belts, mother-of-pearl-handled pistols in their own leather holsters, harmonicas, guitars (with Roy Rogers or Zorro pictures on them), and drums were often enough to set the mood for an afternoon of make believe.

And then there was Superman . . . and that's just the fifties.

By 1962, girls could get official Barbie costumes, complete with an itchy blonde wig with ponytail and curled bangs. The Barbie costumes were mostly reworks of old standards—bride, nurse, ballerina, drum majorette—but there was a prom queen and a fairy princess thrown into the mix.

Boys (and many girls) could wear *Combat!* and camouflage ensembles and carry rubber bayonets, plastic hand grenades and bazooka launchers, and canteens. Other outfits included Batman and his utility belt, Napoleon Solo or Illya Kuryakin from *The Man from U.N.C.L.E.*, a Green Beret, or James Bond with all the spy paraphernalia.

But outfits required accessories for maximum make-believe power, so toy cigarette lighter guns, sniper guns with silencers, ray guns from TV shows like *Lost in Space,* and more entered the picture . . . which brings us to our next section.

Toy Guns

You can't have costumes—especially Western ones—without the six-shooters and rifles so prominent on those bloodless TV shows, right?

At first, toy gun sets came with dummy bullets that were fitted into tight holders, sewn or molded into the holster. They looked nice on the belt and sometimes could be forced into the gun, but they lacked firepower.

Toy guns of the late '50s.

Most of us remember clearly the pungent smell and sharp sound of caps—toy cap guns have actually been around since just after the Civil War. The early ones were made of cast iron and used percussion caps, while those that Boomers remember were made of zinc alloy and used rolls or disks of caps. But the real innovation came in 1950 when Nichols Industries figured out how to make a toy gun with a reloadable cartridge. Play cowboys could load the Stallion 45 with bullets, just like real guns!

Funny story about the brothers who started Nichols Industries: Talley and Lewis Nichols made war material, but after 1945 they needed to switch to peacetime products. They decided to make cigarette lighters, a very popular item back then. Just as they were tooling up for a production run, the federal government flooded the market with 15 million surplus lighters they'd been holding onto throughout the war. The brothers figured there was no way the government could have a surplus of toys, so they switched to making cap guns.

Other companies also jumped into the toy gun market. Lone Star Products produced real-looking, die-cast metal guns called the Frontier Scout, Sharpshooter, Cobra, and Ringo Ricochet. Marx brought out plenty of copycat guns as well, and companies like Hubley and Wyandotte also put out toy guns with the names and logos of Western heroes on them.

Mattel made some great guns, starting with the Burp Gun, first advertised on *The Mickey Mouse Club* with a commercial that implied it was the perfect gun for shooting jungle animals in your living room. The Burp Gun was "the first fully automatic cap gun in the world." It fired through a roll of caps that unwound and curled off the gun like a cartridge belt would . . . if a cartridge belt were made of paper, that is.

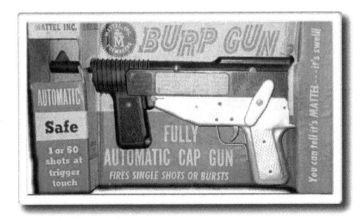

A packaged Burp Gun from the 1950s.

Mattel also made the most popular variety: Greenie Stick-M-Caps. These caps got stuck on the back of toy bullet casings so that your gun made a bang when you shot it. You used the Greenie Stick-M-Caps with Mattel Shootin' Shell models, like the Lone Ranger Rifle. Shootin' Shell guns and bullets—which were gray plastic—depended on spring action for their propulsion.

The Shootin' Shell guns were Fanners with a large hammer so that children could hit—or fan—it over and over: bang-bang-bang-bang-bang . . . you get the idea. Fanning guns came out in 1957, and at $2.98, they cost more than double the amount of other guns. Although just a toy, all Fanners strived for realism: they came in black or metallic (nickel or even gold!), with handles that looked like carved bone, horn, or mother-of-pearl, and the Fanner 50 was the most popular model.

In 1958, toy designer Marvin Glass one-upped the Fanner with the Ric-O-Shay, a gun that made a sound like a bullet ricocheting. The innovation was Glass' idea, but it took a team of engineers, a sum of $64,000, and months of work by his employee Carl Ayala to make that sound a reality, putting it in a prototype pistol. Tempered piano wire made the sound, but mounting it in the gun's handle required precision measurements within one-thousandth of an inch. More months of work followed, and finally the Ric-O-Shay, made by Hubley, was on store shelves for $3.98. Over a million were sold in the first eight months.

As toy guns evolved over the years from using loadable wooden bullets that didn't shoot to cap shooters or fast-action clickers, children's gun savvy grew in sophistication. Observant fans even came to know their TV heroes by their firearms. Paladin of *Have Gun Will Travel* carried a black Colt .44, while the hero of *Wanted: Dead or Alive*—a young Steve McQueen—kept a humungous sawed-off Winchester rifle at his hip. He called it the Mare's Laig, and kids could play with a replica in either a cap gun or dart-shooter style.

Into the 1960s, snub-nosed guns that might have belonged to detectives or secret agents became popular as well, but they still used the Shootin' Shell technology.

Howdy Doody Marionettes and Other Puppets

This one is for the first-wave Boomer cohort.

The Howdy Doody Show debuted on NBC in 1947, and by the mid-1950s over 15 million viewers were tuning in—and not all of them were children. Buffalo Bob Smith served as host, and he was also the creative genius behind the show, which was one of the first TV shows shot at Rockefeller Center in New York City.

Comic books with the puppet appeared by 1949, followed by Howdy Doody food products, clothes, and hundreds of toys, records, books, wallpaper, bubble bath, you name it, all managed by the Kagran Corporation. A group of Wall Street suits smart enough to invest in the new TV-inspired merchandise, Kagran Corporation sold around $40 million worth of Howdy Doody products a year in the 1950s.

In 1952, Howdy Doody ran for President of the Kids of the United States with the slogan: "It's your Doody to vote!" and his platform included two scoops of ice cream in every cone. By November 4th of that year—the real election day—NBC had received 1,294,003 ballots for Howdy. Ike got over 34 million votes to win the presidential election that year, but third party candidate Howdy Doody's showing was more than respectable.

Howdy Doody at his mailbox, circa 1949.

As Christmas gifts go, the Howdy Doody marionette—which went for under three dollars—was the most popular, but Clarabell (with horn) and other characters were available too, as were lower-priced hand puppets topped with washable Vinylite heads that looked eerily like their TV counterparts.

Those puppets from the 1950s (the last *Howdy Doody Show* aired in 1960) sell for hundreds of dollars now. Most prized are the Howdy Doody marionettes, but his sister Heidi Doody, Flub A Dub, Clarabell, and the others all fetch big bucks if they're in good condition, especially if the packaging is still with them. Wristwatches and wind-up tin toys have likewise brought prices in excess of $1,000—if they are authentic.

A Charlie McCarthy dummy from 1961.

And what about Charlie McCarthy, the marionette creation of Edgar Bergen? He predated Howdy Doody by a couple of decades, and was very popular too.

Bergen was a vaudeville performer who got his own radio show during the Depression. You might think the magic of ventriloquism would be stymied by radio—after all, listeners couldn't *see* Charlie McCarthy; they could only hear the two voices that both came from Edgar Bergen. But the audience didn't care. The show was popular and Bergen and his creations were radio show fixtures for nearly twenty years, ending in 1956. He also showed up on television and in film.

Bergen's inventive humor and talent made up for visual loss, and he added other characters to the show, including Mortimer Snerd. They all had their own style, and guest stars like Mae West and W. C. Fields kept the repartee funny and even a little racy—in a way that went right over our heads as kids.

Bergen was the father of Boomer baby Candice Bergen, who was an early guest on her dad's radio shows. When Edgar Bergen retired in the late 1970s, he gave his Charlie McCarthy marionette to the Smithsonian Institute, where you can see it today.

Easy-Bake Oven

The Easy-Bake Oven was Kenner's first big success, and it took playing house to a whole new level. The toy sold for $15.95—quite a lot in 1963—but that didn't deter the little girls who had to have it; half a million were sold the first year. The bright turquoise oven was used to bake the little cake mixes in foil packs that accompanied it, and within two years, junior chefs could also make popcorn, birthday cakes, and mini Kid Dinners that looked like tiny TV dinners.

Just how did the Easy-Bake Oven work?

The junior appliance heated food with a simple 100-watt bulb that couldn't be accessed without removing the screws and rear plastic plates from the oven—which required adult skills—making it safe for children. Kenner sold five million of their invention by 1967 to the delight of the company and of numerous little hostesses, wives, and mommies in training.

A little bit of history: Kenner Products was started by three brothers in 1947, making it a true blue Boomer company. The three owners were named Albert, Philip, and Joseph Steiner, and the company's name came from the Cincinnati street where the first factory sat.

The oven itself was invented by Ronald Howes, who once noticed that New York City food vendors kept their food hot with heating lamps. Howes' other inventions involved electrostatic printers and defense industry weapons, and he continued to work for Kenner to help refine other toys. But he is remembered mainly for the Easy-Bake Oven that everyone wanted, through all its color and style changes.

A 1963 Dad plays with his daughter and her new Easy-Bake Oven.

In 1967, the Steiners sold their toy company to General Mills. As GM owned the Betty Crocker brand, they soon began creating miniature Betty Crocker cake mixes for the Easy-Bake Oven. In 1969 they changed the oven color to avocado green; the next year, they released the new Super Easy-Bake Oven in harvest gold—and double in size, with *two* light bulbs to cook the food.

General Mills acquired a couple other toy companies—Rainbow Crafts (which made Play-Doh) and Parker Brothers—then merged them all together as Kenner Parker Toys. In the mid-1980s, GM put the toy division up for sale, and Hasbro eventually ended up owning the company. The Easy-Bake Oven, now made by Hasbro, is still a big seller—by 2011, 23 million had been sold.

Space Toys

Unless you count Robert the walking, talking robot, or the Buck Rogers' Sonic Ray Light Gun that sparked and buzzed, toys celebrating space travel and the future didn't really become popular until the 1960s. It was then that flying saucers, rocket launchers, and robots with names like "Mr. Atomic" and "Mr. Machine" began showing up under trees.

Mr. Machine, from Ideal Toys, was one of toy designer Marvin Glass' first big hits. It stood 17 inches tall, had a red top hat, a blue wind-up key, and colored gears inside that turned as Mr. Machine moved across the floor. Glass—the creator—went on to bring us some of the top games of the 1960s, like Mousetrap, Operation, and Lite-Brite. But Glass was predominantly an idea man; the real designers of Mr. Machine were Leo Kripak, a former watchmaker, and Burt Meyer, who worked with Glass on most of his big successes.

A store display of alien monsters, c. 1952.

The *Lost in Space* robot, helmets, ray guns, and laser guns soon joined Mr. Machine, along with Mighty Zogg, Commander in Chief of the Zeroids, who came with dyno-arms and flashing lights. GI Joe had already been introduced, proving there was money in action figures, so in 1966 Mattel brought out Major Matt Mason, a moon-based astronaut, as well as members of Mason's crew—the alien Callisto and the evil Captain Lazer.

Lest you think those were the only products for the wanna-be astronaut, Astro Bases and Space Stations, three-stage rockets, moon copters and travel vehicles, Space Walker shoes (with giant springs on the bottom), and even Space Faces also lined toy store shelves. Don't recall Space Faces? They were a Mr. Potato Head toy with alien antennae, button eyes (or were they weapons?), and Frankenstein neck knobs to stick on your hapless carrot.

Chapter Nine

GAMES, CRAFTS & INDOOR TOYS

Early Boomer Games (through the 1950s)

Scrabble

An out-of-work architect named Alfred Mosher Butts (stop giggling!) started working on a word puzzle game in 1931, a very dismal year for job seekers. "I got the notion that I could invent a successful game," Butts said. "Nothing else occupied my time, so I decided to give it a whirl."[14]

As he tinkered with "it"—the game wasn't called Scrabble until the late 1940s—he counted up the number of times letters appeared on a newspaper's front page to set the point values of each letter. That, he said later, was inspired by an Edgar Allen Poe story, "The Gold Bug," in which a secret code is deciphered by figuring out which letters are most commonly used in English. He called his work-in-progress Lexiko.

As years passed, Butts went through several versions of the game before he came up with the setup we now know—a board that links words as in a crossword puzzle. By the mid 1930s, all the game companies he'd queried refused his game because it was too highbrow and intellectual. Butts made copies of his game and sold them for $2 each, but eventually he found a "real" job and gave up on Lexiko.

So it wasn't until 1948—the Boomer Era—that a friend named James Brunot offered to go into business with Butts and manufacture the game. That's when Lexiko finally got its name: Scrabble. Butts got a small royalty—two-and-a-half cents a sale—and Brunot produced the games.

Brunot set up manufacturing in his own living room. His wife didn't mind as the couple had a dream of escaping city life and moving to the country, and they hoped that Scrabble would open up a path to do just that. Although they assembled and sold over 2,200 games that first year, however, they actually lost money.

But the slow start didn't phase the couple. Because they couldn't afford advertising, they relied on word of mouth—and it worked. The raves of happy customers caused sales to double every year for the first four years; by 1951, 9,000 games were sold. Using a stamp machine, the Brunots' output peaked at twelve sets an hour to meet the demand.

Scrabble reached a tipping point in 1952 when orders for thousands of games a week started pouring in. An urban legend credits a Macy's executive—Jack Strauss—with falling in love with the game while on vacation and getting the chain store to buy it. Whatever the explanation, the bottom line was this: 9,000 games sold in 1951 . . . and 59,000 games sold the next year.

Brunot was swamped. Even though he hired more help and farmed out the boards to a game producer—Selchow & Righter, makers of Parcheesi—his maximum output was 6,000 games a week. Selchow & Righter realized that Scrabble had become a hot commodity, and they wooed Brunot for the rights to manufacture the entire game.

Brunot sold, but he retained the rights to make "deluxe" Scrabble sets—the ones with the red leather-like cases. Then he sold rights to make a lowdown dirt cheap $2 game to another firm, changing the name to Skip-A-Cross.

Back then, the $10 Deluxe set made in Brunot's workshop had white plastic tiles, while the ordinary set from Selchow & Righter, which cost around $3, had wood tiles. In 1953—the magic year for Scrabble—everyone had it on their Christmas list, and around 800,000 of the $3 sets sold. By 1954, the number had climbed to over 4.5 million.

Butts and Brunot lived comfortably and both sold their interest in Scrabble to Selchow & Righter in 1971. Butts made over a quarter million in that deal, and Brunot walked away with $1.5 million. Selchow & Righter sold their business to Coleco in 1986, and when Coleco went bankrupt, Hasbro acquired Scrabble and their other product, Parcheesi.

Games were licensed and sold all over the world; Braille and children's versions came out, and very early on, people started playing cuss-word Scrabble. Even celebs like Darryl Zanuck, Elia Kazan, Bennett Cerf, Oscar Hammerstein II, and Prime Minister Nehru of India loved Scrabble, adding to its popularity.

To this day, the Scrabble phenomenon keeps growing. In the 1970s, Scrabble tournaments as well as national and international championships started up, and of course there are video Scrabble games for every platform.

Candy Land

A "sweet little game for sweet little folks," the box reads . . . and Candy Land also comes with the world's sweetest backstory.

You may not remember the days when the word *polio* carried a gut-clenching aroma of terror, but your parents and grandparents do. During that time, the fear actually became so great that parents stopped taking their kids to public parks and swimming pools. No one knew how the disease was transmitted, and it crippled indiscriminately, ruining childhood and leaving people to lie—often for years—in iron lungs. Scariest of all, the number of cases started to rise during the late 1940s and into the '50s, and although polio threatened everyone, children were afflicted most. Boomers were the first generation of children to grow up without the worry of polio because of the Salk vaccine—which was tested in 1952 and released to the world in 1955. By 1957, the number of polio cases had plunged.

What does that have to do with Candy Land?

A retired school teacher named Eleanor Abbott was stricken with the disease and ended up in the polio ward of a San Diego hospital in the 1940s. Many of her fellow patients were children

—some too young to read. Abbott developed the game for them. To play Candy Land, all you had to know was colors.

Because it was so popular, she took a sketch of the game—drawn on butcher paper—to Milton Bradley. They were interested and did a small test run, then a larger run. As a result, Eleanor Abbott was given a big check that she spent on school supplies and equipment for the kids in the polio ward. The royalties were apparently given to charity, but Abbott herself disappears from the historical record.

The early Candy Land games came with wooden pieces; in fact, Milton Bradley used painted chess pawns as game pieces for that first, limited test run (the plastic gingerbread man tokens didn't come along until 1960). Very early Candy Land game boards even showed a boy with lines on one leg, possibly hinting at a brace. Perhaps this was a bow to Abbott, or maybe it was a subtle hint that the game could amuse children who were sick or immobilized.

The sets from the 1950s pictured cartoon tots with skirts so short their panties showed, which was considered quite normal and wholesome back then. Through the Boomer years, the only update to the Candy Land box was the clothing on the kids, and little more.

The game box produced from about 1955 to the early 1960s.

Hasbro bought Milton Bradley in the 1980s, and they still make the game today. Candy Land boxes on Hasbro's website feature a cartoonish image of smiling King Kandy, but other 21st-century packages feature a fairy-like Princess Lolly and fantasy characters. Dora the Explorer sets are available too.

Over the years, however, two things have stood the test of time for this sentimental favorite: the original rules of the game, and the candy cane stripes that spell out the Candy Land name. And since the game's introduction in 1949, 40 million Candy Land sets have been sold, leading Milton Bradley to record sales. Fun fact: In 1958, the company outsold rival Parker Brothers for the first time to become the biggest game company in the US.

Clue

In the years before World War II, a young pianist named Anthony Pratt performed in country hotels. There was no TV back then, so for entertainment, hotel guests played games. "Murder" was popular, a game where all the hotel guests and a few of the employees acted out roles and guests had to solve a crime (it's still played today).

Pratt had to abandon his musical career for the war effort, but he drew on his memories of playing Murder and designed a board game with the same name. He patented it as soon as he could and sold it to the venerable Waddingtons, a British company founded in the 19th century.

Murder weapons of an early Clue game.

Waddingtons came up with the name Cluedo, which is actually a pun on the word Ludo—the ancient game we call Parcheesi. Ludo is also the Latin word for "I play" and in the 1940s, educated Brits knew that, giving it an extra subliminal boost. Waddingtons made a few other changes too, such as the addition of the hapless Mr. Boddy—absent in Pratt's original design, where a different character played the victim in each game.

Clue came to America in 1949, advertised as "the great new Sherlock Holmes game." An original 1949 box with that phrase is very collectible, as is the original rope, which was made of real rope instead of plastic.

About 150 million games of Clue—or Cluedo—were sold in more than 75 countries over the next fifty years. Waddingtons remained the owner of the game; however, Parker Brothers manufactured Clue for the US and other countries.

After Pratt sold his game, he went into civil service. Then with the help of a final check from Waddingtons for all the international rights to the game, he opened a tobacco shop. He lived a quiet life until his death in 1994—the same year that Hasbro bought Waddingtons.

Magic 8 Ball

A black, oversized pool ball that foretold the future . . . how did that become a must-have toy?

Invented by the son of a clairvoyant named Mary Carter—a psychic who counted Sir Arthur Conan Doyle, the creator of Sherlock Holmes, among her visitors—the original ball started out as a cylinder. Albert Carter called it the Syco Seer and patented the tube that eventually became the fortune-telling mechanism of the Magic 8 Ball. Here's how it worked:

A "liquid-filled dice agitator"—as the tube was called on the patent—allowed a multi-sided die to float in the thick liquid in the tube, and each side of that die had an answer to a yes/no question. When you turned the tube over, the die floated to the top and one side became visible, showing the answer to your question.

Carter teamed up with Abe Bookman to form Alabe Crafts (Alabe was a combination of the two first names Al and Abe). In 1946, they produced the Syco Seer as a seven-inch-tall tube. The toy was popular—a *New York Times* article by none other than Gay Talese reported that half a million were sold—but its inventor died only a year later. Of Al Carter, Abe Bookman said, "When he was sober, he was a genius."[15]

Apparently, he wasn't sober often. Carter lived in flophouses until his drinking took the ultimate toll. After that, Bookman tweaked the Syco Seer, dropping the tube into a classic "crystal" ball. Brunswick Billiards of Chicago saw it and asked if Alabe could turn the crystal ball into a billiard ball for use as a promotional item. That was in 1950, and the 8-ball form sold so well that the toy has not wavered from that design since.

The Magic 8 Ball has made guest appearances on *The Dick Van Dyke Show*, *The Simpsons*, and *Murphy Brown*; it's also been marketed as a keyring ornament and clothed in bright pink. As for its company history, Ideal Toys bought the Magic 8 Ball in 1970, Tyco bought Ideal in 1987, and Mattel bought Tyco in 1997.

Colorforms

This favorite was created in the low-rent, Upper West Side apartment of Harry and Patricia Kislevitz, poor but happily married art students, who came up with the idea of putting scissors and a big roll of thin vinyl in the bathroom for party guests to cut and play with. Since the vinyl would stick to the semigloss paint, the party's action moved to the bathroom in no time, where guests created Matisse-like masterpieces for hours on end.

The success of their experiment led the Kislevitzes quickly into marketing their idea as a toy, and their first order for 1,000 sets came from F.A.O. Schwartz. The earliest Colorforms sets were simply shapes—triangles, circles, and rectangles in white and four other colors—but it wasn't long before the Kislevitzes were expanding. Another store, Bonwit Teller, wanted exclusive rights to the toy, but the Kislevitzes refused, hired a sales force, and built their own factory. In 1957, they became one of the first toy companies to license cartoon characters, introducing Popeye Colorforms.

"No scissors, no glue, no mess—nothing but fun," said the early ads on *The Mickey Mouse Club*. Soon Beany and Cecil, Bugs Bunny, and Mickey Mouse Club characters—both real and animated—were the subjects of Colorforms sets. Dennis the Menace, space creatures and dinosaurs, and Miss Weather—who came with a wardrobe for sunshine, rain, wind, and snow— all made for "more fun to play the Colorforms way."

With the success of previous characters, it should be no surprise that the toy has evolved to feature current beloved icons such as Harry Potter, Dora the Explorer, SpongeBob SquarePants, and the Transformers.

Harry Kislevitz retired in 1988 and two of his and Patricia's six children took over the business; by 1990 a billion sets had been sold. But because Colorforms aren't big-ticket items, the company wasn't able to compete against glitzier toys and video games. As a result, the Kislevitz boys—Joshua and David—sold their company to Toy Biz in 1997 but stayed on as vice presidents. A year later, University Games bought Colorforms, keeping the brothers in their executive positions. Joshua remains president of Colorforms to this day.

Mr. Potato Head

Mr. Potato Head was the first toy to be advertised on television, on April 30, 1952. The ads, shown on local TV shows, were also some of the first aimed at children instead of their parents.

In response, Mr. Potato Head sales for that one year jumped to $4 million. But who dreamed up the idea of sticking plastic ears, eyes, mustaches, and all the rest onto a spud?

A guy named George Lerner, who thought turning vegetables into funny faces would be entertaining, that's who. Lerner had partnered with his friend Julius Ellman to form a toy development company called Lernell, but in the late 1940s, they couldn't sell the idea to anyone. Stick plastic eyes into a potato? Please.

A breakfast cereal company finally offered Lerner $5,000 to create little packages of "Funny Faces" that went into cereal boxes as free giveaways. Lerner took the money and produced the packets, but he didn't abandon his original idea. He scored a meeting with Merrill Hassenfeld, where he showed him a lunchbox full of the plastic face pieces.

Hassenfeld—son of one of Hasbro's original Hassenfeld brothers—loved the idea. He envisioned the stickpin-like noses and eyes as something that could go into the lunch boxes and pencil cases that his company still made, thinking maybe it could help them move beyond kits and cases and make toys that were fun.

Did it ever!

Hasbro bought the rights to "Funny Faces" from the cereal company, paying them $7,000, which covered their payment to Lerner and compensated them for their trouble. Then Hasbro partnered with Lerner, writing him a check for $500 against future royalties of 5% per kit—about a nickel per sale—and went into production.

Hasbro dreamed up the Mr. Potato Head name, and Mrs. Potato Head came along a year later. That first year—1952—was huge for Hasbro and Lerner as the company took an unprecedented leap of faith when they advertised Mr. Potato Head on TV.

Believe it or not, no one—not Crayola, Tinkertoys, or even Parker Brothers—had ever done that before. Mr. Potato Head's was the first toy commercial ever, in glorious black and white. And as a result, one million Mr. Potato Head toys sold that first year.

For the first dozen years, the Mr. Potato Head toy was a kit with plastic and felt facial features and body parts only, and the price was around a dollar. Parents supplied the body—the potato, carrot, tomato, squash, lemon, or whatever fruit or veggie that worked—and most of us quickly learned which ones could get quite messy. The plastic potato body didn't debut till 1964.

The industry was beefing up toy safety back then, and plastic points sharp enough to dig into a spud were *out.* But that didn't slow sales, so play kits featuring Mr. Potato Head and his

Tooty-Frooty Friends (who had plastic cucumber, bell pepper, and orange faces) hit the stores in time for Christmas.

You may be surprised to know that Mr. Potato Head's first plastic visage was half the size it is now—in 1964, he came with a full body: arms, hands, trunk, legs, and feet. Today, his potato head rests directly on plastic shoes, and arms can be inserted directly under the ears. As for the facial features, they are now five times as large as they were in the 1950s.

Do you remember when Mr. Potato Head had a pipe? That was dropped in the late 1980s when Mr. Potato Head quit smoking and became a "spokespud" for the American Cancer Society. In fact, during the Great American Smokeout of 1987, he handed over his pipe to the Surgeon General, C. Everett Koop, and accepted a note of congratulations from First Lady Nancy Reagan as well as an award from Arnold Schwarzenegger.

As of his 60th birthday in February 2012, over 100 million Mr. Potato Heads had been sold. Since he's now a big-time movie star in the *Toy Story* franchise, that number will likely continue to rise.

Cootie

Know where the word Cootie comes from (as in "Oooh, you've got cooties!")? Someone made it up during World War I, when the soldiers huddled in trenches had to endure lice in addition to being shot at. The lice were the cooties and the word caught on.

By 1915 a Cootie game was invented—but it was nothing like the game Boomers played. In the early game, the object was to trap the tiny cooties in a box. The Roaring Twenties saw a new Cootie game that involved drawing a bug with six legs—kind of like Hangman, only you tossed dice instead of guessing letters. In the 1930s, that game developed paper pieces.

But when the Boomer era came along, a man named Herb Schaper whittled a fishing lure that looked more like a toy bug than anything fish would bite at. So he

The first Cootie game, released during World War I.

took it to his Minnesota shop and discovered that the kids liked it. He ended up carving a couple hundred of the bugs before he figured out how to make that bug a game—by carving bug legs and pieces that had to be assembled, rather than the whole bug. The year was 1948.

Within a year the W.H. Schaper Manufacturing Company was formed, and Herb had created plastic molds to match his wooden bug parts. Dayton's Department Store of Minnesota agreed to carry the toy, and by the end of 1950, 5,000 sets—or 500, depending on who's telling the story—were sold. In any case, the toy was a hit. An incredible 1.2 million Cootie games sold across the country in 1952.

Schaper loved bugs, and he went on to design the games Tickle Bee, Tumblebug, and Ants in the Pants, as well as non-bug games like Don't Spill the Beans and Don't Break the Ice—all for preschoolers. Tyco bought Schaper's company in 1973, and in 1986 Milton Bradley—by then a division of Hasbro—took over. The game is still made today, only with bugs that are brighter and cuter than the originals.

Yahtzee

Back in 1956, a rich woman approached successful game company manufacturer Edwin S. Lowe, asking if he would make one thousand sets of a dice game she and her husband played on their yacht. The sets were for their friends (apparently, money was no object and they had lots of friends).

Lowe was a lucky guy when it came to games. Twenty-five years earlier, he'd stopped at a carnival while on a sales trip. The stock market had just crashed and Lowe's small company was in trouble; no one was buying his toys.

The teenaged Lowe needed cheering up, but the carnival wasn't a very cheerful place—until, that is, Lowe spotted a crowded table where a pitchman was leading a game called Beano. Everyone had a card with numbers on it, and whenever the barker called out a number, players used a bean to mark their cards.

Beano inspired Bingo and Lowe's company was saved from bankruptcy. Twenty-five years later, he thought this new yacht game could be just as big a hit. Was the lady interested in producing and selling the game? No, but she loved the idea of sharing her yacht game with thousands of people. She told Lowe he could manufacture it, and he made her a thousand sets for free.

Lowe named the game Yahtzee, but buyers didn't jump on it at first—rolling dice to get certain combinations just didn't *sound* like fun. So after wasting tens of thousands of dollars to promote the game, Lowe had a brainstorm. He offered to provide food, drink, and free game sets if the corporate toy buyers and store managers would host Yahtzee parties in their homes. Winners would get a free game as a prize. That got sales rolling. Party guests discovered that the game was fun; buzz started, and soon Yahtzee was a top toy.

After selling 40 million sets over the years, Edwin Lowe sold his game company to Milton Bradley in 1973 and retired; he died in 1986. And who makes Yahtzee now? Hasbro—Boy oh boy.

Late Boomer Games (1960 and Beyond)

Life

Milton Bradley brought out this game in 1960 to celebrate their Centennial—that's right, the game-making company was 100 years old.

Funny story how the company started . . .

Mr. Milton Bradley started a lithography business in 1860, and one of his first big jobs was to produce lithographs of Abraham Lincoln, who was running for president. When Lincoln won the election and grew a beard, demand for the earlier, clean-shaven Lincoln pictures stopped. Bradley was going to sell his equipment and get out of the business when Life (with a capital L) became a spark in his mind.

He started making games, but being the early Victorian era, games were not very popular. They were considered time-wasters and often involved gambling. So Bradley's game, called The Checkered Game of Life, stressed righteous living and sobriety. He developed a spinner so that no wicked dice had to be used to move the players forward, squares represented virtues or vices, and the goal was to win by acquiring virtuous points.

Bradley took a sales trip to New York and was soon shipping games as fast as he could make them—40,000 Life games were sold by the eve of the Civil War.

The Checkered Game of Life was updated and sold into the 20th century, but it eventually retired. By the 1920s, the game seemed old-fashioned; no one was interested in such a puritanical set of rules. Milton Bradley's company endured, though, passing to his heirs and then to heirs of his friends, and finally—during the Depression—to businessmen who kept it afloat.

On the eve of its 100th birthday, the Milton Bradley Company dusted off the Checkered Game of Life and redesigned it to suit a modern audience with the following alterations:

- The checkerboard was out, and a 3D plastic landscape replaced it.

- Instead of landing on virtues and vices, players hopped on squares enabling them to acquire kids, cars, and big bucks—or gamble, get cheated, and lose those bucks.

- The goal of the original game was a Happy Old Age. The goal of the Boomer version: make the most money and avoid The Poor Farm.

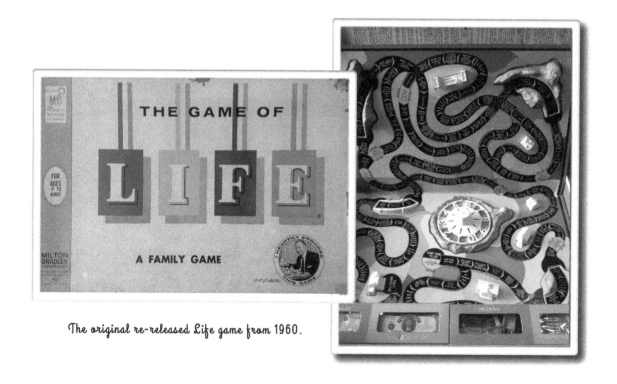

The original re-released Life game from 1960.

Ever wonder why TV personality Art Linkletter's picture was on the $100,000 bill? Well, the designer of the new game, Reuben Kalmar, knew that Linkletter had not one, but two hit shows running on two different networks in 1960 (*People Are Funny* on NBC and *House Party* on CBS). Kalmar figured the TV star could promote the new game on both shows. Milton Bradley struck a lucrative deal with Linkletter, advertised the game on two networks, and paid him in real money. In addition, they put Linkletter's picture on the game's $100,000 bills.

Of course, the 1960 game is not the one you'll find on toy store shelves now. Updating a game must be addictive—or at least, profitable—because today's game of Life comes in different versions to please fans of *Star Wars, Pirates of the Caribbean, The Wizard of Oz, SpongeBob SquarePants,* and more.

By the way, the Milton Bradley Company remained in private hands for 124 years, but Hasbro bought it in the 1980s.

Mouse Trap

The next few entries might well be subtitled "The Games of Marvin Glass."

Glass was a quirky, brilliant guy who refused to study children when he designed toys—he was afraid they would blab about the toy and let his competitors get the jump on him. Quirky, yes . . . and a bit paranoid.

He was an idea man and a very successful one, but you might wonder: Why didn't Glass make the games himself? Why, when he was an incredibly prolific and popular designer, didn't he sell his designs to other companies? There was actually a very good reason.

Earlier in his career, Glass designed and manufactured a flop: not a toy, but a Christmas tree ornament that looked like a stained-glass window. He invested over a million dollars in the product, lost that, and went into debt to the tune of $300,000—a big amount now, but a stupendous sum in 1949.

Glass survived. One of his quirky traits was that he never gave up.

While living on borrowed money, Glass designed a small toy called the Busy Biddee, a pocket-sized chicken that laid five white marbles like eggs. Another toymaker produced it, selling more than 14 million units. After the royalties paid off Glass' debts and gave him a fresh start, he never ventured into manufacturing again. Instead, he became a designer and consultant, putting an estimated 500 new toys on the market between the time he created Mouse Trap in 1963 and his death in 1974. One magazine story about him began, "Manufacturers pay him $1,000 a day plus expenses merely to have him inspect their pilot models and answer one question—"Should we make this?"[16]

Mouse Trap was a huge hit, one of the first 3D games that built itself up from the classic game board. The point of the game was the construction of a surreal, bizarre mouse trap that every player's mouse had to avoid. Mouse Trap shook up the industry because it reshaped the rules about what made a good game, and though it had tons of little pieces that got lost quickly, it was fun while it lasted.

The game owed a lot to Rube Goldberg, a famous cartoonist who used to draw wild, complicated inventions (you can see some of them at RubeGoldberg.com). Glass told designers at his company—MGA, for Marvin Glass Associates—that he wanted to create a toy that worked like a Rube Goldberg drawing, and Mouse Trap was the result.

In 2009, a gigantic Mouse Trap was built at a fair in San Mateo, CA.

After seeing the game, Goldberg's publisher asked the game designer for a royalty, since it was so similar to his contraptions. Glass ignored the request. Mr. Goldberg was already 80 and not interested in pursuing legal action, so there the matter rested.

After creating it, MGA offered the game to Milton Bradley, who passed on it. MGA then went to Ideal—the company that made Teddy Bears and dolls. Ideal had been branching out into other areas and had bought Glass' previous toy, Mr. Machine. They made lots of money from it, so their relationship with MGA was a good one. Mouse Trap was Ideal's first foray into the game industry, and it became a phenomenal hit. More than a million games sold before Christmas in 1963, the year it was introduced.

And—like so many other great toys—it's now made by Hasbro, via a sale of Ideal to CBS Toys, then to ViewMaster International, then to Tyco Toys, which merged with Mattel in the late '90s—but it's not made by Mattel now because the rights to Mouse Trap and a few other games were then sold to Hasbro.

Hands Down

The must-have game under the tree in 1964 was another Marvin Glass invention produced by Ideal, based on the card game Slap Jack.

Hands Down used cards too, but the slapping got done on the Slam-o-matic, a blue plastic box with a pink, yellow, green, or reddish-orange plastic hand for each player. It was loud, and that was the point.

A secondary point was to avoid being the last person to slap the machine. The Slam-o-matic was brutal in its judgment, with the color and number of the slowest player displayed on top after a slapping spasm. And a third point was to fake out the other players by reaching to slap, and tricking *them* into slapping. That way, the fooled players lost cards.

With all that abuse, it's a wonder that the Slam-o-matics lasted through Christmas vacation, but surprise, surprise, surprise—as Gomer would say—they did.

Operation

How many Boomers became nervous wrecks because of this game?

A college student named John Spinello developed this toy as a class assignment, and Spinello's grandfather just happened to work for Marvin Glass' toy design firm, MGA. Hence, Grandpa got Spinello an appointment with Glass.

Glass could be loud and abrasive, as many geniuses are. When Spinello put his game on Glass' desk, Glass called it "a piece of @*&!" and told the young man to get rid of it. But when he tried the toy and the buzzer went off, Glass jumped up and said, "I love it! I love it!"

The game was called Death Valley, and it had nothing to do with doctors or body parts. As originally designed, players were pioneers in covered wagons going through a desert. They looked for water in holes and wells—but the little compartments were empty back then.

Whether you call it Death Valley or Operation, the game is made with two metal plates only a quarter-inch apart. One plate has a positive charge and one a negative charge. The game, as Glass first saw it, had a 12-volt lantern battery and a 6-volt bell hooked up inside the box. If the tweezers touched the sides, the bell went off.

Glass paid Spinello $500 for the game and promised him a job after college. MGA then tweaked the toy a bit and sold it to Milton Bradley. It was still a game about plodding through a desert at that point, but Milton Bradley altered the concept. Operation was born, and the guy with the bright red nose was named Cavity Sam.

Glass is listed as the inventor on the patent applications of Operation (actually, of Death Valley), and many other games, but his real contribution is debatable. He was the idea man who ran the company, but he was backed up by a team of engineers and designers who did most of the work.

Nothing wrong with that. Glass' lifestyle was legendary; in fact, *Playboy* magazine did a photo spread of his Evanston, Illinois, home in 1970. Glass had remodeled a century-old carriage house and filled it with artwork by Picasso and Dalí. Two rooms were paneled in rosewood, with each wall's paneling cut from the same tree so that the grain patterns would match. He also dug into the ground to add a Roman tub that seated eight, with a Jacuzzi, drink dispenser, and mirrored walls. A sauna filled the next room. Glass liked to party, and he had the perfect venue for his soirées.

By most standards, Glass and his company were incredibly successful, but Glass is quoted as saying:

"I consider myself a complete and utter failure," "I'm a frustrated man," and "I never wrote a play or a book or relieved anybody's suffering for an hour."[17]

Not that Glass was an altruist. He partied hard, smoked three packs a day, lived on junk food and four or five hours of sleep a night, obsessively collected the trappings of a rich man but never enjoyed them, and—sadly but not surprisingly—died relatively young at the age of 60.

Milton Bradley, maker of Operation, bought a lot of games from MGA over the years. According to some, Glass products and designs accounted for a quarter of Milton Bradley's sales, which tripled between 1963 and 1968.

In the 21st century, you can buy Operation in its original version—or you can operate on Buzz Lightyear, Shrek, Homer Simpson, Spiderman, Iron Man, Mater (from *Cars*) or SpongeBob SquarePants. In Great Britain, you can even buy the *Dr. Who* version. All these are courtesy of Hasbro, who took over Milton Bradley in 1984.

If you want to learn more about Glass' eccentricities, the security surrounding his toy business, or his wild lifestyle, a former MGA employee put up a website called MarvinGlass.com. Glass is also mentioned in many books and magazines, and a Google search will turn up some interesting articles.

And that job Spinello was promised? He never got it but stayed in the Chicago area, working as an industrial designer, and today his grandchildren play the game he invented.

Mystery Date

The Mystery Date game was another example of how Milton Bradley's sales went up whenever they bought ideas from Marvin Glass Associates.

Henry Stan of MGA designed this as a girlie game. The game pieces and the box looked like Barbie, the dates looked like Ken, and the game cards were fashion ensembles to wear to the prom, the beach, to ski, or otherwise hang out. The date hid behind a plastic door in the middle of the board where he might be dressed in a tuxedo or goofy-looking nerd clothes.

The game came out in 1965, got updated in 1972, and faded away with the end of the Boomer teenage years. In 2000, Milton Bradley modernized it for the 21st century, but it's still a girlie game. If you have the original, whole game sets with the box are selling to collectors for hundreds of dollars today.

Rock'em Sock'em Robots

Are you getting tired of hearing about Marvin Glass? I hope not, because this 1965 hit is his too.

Glass and another designer, Burt Meyer, got the idea of Rock'em Sock'em Robots from an arcade game and worked on it for months. Like so many of his games, and like Glass himself, it was loud and confrontational.

Originally, the fighters were human boxers, but in April 1962, welterweight champ Benny Paret slipped into a coma and eventually died after being beaten at Madison Square Garden in a televised fight. Almost exactly one year later, boxer Davey Moore died hours after losing his world featherweight title bout at Dodger Stadium in Los Angeles.

After the second death, there were calls to ban boxing entirely. Even the Vatican newspaper *L'Osservatore Romano* chimed in, referring to boxing as "morally illicit." Glass wanted to drop the game, but Meyer suggested making the combatants robots, rather than men. Seeing a robot's head fly back is cool, but seeing a boxer's head do the same thing? Creepy.

The old black and white commercial is on YouTube if you want to refresh your memory, but here's a sampling of the dialogue:

"The Blue Bomber's block is knocked off!"

"His block is knocked off?"

"Sure!" the adult announcer laughs. "But you can press it back on again!"

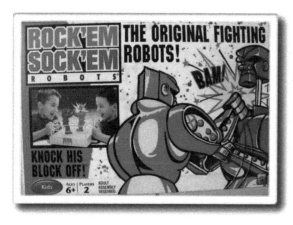

The robots have gotten smaller, but the box hasn't changed much in nearly 50 years.

With robots, it's funny. Even if the robots have names, like Red Rocker or Blue Bomber.

The robots' heads compress a spring, and jarring them by an eighth of an inch with a well-landed punch sets the spring free. Glass and Meyer's original idea had been to have the humanoid boxers fall over, so spring-loaded robot heads made their design work easier.

Marx Toys made Rock'em Sock'em Robots back then; Mattel makes them today—in a slightly reduced size, but with the same retro-looking box.

Twister

It's hard to believe today, but Milton Bradley Company almost missed the boat on Twister. How? Because they didn't take it to the springtime New York Toy Fair in 1966, where most buyers picked their Christmas inventory. They seemed to have reservations about the game, perhaps because there wasn't much in the box—the game consisted only of a plastic sheet and a spinner.

Where did the game come from in the first place?

Nope, not Marvin Glass.

Originally called King Footsie, the game was invented by an ad man named Reyn Guyer, who developed it for Johnson Wax, the shoe polish folks. The Wisconsin-based company asked Guyer to create a giveaway that kids could get for sending in magazine coupons.

Guyer said he created the game we know as Twister and after testing it, realized he was on to much more than a simple giveaway—so he swapped. He gave Johnson Wax some color patches to stick on shoes and took his game, which he called King Footsie, to the 3M Company. They passed.

Guyer then hired professional game designers Charles Foley and Neil Rabens. They helped fine-tune the game, which Rabens dubbed Pretzel. How big a part each man played is a matter of debate, as each of them later claimed credit for inventing Twister. But no matter the source of its genius, Milton Bradley bought it, changed the name to Twister (turns out there was already a toy named Pretzel), went into production . . . and then scratched their heads over how to promote it. Players had to reach through and around and often fall on top of each other —not the most comfortable image for a game in 1965.

Sales dragged for a few months. Even Sears, one of the biggest retailers in the country, refused to carry it. With great disappointment, Milton Bradley decided to stop production— only they forgot to tell the PR people.

The public relations staff were basically a small firm who'd sent out a dynamic woman named Mickey Mackay to promote Twister. It was kind of a trial run as Mackay's firm wanted to handle PR for all of Milton Bradley.

Because Mackay never got the word that Milton Bradley was going to cut Twister, she took the game and a cute model in tights to the NBC studio where Johnny Carson taped *The Tonight Show*. Why a model in tights? That became obvious when Mackay demo'd the game. Once the show's writers saw the model bending and sprawling and realized the comic potential, they wrote the game into that night's show.

Carson's guest that evening was Eva Gabor (her sitcom *Green Acres* was in its first year), and she wore—as usual—a low cut gown. Game on! After watching Carson and Gabor down on their hands and knees playing the game, the audience made Twister an instant hit. Milton Bradley sold three million Twister games during its first year of release.

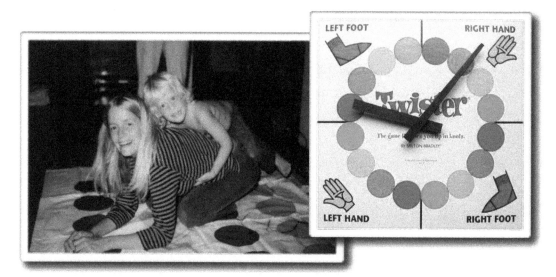

Playing Twister in 1972.

After that, Mackay arranged to have New York's Madison Avenue closed to traffic one day so mobs of people—encouraged by mini-skirted models—could play Twister in the street. It rained, but that didn't stop anyone from playing. Another time, Mackay brought 400 Twister mats to a Fort Lauderdale beach, set up crane shots, and called in the media. And the fun never ended.

A few years later, Guyer created another hit: the Nerf ball. He was trying to perfect a caveman game in which lightweight "boulders" were used to clobber opponents, when he suddenly realized that the boulders—made of open-celled polyurethane—would make a great indoor ball.

But because the Nerf ball didn't debut until 1970—and was aimed at younger kids—most Boomers were teenagers by then, so that's all we'll say about the Nerf.

Creative Toys for Our Brilliant Little Minds and Fingers

Play-Doh

The first Play-Doh, a white, clay-like substance, was marketed as Kutol's Wallpaper Cleaner. Back during the Depression and even before, that product was in high demand. Coal heating systems and lots of smoking coated wallpaper with grime and it was hard to clean. So Kutol Chemicals, a Cincinnati company that made soap and cleaning products, came out with a cleaner that would rub the dirt off without harming the color or pattern on the wallpaper.

Flash forward to 1949. Right after his father's death in a plane crash, young Joseph McVicker—who worked for his father's Kutol Chemicals—was stricken with Hodgkin's disease at the tender age of 25, and while he battled for his life, the business nearly went down the toilet.

Meanwhile, McVicker's sister-in-law Kay Zufall was teaching nursery school in New Jersey. She read in a magazine that children could make Christmas ornaments out of wallpaper cleaner, and danged if wallpaper cleaner wasn't one of the products turned out by Kutol Chemicals.

By now Joe—who'd been sent home to die—was actually on the road to recovery and trying to save his father's company. Kay told him of her discovery and he flew to New Jersey to watch her toddlers in action. Afterward, he flew

Joseph McVickers

back to Cincinnati ready to rebrand and launch a product that his dad had made for 20 years.

Joe's uncle, N.W. McVicker, had created the wallpaper cleaner to begin with and was called in to help rework it. He removed the detergents in the clay and added an almond scent to make it smell more appealing. Joe called it Rainbow Modeling Compound, but Kay Zufall stepped forward to save the day again. She thought the name was all wrong and came up with a new, catchier one: Play-Doh.

Joe took his Play-Doh to Cincinnati schools and to the school board, believing that schools—not retail consumers—would buy the stuff. Kutol originally packaged it in one-gallon cans with lids of red, blue, or yellow—like the Play-Doh inside. Soon, all the schools in the area were using it.

Joe then started selling it at education conventions, which led to demonstrations for toy store owners, which led to nationwide sales. Kutol Chemicals then set up a new subsidiary: Rainbow Crafts. A few retirees recall when Play-Doh first was first packaged in 7-ounce cans; the color white was added in 1958 to the red, blue, and yellow to make a four-pack.

The official Play-Doh website, however, says that Play-Doh first came in white only, and that the other three colors were added in 1957. If a time machine ever becomes available, perhaps its first trip should be to the Kutol Chemicals warehouse of 1956 or '57 to settle the burning question of Play-Doh coloring.

After Joe met with Captain Kangaroo—Bob Keeshan—Play-Doh found a home on TV. Joe was quite a salesman, but as he told the Captain: his new company had no money for advertising. Joe promised Keeshan 2% of sales if he'd put Play-Doh on his show twice a week, and the TV star agreed. *Romper Room* and *Ding Dong School* followed.

In four years, Rainbow Crafts was selling $3 million worth of Play-Doh a year. McVicker hired chemist and researcher Dr. Tien Lui to improve the product, and while some sites credit Dr. Lui with adding color, what he actually did was figure out how to keep Play-Doh from losing its color when it dried.

As a boost to the creative experience, the Play-Doh Fun Factory came out in 1960, the brainchild of a couple of engineers—Bob Bogill and Bill Dale—who came to the Play-Doh factory with the idea for a toy rocket. They were given a tour of the plant and watched giant extruders pump out Play-Doh and cut it off into can-sized bites. The duo went back to their drawing boards and designed the Fun Factory. It was a case of art imitating industry.

Kenner Products merged with Rainbow Crafts in 1971. Former partners held onto Kutol Products (it's still around) and wanted to keep Rainbow Crafts, but it was Joe McVicker's decision, and he accepted $3 million for it from Kenner.

Tonka acquired Play-Doh in 1987—by then it came in plastic, not cardboard, cans—and Hasbro bought Play-Doh in 1991.

A few trivia bites:

- By 2011, 700 million pounds of Play-Doh had been sold.

- The eight-color palette that became so popular was not introduced till 1983.

- It now comes in glitter and glow-in-the-dark colors with all sorts of play sets.

- The mascot on the package, who morphed from a pointy-eared elf to a pint-sized artist with a beret to a kid with a baseball cap turned backwards . . . His name is Play-Doh Pete, but he seems to be missing from most Play-Doh sets these days.

The Play-Doh mascot in the '50s, '60s & '70s (when Kenner bought the company).

In 2006, to celebrate Play-Doh's 50th Anniversary, Hasbro released a Play-Doh perfume. Yes, it smelled like a new can of Play-Doh and sold for around $19.

Models

Plastic models were another big hit of the 1950s.

For decades patient, industrious souls—and even some children—made models of planes, cars, guns, and ships, but these were of wood or metal. Balsa wood was an early favorite for model plane makers, but it required sanding and shaping, and most kids didn't have the skills for that. Model-making was an art for collectors and dilettantes . . . until 1951, that is.

That was the year Revell (whose name comes from the French verb "to awaken")—followed quickly by other companies—developed plastic injection models that were not only quick and easy to assemble, but incorporated incredible detail.

Lewis Glaser was the founder of Precision Specialties of California, which during World War II manufactured round, almost flat compacts that held powder and a mirror and slipped into ladies' purses (you see them all the time in old movies, but not so much now). By the mid 1940s, he was also making pull toys that looked like they walked off a *Toy Story* drawing board. Plastic model kits followed.

When Glaser changed his company name to Revell and brought out his first successful plastic model kit—Jack Benny's 1913 Maxwell automobile, a car made famous by Benny's radio and TV show—the 69-cent model flew off the shelves of Woolworth's, who sold these "Highway Pioneers" exclusively.

In time, he introduced other models: Stanley Steamers, Stutz Bearcats, turn-of-the-century Cadillacs, Model Ts. Who could resist? Revell soon made more cars than Ford, GM, and Chrysler combined, all with painstaking details that could require up to 7,000 hours in the design stage.

Another company, Monogram Models of Chicago—started by Bob Reder and Jack Besser in the 1940s—made balsa wood models of modern military planes and ships, especially the types of destroyers and cruisers that all kids and their Dads knew from World War II. Monogram switched to plastic in 1953, calling their products "Plastikits." Their first model was the Midget Racer—a hot rod, if you will—but the World War II fighting machines were soon available in plastic as well.

In 1953, Revell introduced a plastic model of the *USS Missouri.* Jet airplanes, submarines, tanks, ships and more followed. Before the end of the 1950s, Revell even issued "near-future" space vehicles, like a Space Station and Moon Ship. The most elaborate models—those with around 150 pieces—cost three bucks, and the boxes of these models, showing artwork of the plane in flight or a ship on the high seas, are considered valuable and collectible today.

A completed model of the USS Missouri, which Revell debuted in 1953.

By the mid-1950s, *Boys' Life* magazine reported that a full 80% of American boys were making models, and sales went from less than $1 million a year to over $60 million (that figure was for all model-making companies, not just Revell, and included those that produced balsa wood models).

The accuracy of each plastic model was a big selling point. Revell, for example, started by crafting a master model, then taking photos of every part of it and comparing those to photos of the original vehicle. The goal was that no one would be able to tell whether the photo was of the model or the real thing. The master model was then broken down, and thousands of hours were devoted to creating molds for each part—not separate molds, but a large multi-faceted steel mold that allowed all the different parts of each model kit to be made at once, in less than half a minute. That way, 150 kits could be turned out every hour.

In fact, in 1961, a Revell model of the Polaris guided missile submarine was examined by Admiral Hyman Rickman of the US Navy. His opinion? The model was tantamount to releasing classified information to anyone with $2.98 to spend!

Later Boomers will remember models of the "Rat Fink" and other specialty cars designed by Ed "Big Daddy" Roth. Revell signed a contract with Roth, who was a cult hero famous not only for his custom cars, but for the cartoons and airbrushed t-shirts he created. In the artwork, Roth's cars were driven by monsters and the giant Rat Fink.

The models featured both fanged monsters and cars like the Surfite, with a surfboard where the passenger seat should be. Roth got a penny for each sale, which in 1963 alone amounted to $32,000 in royalties. The real

Car and model designer
Ed "Big Daddy" Roth in the 1980s.

Surfite car, not the model, even made a guest appearance in the film *Beach Blanket Bingo*.

Not to be outdone, Monogram Models hired their own funny car designer. Tom Daniel created fantasy cars like the Li'l Coffin, based on a 1932 Ford Sedan with a 1954 Desoto engine. The model came with a skeleton that leaned against the car.

Revell became a publicly-traded company in 1965 and got into the slot-car racing field, which seriously hurt the company a few years later. Monogram, meanwhile, stayed private and tried to please both adult and child model makers. In the late 1960s, Monogram introduced their Snap-Tite line for children: models that didn't need glue as the pieces just snapped together. Right after that, Mattel acquired the company.

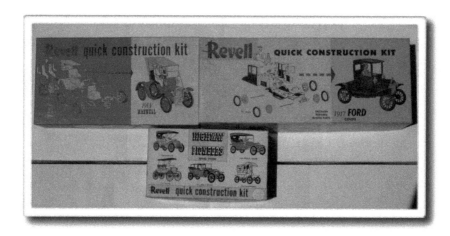

Revell introduced Highway Pioneers Quick Construction Kits (with plastic drivers) in 1953. These are c. 1955.

Revell merged with Monogram Models in the 1980s—Mattel put the latter back on the market—and the new company was moved to the Chicago area. Binney and Smith, makers of Crayola, owned them from 1994 to 2007, then Revell was purchased by the employee-owned company Hobbico in 2007.

And Big Daddy Roth, after decades designing cars and characters that now decorate surfboards, show up in tattoo parlors, and hang in fine art galleries, passed on in 2001.

Paint by Numbers

"Every man a Rembrandt" promised the box, and in 1953, Paint by Numbers kits took over the holidays and sold millions.

How were these popular kits born?

Max S. Klein acquired a Detroit company called Palmer Paint around 1950 and subsequently hired a young man, Dan Robbins, to design packages for him. Robbins came up with a great idea for paint kits: code each little paint pot with a number and sell them with a canvas already drawn, with paint numbers in every space. To show how it would work, Robbins created a prototype: an ultra-modern, abstract picture. Klein got the idea but told Robbins he wanted prettier pictures.

Robbins complied, but there's a funny story about that first abstract picture. Klein and Robbins included it in their first catalog of paint kits. A customer bought a kit and entered a completed copy in a San Francisco art show—and won first place.

Klein and Robbins called their new kits Craft Master, but no one cared. The sets just didn't sell well. But after two years passed, they suddenly took off—partly because Macy's started stocking them, and partly because of that abstract, award-winning painting that got so much publicity. Twelve million were sold between 1951 and 1954, and soon Robbins was supervising twenty-five artists who created new picture kits. To this day, he is probably the most exhibited artist in the world.

Mad Magazine's September 1958 cover satirized the Paint by Numbers fad.

Everything from smaller pictures of puppies and roses to large canvases with up to ninety colors of paint for luxurious landscapes abounded; reproductions of great works of art were popular too. Craft Master's version of DaVinci's *The Last Supper*, priced at $11.50, was their all-time best seller.

Compelling story behind *The Last Supper* picture: It was created by the first artist Robbins hired, Adam Grant. A Catholic immigrant from Poland, Grant had survived Hitler's death camps because he could paint. He created portraits of camp officers, still-life pictures, and even birthday greetings—all on demand, of course, because his life depended on pleasing the Nazis with his work. After the war ended, he came to Detroit and went to work for Ford Motor Company, until Robbins brought him into the Craft Masters fold. Later, Robbins hired an art school graduate from Baltimore named Peggy, who soon became Mrs. Grant.

Adam Grant composed The Last Supper for Craft Master.

With regard to promotion, Ozzie and Harriet sold the sets on TV, and the fad became so popular that one of President Eisenhower's secretaries, Thomas Edwin Stephens, distributed Paint by Numbers kits to White House visitors and administration officials, including cabinet secretaries. Soon, he had enough completed paintings to mount a show in a West Wing corridor. Decades later, the Smithsonian exhibited the paintings, including works by such well-known public servants as Claire Booth Luce and Henry Cabot Lodge, Jr., as well as celebrities like Ethel Merman.

Despite the craze, however, academics and artists worried from the start over what the fad said about Americans: "Filler-inners of numbered pictures," sneered Russell Lynes in *Life*, while art historian Alfred Werner whined about "paintitis." Not so long ago, such paintings were dumped in garbage cans or sold for a quarter at garage sales. Now, however, they're collectible and highly sought after.

If you're interested, check Ebay—or better yet, the PaintbyNumbersMuseum.com.

Visible Man

The Renwal Company—Renwal Products, Renwal Toys, and other iterations—started in 1939 when a man named Irving Lawner spelled his name backwards and began distributing kitchen gadgets. Within a year he sold Renwal to his top two salesmen, and after World War II Renwal came out with two very successful lines of plastic toys: replicas of planes, like the P-47 Thunderbolt, and dollhouse furniture.

Sales were healthy until Renwal decided to try its hand at metal toys and compete with Matchbox. The effort did not go well, so after that debacle in the mid-'50s, the owners sold the company to two company officers, L. S. Wetzel and Irving Lubow. While recovering from the financial losses of the metal toy experiment, they found themselves facing increasing competition from Japan. So Lubow brought in new toy designers—including a man named Marcel Jovine.

Jovine had been a soldier in his native Italy during the war, was captured by Allied forces in North Africa, and shipped to a POW camp in Pennsylvania. American POW camps were not as awful as those in other countries, however, and this one brought in entertainers. Before the war ended, Jovine had fallen in love with a singer and pianist named Angela D'Oro, who performed at the camp.

The exhibit of educational toys from the 1950s and 1960s showcased the Visible Man.

Once the peace treaties were signed, Jovine was shipped home, but he turned right around and came back to America to marry D'Oro. The only problem was how to make a living.

Because he was a sketcher and sculptor, though not formally trained, he fell into the toy business. Ideal Toy Company bought one of his creations and named it the Blessed Event—a baby doll made of plastic that Jovine himself cooked up—literally. He brewed and perfected the rubber and plastic formula on his kitchen stove. The royalties from that toy paid for his growing family's home in New Jersey.

Shortly after, he began working for Renwal producing models. As Irving Lubow recalled, "About the time of Sputnik, [Jovine] ran out of assignments, so I suggested he ought to spend some time in the library thinking up possible products we could develop on scientific themes."[18]

The library was a fine arsenal of ideas, but upon visiting the American Museum of Natural History in New York one day, Jovine saw a life-sized figure of a woman with all her internal organs. Sparked by the exhibit, he was inspired to create what eventually became the Visible Man and Visible Woman.

Renwal loved the concept and envisioned a whole line of educational toys, unveiling the new model with a full-page ad in the *New York Times* of July 7 and 11, 1959. A huge drawing of the model was surrounded by text that began, "You are looking at a miracle, the human body." The rest of the text was rather dull—mentioning months of research . . . precisely detailed . . . blah blah blah, ending with "You owe it to your children." The bottom quarter of the page was covered with a list of stores that would sell The Visible Man to worthy parents for just $4.98.

Basically, the Visible Man was a 1:6 scale model of an unsexed human male, with his organs and bones made to be removed and put back into position. Not all retailers got on board, however; the yuck factor was a bit much for some. But no one could deny the intrigue of the package's wording: "THE WONDERS OF THE HUMAN BODY REVEALED." Even the booklet included in the box was supposedly double-checked by a team of doctors. Ultimately, the Visible Man was a huge success, and for three years, Renwal could not keep up with demand.

Visible Woman came next, with the "Miracle of Birth" packaged separately inside the box. A label alerted parents about the enclosure, which consisted of eight additional plastic pieces that showed pregnancy in the seventh month of gestation. If it offended them, they could simply remove the packet from the box.

Next came the most successful product of all: the Visible V-8 Engine. After that, there were Visible Pigeons and other animals, a Visible Auto Chassis, and a Visible Airplane Engine, but none of them really took off as the previous Visible sets had. Renwal tried other educational toys, like a Botany Kit, but in 1968 the company was sold. It had its ups and downs, reissued the most popular Visible models, but finally folded for good in 1976.

As for Jovine, he left the world of toy and model making in the late 1970s to design coins, civic seals, and medals. He sculpted and created molds for the Winter Olympic medals in 1980, and one of his designs was even used by the United States Treasury for a special five-dollar gold piece to commemorate the bicentennial of the Constitution in 1987. When he tired of that pursuit, he moved to another, that of sculpting famous racehorses.

Ant Farms

Milton Levine—also known as "Uncle Milton" (not to be confused with Milton Berle)—began making Ant Farms in 1956. Before that venture, Levine had grown up on a Pennsylvania farm, fought in World War II, and married a French girl he met in Cherbourg when she was playing piano in a USO club. With his brother-in-law, E. J. Cossman, he started a mail-order novelty business in Pittsburgh and moved it to California in 1952.

Levine got the idea of the Ant Farm at a picnic where ants were the uninvited guests. He'd loved collecting insects as a child, and since he had his mail-order business (called Cossman & Levine), he and his partner designed the toy. They figured they'd need around $18,000 to go into production with their first design—an outrageous amount in the early '50s—so the men had to iron out some problems, do a little research, and reduce costs before they could move forward.

First, Levine and Cossman ran a two-inch ad in the *Los Angeles Times* to see if there really was a market for Ant Farms. The result was overwhelmingly positive, so the men went into production mode.

Making the plastic-sided farms would be easy, but ants had to be collected. Each farm required 25 to 30 of the little buggers, and it turns out there's only one species of ants that will tunnel in daylight: red harvester ants. Watching the ants tunnel was pretty much the point of the Ant Farm, so red harvester ants it was.

After a few false starts, Levine signed a contract with the Gidney family, paying them a penny an ant for all they could provide. It sounds strange, but in those early days the Gidney family invented special equipment that vacuumed up the ants for delivery to Cossman & Levine.

The first Ant Farms were only six by nine inches but they soon increased to ten by fifteen. Once mail orders were coming in, toy stores wanted to stock Ant Farms too. Live ants couldn't just sit in boxes on shop shelves for weeks or months, however, so the new business designed a mail-in certificate for the six-footed critters. The company slogan became, "You take the farm, we mail the ants."

Sales took off, especially after Cossman was a guest on *The Johnny Carson Show* and managed to amuse the audience for thirty minutes with the Ant Farm. Levine's young son Steven even got into the family business, appearing on children's TV shows with the toy.

Decades later, another supplier—who preferred to remain anonymous—took over the task of gathering the ants. A grown-up Steven Levine claimed that the new supplier did not rely on mechanical equipment, but instead used straws in the desert. The ant pickers would find an ant hill, stick a straw into it and blow. Then they scooped up all the ants as they scampered away.

Was he serious? You can never tell when ant impresarios talk to the media. There've been many ant suppliers over the years—sometimes as many as 35 contractors at a time. As to methodology, maybe it's best not to ask too many questions.

Note: Federal regulations have always dictated that no queen ants can be shipped by mail; properly cared for ants in an ant farm, however, can last for one to three months, after which more can be ordered ("properly cared for" means no shaking as ants can die of shock).

After buying out his brother-in-law's share in the 1960s, Levine renamed the company Uncle Milton Industries. Apparently, whenever he introduced himself, people would ask, "If there are so many ants, where are all the uncles?" So he started calling himself the uncle.

The term "Ant Farm" is trademarked by Uncle Milton Industries, as cartoonist Scott Adams found out when he used it injudiciously in his *Dilbert* comic strip. Uncle Milton's lawyers wrote Adams a letter demanding he apologize and not use the term anymore. And just for the record, a colony of ants in a habitat with transparent sides can be called either a formicarium or a vivarium or even an ant habitat, but Ant Farm refers specifically to the kit made by Uncle Milton Industries.

For awhile, at least, Ant Farms were assembled in Los Angeles area communities by handicapped workers, which won the elder Levine a Man of the Year award in 1986.

Milton Levine lived into his 90s and over 20 million Ant Farms were sold during his lifetime. Just before he died, his company was sold to a private equity group which still runs it under the Uncle Milton name.

Etch A Sketch

Maybe make that *L'Etch A Sketch*. That's right, the toy is French.

Electrician Andre Cassagnes developed the L'Ecran Magique or Telecran, which he displayed at the 1959 International Toy Fair in Nuremberg, Germany.[19] Sadly, it wasn't successful, but the next best thing happened when Ohio Art decided to buy it from Cassagnes for $25,000 and change its name.

Within a year, the toy debuted in summer with a $2.99 price tag, and holiday demand for the Etch A Sketch was so high that Ohio Art continued production till noon of Christmas Eve.

Ohio Art Company, by the way, was founded over a century ago by a dentist who successfully designed and made metal picture frames. A few years later, he added metal tea sets for little girls and other stamped metal toys, but nothing took off like the Etch A Sketch did.

So how does this magic toy work?

The knobs actually control one stylus, which draws a design on the back of the glass screen. Aluminum powder and plastic pellets coat the screen, and as the stylus passes through it drags the aluminum powder, which is held in place by static changes. Shaking the Etch A Sketch mixes up the pellets and powder once again.

The toy got a bum rap in the late 1960s when a child fell downstairs while holding an Etch A Sketch, and the glass broke in the fall and cut her. Minneapolis lawyer Allen Saeks represented the family, who claimed faulty construction and sued Ohio Art. Technically, Saeks lost the case, but Ohio Art was the real loser: an estimated $2.5 million in sales evaporated. Ultimately, they redesigned the toy, and today the screen is plastic, not glass.

Using the classic toy, an artist called Etcha posts amazing pictures on the Internet.

Ohio Arts moved manufacturing to China in 2001, devastating the folks of Bryan, Ohio, where the Etch A Sketch factory had operated for 40 years. One hundred workers lost their jobs, though many found work in other divisions of Ohio Art.

Some have been quoted as saying the town lost its heart that year.

Creepy Crawlers & Incredible Edibles

One day, Mattel product development specialists Fred Adickes and Floyd Schlau were fiddling with a pink substance used in doll manufacturing called plastisol, a PVC compound that turned from liquid to goo easily. Ever-curious and inventive, they wondered what else could be done with it.

Adickes' job in the 1960s was to come up with new toys for boys, and when he and Schlau turned the plastisol into "plastigoop" and poured it into metal molds to make worms and bugs, Thingmakers and Creepy Crawlers were born.

Starting in 1964, parents could buy kids a Vacu-Maker kit that included the Thingmaker heating unit, bottles of different colors of plastigoop, and metal molds for toads, centipedes, dragonflies, moths, spiders, bats, lizards, worms, scorpions—the works. The kit also included plastic sheets and templates to make wings to glue onto the bugs.

Once you had the plug-in Thingmaker heater—which reached a temperature of 300 degrees —other accessory packs of molds and goop were available. And of course, more varieties of mold sets followed: you could ask for the Giant Creepy Crawlers, the Fright Factory (make your own vampire teeth!), the Creeple People, or—if you were really, really skittish—Fun Flowers. By 1969, Mattel was even selling molds for Peanuts characters, followed by a few comic book heroes.

But let's not leave the '60s yet. Two years after Creepy Crawlers debuted, Mattel introduced Incredible Edibles. This was also an Adickes-inspired creation for which he said he originally used pancake mix and green food coloring in the molds.[21] Several people loved it, but Jack Ryan, in charge of Mattel's R&D division, insisted the edible concoction had to jiggle. The result? Ryan had his chemists develop a gelatin-based formula called Gobble-DeGoop, with flavors like licorice, butterscotch, mint, and root beer.

Incredible Edibles came with a half-dozen tubes of Gobble-DeGoop, and the molds were cooked in the clown-faced Sooper Gooper oven. Though the clown's wooden nose served as a handle, it got too hot to touch at times. But no matter, the end product—which came out slightly gummy—was the important thing, and kids loved it.

The methodology for making any of these noxious treats would probably send most 21st-century parents to the Consumer Products Safety Commission website. The instructions went something like this:

1. Pour the goop into a mold, and put that mold on top of an electric heating unit.

2. When the goop starts to smell, use a pair of tongs to pick up the mold and put it in a tray of water to cool it.

3. The mold sizzles as it hits the cold water.

4. Use a knife-like tool to remove the set goop from the mold.

Sound like a lawsuit waiting to happen? Well, Mattel pulled the product off the market sometime in the early '70s—but not because of safety concerns over hot ovens, toxic smells, or knives. Nope. It was over concerns for kids with diabetes.

Incredible Edibles were advertised as being delicious and sugar-free. No one remembers them as delicious, but technically the sugar-free part was true. The Goop, however, was starchy, which was just as bad for diabetics.[20]

The toy made a comeback in the 1990s when a different manufacturer sold Creepy Crawlers packaged with a safer, plastic heating oven. And Plastigoop? It's still sold by several suppliers and can be procured through the Internet.

Spirograph

Denys Fisher of Great Britain introduced his Spirograph drawing tool at the International Toy Fair in Nuremberg in 1965—the same big fair that saw the debut of the Etch A Sketch six years earlier. (As a side note for those who like this sort of trivia, Nuremberg's International Toy Fair is the biggest trade fair for toymakers in the world. It's been held every year since 1950, lasts for six days, and about a million products are on display each year.)

Now, back to the Spirograph. Fisher, an engineer, made the product initially for industrial—perhaps even military—use, then realized it would make a great toy. He manufactured it in England, winning Toy of the Year-type awards, and in 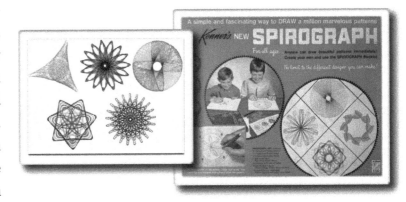 1966 he sold US distribution rights to Kenner. More awards followed, and a few years later, Hasbro—by then part of General Mills—bought Fisher's entire company.

It was a complicated toy to use with all the plastic gear-like stators, but it sure made pretty designs. You clamped or pinned the paper in place, fit the smaller gears into or outside of a large hoop, and put a colored pen or two into the holes centered in the gears. In a few minutes, you had created beautiful art—or at least, something your Mom would treasure.

As inspired as it was, the Spirograph was actually not a completely new idea. Here are some examples of earlier spiral-based toys:

✦ In the very early 1900s, a toy called the Marvelous Wondergraph hooked up wooden wheels (not gears) with wires to a penholder to make spirographic pictures. Once it was all set up, the child simply turned a crank.

✦ Northern Signal Company produced Hoot-Nanny: the Magic Designer in the late 1920s. It used metal discs and pencils to make the same detailed wheels and designs as the later Spirograph. By the 1940s, the Hoot-Nanny name had been dropped, but the Magic Designer was still available, now with an Aladdin-like character on the box. Creative Playthings and Lakeside Toys produced the Magic Designer right into the 1960s.

✦ The Dizzy Doodler from Carter Craft was similar, and came out in the post-World War II era.

✦ Marx Toys had a Design-All or Design-O-Marx toy in the 1960s that used plastic gears and colorful pens, very similar to the Spirograph.

Regardless of its status of innovation, however, the Spirograph was a marvelous toy if you were patient enough to get the hang of it.

Lite-Brite

This toy owes its inspiration to an over-the-top window display along Fifth Avenue in New York, where Marvin Glass, Burt Meyer, and Henry Stan walked during a break from the 1966 Toy Fair. When they saw the thousands of tiny lights used to compose the arrangement, they immediately thought: *toy!*

Their second thought was that such a toy would be impractical and expensive to produce. But right on the spot, Meyer came up with the idea of using one bulb to backlight the many plastic pegs that make up a Lite-Brite screen. That alone reduced the cost, so when the MGA guys returned to their headquarters in Chicago, they got to work.

About those headquarters . . .

Someday, someone will no doubt write a smash bestseller about Marvin Glass and his many idiosyncrasies. We've already mentioned that he was manic, egotistical, hedonistic, driven, ostentatious, manipulative, and more, but another adjective often mentioned is paranoid. Glass was a nut about security.

The MGA Headquarters looked like a prison and was called "the fortress." Closed-circuit cameras tracked all the comings and goings of employees and visitors, and the doors had triple locks on them that were changed periodically, and only three full sets of keys existed. Employees were sworn to secrecy way beyond the standard non-disclosure agreements, and they were forbidden to discuss any toys under development with their families or spouses. The inside decor, however, belied the trappings of the outside. Paintings by Dalí, crystal chandeliers, and a chef who prepared Chinese dishes for the execs and their guests made for an elegant work environment that one wouldn't have guessed existed from the looks of the fortified exterior.

Legend has it that when Glass arrived at the New York Toy Fair, he brought his latest inventions by armored truck. At times he handcuffed his briefcase to his wrist. He even paid for prototypes to have their own seats on the plane next to the executives—they were never checked in as baggage.

But the Lite-Brite did not have to make that trip to be sold. Glass was so certain about the magic of this toy that he invited Merrill Hassenfeld—head of Hasbro—to the fortress in Chicago. Burt Meyer confirms the story that once the guest was seated in a conference room, the lights were dimmed and the Lite-Brite was turned on. One peg was already pushed into the black paper; Hassenfeld picked up a second peg and pushed it in. His eyes and smile became as bright as the toy. A deal was made within the hour.

As you already know, Glass lived hard and died relatively young (it's surprising how young sixty seems to Boomers these days), but Burt Meyer—whose name has been mentioned almost as often as Marvin Glass'—was blessed with a stronger constitution. He biked coast to coast across the US in 41 days; he skied to the North Pole at 69, one of the oldest men to do so. He's also a pilot and was still flying at 85. What's more, after MGA disbanded in 1988, Meyer rounded up other ex-employees, founded Meyer/Glass, and continued to create toys for the next generation, right into the 21st century. He is a happily retired toy designer as of this writing.

When the Chicago Toy & Game Inventor Group presented Meyer with a Tagie Award honoring a lifetime of toy-making achievement, Meyer acknowledged that the Lite-Brite was his favorite invention.

Chapter Ten

Dolls and Figures

Let's start with a disclaimer: not all dolls are for girls, not even girlie dolls. With that in mind, this section commences with the first action figure, which—even though no one wants to call it a doll—is kind of hard to pigeonhole into any other slot. He's tough and manly, but in his original incarnation he stood only a bit taller than Barbie, moved his arms and legs, and the company that introduced him made millions off his additional clothes and accessories. We're talking about none other than:

GI Joe

This quintessential tough guy was born when toy designer Larry Reiner and toy agent and pitchman Stan Weston envisioned a foot-high toy soldier and brought the idea to Hasbro with the goal of boosting sales with dozens of accessories: battle armaments, equipment, uniforms, you name it. He would be just like Barbie, but with a major exception: he wouldn't be marketed as a *doll*.

Hasbro president Merrill Hassenfeld was out of the country at the time, but Creative Director Don Levine championed the idea. By the time Merrill returned, Levine presented him with a whole merchandising kit for the toy and Merrill loved it. But it was by no means a sure thing—if anyone called it a doll, Hasbro was sunk. Boys did not play with dolls.

Everyone realized that throwing their resources into the making of such a toy line could bankrupt Hasbro. It meant moving production overseas to reduce the cost of creating the flexible joints and durability that GI Joe required—far beyond what most dolls had in those days. The cost to make and market the toy would be $15 million in 1963 dollars, and Hasbro was not a big company back then, in spite of the success of Mr. Potato Head. In fact, they had just lost $5 million on the Flubber debacle.[22]

1964 GI Joe in a mint Green Beret outfit.

Despite the risk, Hasbro went ahead and rolled out four GI Joe figures in 1964: Action Soldier, Action Marine, Action Sailor, and Action Pilot. Of course, they represented the US Army, Marines, Navy, and Air Force and sported uniforms identical to the real thing, in miniature. All even had the dashing and manly scar on their cheeks.

Why all four at once? Simple: Hasbro was worried about imitators. If they produced an Air Force pilot, another company might get the jump on them with a Navy frogman. In fact, so great was their concern that employees and executives were sworn to secrecy over the project, and GI Joe was referred to as "the robot," even at work.

Action Sailor on Shore Patrol.

Just before the toy went public, Larry Reiner and Stan Weston were offered a $100,000 one-time payment or another deal that would've included less cash up front, but a percentage of the sales. They weren't happy with the 1% royalty in that second offer—the industry standard was much higher—but Hasbro argued that it had sunk so much borrowed money into GI Joe that they couldn't pay more.

So Reiner and Weston took the $100,000 cash and split it between them. The irony? Had they accepted the 1% royalty instead, they would've made $150,000 the first year alone.

Hasbro, now owning all rights to GI Joe, moved on to the New York City Toy Fair, the biggest US event of the toy industry. But . . . The toy bombed. Buyers just weren't interested. A foot-high figure was a doll, the buyers insisted, and *boys did not play with dolls.*[23]

But the buyers were wrong.

In summer, Hasbro started running daily commercials in New York City, then they went nationwide with the ads. Egged on (just a little) by the patriotic marching song on the commercials—a throwback to Irving Berlin and World War I—consumers flocked to Woolworth's and the few other chains that were brave enough to stock the toy. Two million were sold between summer and Christmas in 1964 for a total of $5.3 million. The next year, sales skyrocketed to $23 million.

Little boys loved GI Joe and his accessories to the tune of $40 million in its initial two years. Even the first GI Joes had loads of outfits to collect—from weapon sets, parachutes, tents (which came with a machine gun and tripod), military parade uniforms, frogman outfits, and more. The early GI Joe Action Marine Beachhead Assault Field Pack set, for example, came with an M-1 rifle, bayonet, hand grenades, cartridge belts with snap-open pockets, field pack, canteen, shovel, and shovel cover.

Sales dropped off sharply in the late 1960s, due to the Vietnam War and competition from other action figures that weren't soldiers. But rather than just dump the toy—which boys still loved, even if their parents had qualms about "war toys"—Hasbro repositioned the action figures as Adventure Teams made up of several "GI Joes: Men of Action."

So by 1969, parents were buying their kids GI Joe astronauts and deep-sea divers. Soon GI Joes were marketed exclusively as teams of adventurers and explorers. Each was still called GI Joe, though. As Hasbro's associate marketing director put it: "We could not change that, because some buyers would not have bought the new toy without the old name."[24]

As Joe evolved, he became a test pilot or a treasure hunter, a spy or a marine—there was even a talking version. When an African-American Joe made his appearance in the Adventurers group, sales increased again. Hasbro sold adventure kits that came with a comic-type booklet and all the equipment needed to accomplish the mission. By 1974, the action figures had features like Kung-Fu grip and speed like the Six Million Dollar Man.

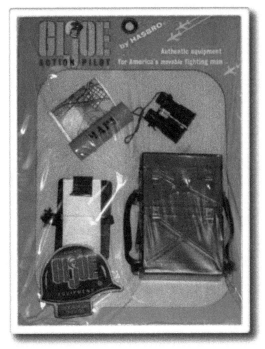

An early accessory package for Action Pilot.

Sales hit $26 million in 1973—his best year ever. But as interest dwindled over the coming years (you can blame George Lucas and his *Star Wars* action figures who boldly took over the market), GI Joe was finally retired . . . put out to pasture . . . dumped . . . and well, dropped from the market completely in 1978. However, you can't keep a good man down. Led by Stephen Hassenfeld—son of Merrill—Hasbro resurrected GI Joes as Real American Heroes in 1982. The new toy was much smaller, just under four inches tall, but it was promoted through a Marvel comic book and soon had a Saturday morning cartoon series, a movie, and video game tie-ins. Sales of the action figures grossed $50 million that year alone, and they continued to rise to $185 million by 1986. The additional merchandise—lunch boxes, clothes, and video games—added to the pot. By 1990, the larger, original-sized Joe was back in stores, but that takes us beyond the Boomer scope.

Play Family / Little People

The Play Family (which became Little People in 1985) started quietly in 1950, when Fisher-Price began selling the Looky Fire Truck with three tiny figures attached—each with a round head topped with a fireman's helmet. But the official anniversary of the line wasn't set until 1959.

Why the lag?

Because nine years passed before a toy with figures—the same type of round heads on a body that looked like a peg—could be *removed* from the vehicle and played with separately. This innovation was a game changer. The Safety School Bus, which had a clear plastic top half, was released with six removable figures (a seventh figure, the driver, never left his post).

By 1960, the pegs were a family with a child, a dog, and a Nifty Station Wagon (worth up to $600 to collectors, should you find one in the attic). Hats and helmets were dropped and wisps of hair were painted on the round heads. Soon, larger and more elaborate play sets, such as the Amusement Park, came out. By 1965—the same year the toy was first advertised on TV on *The Price Is Right*—the pegs were named Play Family.

In 1968, Fisher-Price rolled out the most popular set—the farm and barn—retailing at $9.99. Farmer Jed and the barn door that moo'd have been part of this set for over 40 years, and over 16 million have been sold.

Next came the house and furniture, the garage with the elevator, and the school with the bright numbers and letters that always ended up on the frig. (Admit it—you'd forgotten that those magnetized letters on the frig came from a Play Family set, right?)

A new name was adopted in 1985, and the Play Family became Little People. Through the decades, the style of the peg morphed from wooden cylinders to plastic. Some years, the toys had triangle or square bases, and in others they swelled and tapered. Play Family and Little People toys can be dated and valued according to these variations, as well as by model numbers.

The entire toy line grew wider in 1991. By then, over 800 million of the figures had been sold, but the old molds were destroyed and new, chunkier Little People filled toy stores.

That may or may not have had anything to do with a court settlement made over a tragic incident that occurred twenty years earlier: a 14-month-old child in Canada nearly died when a

Play Family figure lodged in his throat. His mother tried to force air into his lungs via his nose while his father drove to the hospital. The toddler lived, but suffered severe brain damage.

As a result, in the late 1980s, Fisher-Price got hit with the biggest lawsuit award in toy industry history: $3.1 million (the actual settlement a few months later was $2.25 million).

The lawyer in this case was Ed Swartz, famous as the man who wrote the books *Toys That Don't Care* and *Toys That Kill* (the latter actually featured Little People toys on the cover). Swartz was also the man behind the annual Christmastime list of dangerous toys—in other words, a force to be reckoned with.

Still, the settlement did not generate as much publicity as expected. Though changes were made to the product and warning labels added, Play Family—now Little People—and Fisher-Price endured and are both still thriving today.

 *Ginny*

Ginny may not have been the best-selling doll in the world but her introduction sparked a change in the market. Before Ginny, doll makers sold dressed dolls; after Ginny, the money was in the clothes and accessories. Ginny created the dolly aftermarket, if you will.

The originator of Ginny was Jennie Adler Graves of Somerville, Massachusetts, who started Ye Olde Vogue Doll Shoppe in 1922. Graves' specialty was clothing design, so for twenty-five years she dressed and sold dolls that she imported. In the 1940s sales dipped, so Mrs. Graves designed an eight-inch doll named Toddles, which sold well. Other names followed, and in 1947 Mrs. Graves named a new doll Ginny, after her daughter Virginia.

Although she wasn't that different from her predecessors, Ginny took off. She had "sleep-eyes" that opened and closed and synthetic hair that could be washed and set. But starting in 1954, Ginny could also walk and turn her head from side to side. That same year, accessories like a suitcase and shoe bag were added to handle Ginny's extensive wardrobe. Soon, she had a swing and play set, a wardrobe with sliding doors, and even more furniture.

How successful was the Ginny doll? Well, in 1949, Mrs. Graves and her Vogue Doll company had a sales volume of $239,000. In 1953, sales topped $2 million, and by 1957, $5 million. Vogue even released a 10.5-inch Jill doll in 1957 as a teenaged big sister for Ginny—she had separate wardrobe options and sold well too.

Collectors claim that Jennie Adler Graves changed the way dolls were marketed. She—or more accurately, her company—was the first to develop the lucrative niche in costumes and accessories by selling a doll that was nearly naked with a clothing catalog right in the box. And since Vogue was selling so many outfits for eight-inch tall figures, they were not bothered at all by the glut of imitation dolls that appeared in the 1950s.

Ginny could be dressed as a nurse, bride, or cowgirl; she had everything from pinafores and tutus to kimonos and ball gowns, and in 1955, Ginny even had a Davy Crockett outfit! While the doll itself cost around $2, the ensembles ranged from $1–$5. And to keep them buying, little girls could sign up for Ginny's 12-Star Plan and get a new outfit every month.

By 1963, production of Vogue dolls and their clothes slowed with the emergence of Barbie, and Jill and others were discontinued. In 1969 Vogue stopped making Ginny too—at least in the US. Though vinyl Ginny dolls came from Hong Kong for awhile, the quality was not the same.

The company was family owned until 1972 when it was bought by—of all entities—Tonka. A few years later Lesney, the makers of Matchbox cars and trucks, bought Vogue, sold them, and the buy-and-sell continued until 1995 when an owner willing to bring back the traditional dolls took over. As a result, Vogue Dolls is still around, making Ginny and other dolls and designing new outfits with a decided retro feel—heavy on gingham and flared skirts. You can see them all at VogueDolls.com.

Toni Dolls

Toni—the famed permanent wave company (and if you don't know that, are you really a Boomer?)—partnered with the Ideal Toy Company to create the Toni doll in 1949. A pink-labeled box that looked a lot like the real Toni perm box (although it said "play wave kit") came with the dolls.

The selling point for these dolls was the hair and the faux permanent wave—little girls loved to curl Toni's rooted hair with real papers and miniature curlers, and the "setting lotions" were non-toxic and could be replaced with sugar water.

At that time, Ideal was still being run by Benjamin Michtom, son of the original Teddy Bear creators. Michtom hit upon on a great marketing idea: get other companies to pay for ads! So besides the Toni company, ads for the Toni doll were funded by Dupont, which made the nylon for the doll's hair, and Celanese Corp., which made the doll's body.

The next brainstorm? Have Paris designers make clothes for the doll. In 1951, the houses of Worth, Patou, Paquin and more designed high-fashion outfits for twelve special dolls who then toured the country. The promotion was so successful that Ideal repeated the stunt with American designers.

Two years later, American Character Doll Company (a long-lived outfit founded in 1919) began making the Toni dolls. By the late 1950s you could buy Toni as small as 10.5 inches and as tall as 21 inches, and she came with both little-girl outfits and sophisticated grown-up clothes. Those later dolls, with feet arched to fit high heels, had a baby face but a body with older curves and poses—a bit creepy, truth be told.

Between 1949 and 1956, over a million Toni dolls were sold in varying sizes, many through catalogs like those from Sears.

Flo Selfman has held onto her large Toni doll to this day.

Tiny Tears

When she debuted in 1950, Tiny Tears was unique in that she was made of hard rubber except for her head, which was molded, painted plastic. She came with a pink bubble pipe, which most of us never figured out how to work, but her distinctive features were the small holes in her mouth and in the inner corners of both eyes.

Yup, just like the name says, Tiny Tears shed real tears under the right circumstances. If you filled her little bottle with water and pushed it into her mouth or squeezed her tummy, tears would seep out of her eyes.

Although the first doll was 11.5 inches long, just like the later fashion dolls, Tiny Tears was always a baby, whether life-sized or in miniature. You may remember the little onesie-style romper that most Tiny Tears arrived in; it had pink piping along the edges. A wardrobe of pink and white clothes and little cradles, car beds (nothing like later car seats), and playpens could also be bought separately.

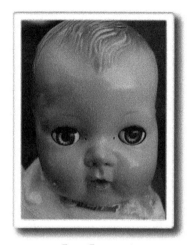

Tiny Tears with tear holes visible.

Throughout the '50s and '60s, the doll's maker—American Character Doll Company—switched from rubber to vinyl bodies and attached wig-hair on the head. The doll came in several sizes (Teeny-Weeny Tiny Tears, anyone? Yes, that was a real name) and in 1959, the manufacturer added eyes that slowly closed when the doll was rocked. She wet her diaper too.

Ideal Toy Company eventually bought American Character Doll Company and released a new version of the doll in the early '70s. The new Tiny Tears cried as soon as she was laid down; otherwise, the Ideal Tiny Tears appealed to '70s parents and kids for the same reason that the TV show *Happy Days* did: nostalgia.

If you still have your Boomer-era Tiny Tears, those with rubber bodies are most valuable to collectors, even though the rubber discolors over time. Brunette Tiny Tears are rarer than blondes, and for your treasure to really keep its value, ensure she's wrapped up and kept out of the sun.

Betsy McCall

This doll started life as a paper doll in *McCall's* magazine in 1951. Millions of mothers got *McCall's* through the '50s, and every issue featured a page with little Betsy, sometimes accompanied by other members of the family. Betsy would appear in her undies with three or four cutout dresses and a paragraph or two to describe an outing or adventure.

The first real Betsy McCall dolls were made by Ideal Toy Company in 1952 and stood 14 inches tall. Five years later, American Character Doll Company, the makers of Tiny Tears, got the license and began crafting small, eight-inch dolls for about $2 each.

A 20-inch Betsy followed. Finally, in 1959, a 36-inch doll with a 38-inch brother, Sandy McCall, came out, imitative of the Patti Playpal doll. Betsy, if you remember, did not look toddler-like, but rather was a slender young girl with thick eyelashes, more of a tween.

The real sales effort—as with so many dolls—went into the wardrobe. Between 1957 and 1960, American Character Doll Company designed over 100 ensembles for Betsy. Another company made white, stenciled Betsy McCall furniture.

The dolls ceased production in 1963 but have been made again since the 1990s by Tonner Dolls . . . just in case you'd like to own another one for old time's sake.

Saralee

In the late 1940s and early 1950, Sara Lee Creech—who was white—noticed that no matter what race children were, their dolls were invariably white. That struck Creech as wrong; she believed little girls should have dolls that looked like *them*.

That might seem a bit anachronistic for a woman of that era, but Mrs. Creech served on

The December 1954 McCalls magazine featured this page for the paper doll.

an interracial council in her small city of Belle Glade, Florida, and her thinking was ahead of the curve. She believed that lovely, dark-skinned dolls who looked like real babies (as opposed to pickaninny dolls, which insulted black children with their exaggerated features) would make young children of any race more tolerant and respectful.

While Creech worked to make the doll a reality, former First Lady Eleanor Roosevelt heard about the project and helped publicize her efforts. Mrs. Roosevelt even brought a group of leading African Americans together—including Jackie Robinson and his wife, writer Zora Neale

Hurston, civil rights leader Ralph Bunche, Mary McCloud Bethune, and others. Amazingly, all of these visionaries came together to discuss a doll's appearance.

Sculptor Sheila Burlingame modeled Saralee's head after studying a thousand photographs of black children—photographs taken by Creech. David Rosenstein, President of Ideal Toys, embraced the idea and agreed that the dolls would be made of fine materials and stick to Burlingame's model.

The Saralee doll came out in time for Christmas in 1951. Mrs. Roosevelt gave her endorsement in popular magazines, and the Sears Catalog included the doll as well.

When she was first sold in 1951, the retail price of the 18-inch doll was $6.89; today, modern replicas of the Saralee doll sell for $100. And the real doll from the 1950s? She's practically priceless.

Uneeda Fashion Dolls

Uneeda Doll Company dates back to 1917, and throughout its long life made hundreds of dolls: movie star dolls in vinyl, cloth and bisque babies, even some famous figures like Charles Lindbergh, the first pilot to solo across the Atlantic in the 1920s. In the Boomer era, Uneeda developed a "teen fashion doll" that beat Barbie to store shelves by three years—and that had equally unrealistic measurements that were anything but sexy.

Debuting in 1957, the TinyTeen dolls sported childish features with practically no neck, a chubby, pouty baby face, and eyes that closed. At the same time, the doll had a curvy waist and slender arms and legs; red polish decorated her fingertips and toenails and her ears were pierced—a very conflicting and mixed message to children. Uneeda might have been on to something with these dolls, but it's just hard to imagine what—the oversized head looked so bizarre on the adolescent-style body.

A second, almost identical doll was Suzette, created by Uneeda to be sold exclusively at W. T. Grant Department Stores. The only difference between TinyTeen and the slightly cheaper Suzette was that Suzette lacked the colored nails and jointed waist that TinyTeen had. The exclusivity agreement didn't last long; soon Suzette was being marketed at Sears and other places. And just to confuse matters, TinyTeen lost the jointed waist and painted nails, which made them virtually identical.

As with other dolls, the outfits were the real money makers. All sorts of lingerie and high-fashion garden party sundresses with elaborate hats—not to mention embellished bridal gowns and veils—were boxed up and sold separately. TinyTeen dolls also came in special editions, like the Blue Fairy TinyTeen in 1962, which had aqua hair and a magic wand.

Long before Barbie hooked up with Ken, TinyTeen and Suzette had Bob—a boy doll with his own wardrobe. Bob could be decked out in silky pajamas, a cowboy outfit, sports clothes, or casual wear—with short- and long-sleeved shirts in plaids to go with his khaki pants.

Soon, Uneeda introduced the larger Dollikin doll, in either a 14- or 19-inch size—with its own wardrobe, of course. Dollikins had up to 16 joints—knees, elbows, ankles, shoulders, etc.—and were often dressed in long sleeves and pants to hide the lines that marked a joint.

Baby-faced Suzette in her lingerie; doll owned by Valerie Myers.

Once Barbie debuted, Suzette and her friends were revamped to match the Mattel babe's proportions, and the giant head was shrunk to meet the size of the doll's contemporaries. After that, Uneeda continued to sell baby dolls, toddler dolls, and more, and in 1960 they were licensed by Disney to create the Pollyanna doll, in sizes up to 31 inches tall, as well as an Annette Funicello doll. They later contracted with Dam Trolls to make the Wishnik troll figures from 1965 into the 1980s.

What happened to Uneeda? They're still around, though the company has changed hands. From the beginning through the Boomer years, dolls were made in a Brooklyn factory, but now they come from overseas. You can check out their modern offerings at Uneedadoll.com.

Shirley Temple Dolls

A huge child star in the 1930s, Shirley Temple was the perfect model for a doll. Earlier, Depression-era dolls were still around, but the ones Boomers remember were produced by Ideal starting in 1958. The reason? The grown-up Shirley Temple now had a TV show, *The Shirley Temple Storybook*. Even though the actress was clearly an adult and wore glamorous gowns on the show, the dolls depicted Shirley as the beloved little girl of classic movie fame. They came with outfits from her films as well as original designs, and since the doll came in five heights, from 12 inches to 36 inches, there were lots of clothes to collect that are still sought after today.

Patti Playpal

In 1959, Ideal needed a new style of doll and came out with Patti Playpal, designed to be the same size as most three-year-olds, about 35 inches high. The perk of this life-size darling was that little girls could put their own clothes on the dolls—but, of course, plenty of dress sets were sold for Patti as well. You may even remember the most popular one: the red and white checked gingham dress with a white pinafore.

Ideal went all out for Patti, employing a soon-to-be famous sculptor named Neil Estern. The artist's goal was to avoid the "vacant detached stare and stylized European look" of other popular dolls and create a doll with the "sparkle of a child's lively personality."[25]

It was Estern's wife Ann, also an artist, who designed both the face paint and the dress and pinafore that Patti Playpal came in. Most significantly, Ann Estern fought for Patti's straight hair. As she told the story, "Up to this point, all the dolls at Ideal had wavy, marcelled hair that made them look as if they had just come from the beauty parlor!" Ann brought an adorable little girl with straight hair to the Ideal Toy folks to prove her point, but remembered that convincing the toymakers was "a huge effort."

Thankfully, she was successful.

Neil Estern created other Playpal family of dolls for Ideal, but only a few years later he became better known for his bronze statues of John F. Kennedy, Fiorello LaGuardia, and other famous men and women, culminating in the seated, caped statue of Franklin Delano Roosevelt and his dog Fala for that president's memorial in Washington D.C.

Patti Playpal set parents back $29.95 in those days, but that didn't deter most—the doll made a million dollars for Ideal during its first year. Soon, though, the dolls could be bought through the Sears catalog for just under $19.

From the beginning, you could get Patti as a blonde, brunette, or redhead, but all the dolls had pale skin. And though many of us remember a walking Patti, that feature came later. The 1959 version did have twistable wrists, but that soon changed as well.

Three different Patti Playpals
show just how special
the doll was.

Patti also had a little sister Penny, who at 32 inches high represented a two-year-old. Other siblings came in varying sizes: Suzy, a 28-inch toddler; twins Johnny and Bonnie, life-sized babies; and finally Peter, a taller big brother for Patti.

The dolls were so popular that Ideal branched out, making child-size dolls of Betsy McCall and Lori Martin, the star of the TV show *National Velvet,* as well as a few others.

In 1981, Ideal reissued Patti Playpal using the original molds—and this time around, they included an African American doll. However, the company that invented the Teddy Bear was sold the very next year to CBS Toy Company, and eventually—through many sales and mergers —became part of Mattel.

Chatty Cathy

Mattel debuted the first talking doll in 1960, causing every little girl named Cathy to be called "Chatty Cathy" whenever she talked too much. Ever wonder how many visits to a therapist that gabby doll was responsible for? Perhaps only the "Betsy Wetsy" namesakes spent more time on the couch.

Trauma aside, Cathy was quite an innovation. You simply pulled a plastic ring attached to an internal string at the back of her neck and she talked! The doll had a phonograph record in her belly, so when her string was pulled, it drew a metal coil wrapped around a pulley, playing a phrase from the record like "I love you." Eleven phrases were voiced by none other than June Foray, the professional voice actress best known for playing Rocky the Flying Squirrel. Over eight decades of working in radio and film, she's played just about everything, from Witch Hazel on Bugs Bunny cartoons to Lucifer the cat in Disney's *Cinderella.*

Remember *The Twilight Zone* episode with the doll that looked and sounded a lot like Chatty Cathy? It was called "Living Doll," and a relatively young Telly Savalas played the wicked stepdad whose stepdaughter brings home a windup doll who tells the man, "My name is Talking Tina, and I'm going to kill you." (It's OK; he deserves it.)

June Foray, channelling her dark side, voiced Talking Tina in that show.

It should also be mentioned that while there is little doubt Foray spoke the words that were replicated in every Chatty Cathy doll that went on sale, another person may have recorded the doll's voice on prototypes, earlier in 1959. That person was Jack Ryan's daughter, Ann P. Ryan (the claims are out there). Ryan, if you remember from the Mattel Corp. history, was the colorful designer of many Mattel innovations, including the talking mechanism in Chatty Cathy. His is the name that actually appears on the patent.

In 1962, Mattel introduced a black Chatty Cathy, along with a new Chatty Baby doll. By then, Cathy's vocabulary had increased to 18 phrases, and the cloth cover over the speaker in her chest was removed. You may remember a bunch of small holes in the doll's vinyl body where the sound emerged.

Unfortunately, the talking mechanism—while innovative for 1960—was not hardy enough to last through the years. Something would eventually snap in the mechanism, and then, no more sound. It's very rare to find a Chatty Cathy from the early 1960s that still speaks today.

Santa brought Chatty Cathy to Cheryl Gardner in 1961.

The doll went out of production in 1964 but came back in 1970, when Mattel reissued the doll and hired actress Maureen McCormick to record Chatty Cathy's voice. The choice was serendipitous as McCormick had starred in a 1964 Chatty Cathy commercial. She shot a "Living Barbie" commercial in 1970 as well, but her most famous role started in 1969, as Marcia Brady in *The Brady Bunch*.

More Babies, More Gimmicks

Remember when Fred and Wilma Flintstone had a baby? Well, danged if Ideal wasn't right there with a cuddly little Pebbles doll in 1963. And what about Baby Secret from Mattel? She would whisper in your ear and her lips really moved. Mattel also came out with Baby First Step, who—first steps apparently being too tame to hold our attention for long—also roller skated.

Moving into the early 1970s we had Baby Alive, who chewed and swallowed and made bubbles. Funny story: When Kenner's designers presented their first Baby Alive to the company president, Bernard Loomis, the doll pooped green gel all over his arm. Some of the men in the room were disgusted. Who would buy a doll that poops? they asked.

Fortunately, Loomis saw the potential in the doll, and the Kenner Baby Alive was the most popular doll of 1973—outselling even Barbie. Remember what you—or your kids—fed her? It was cherry, banana, or lime—or rather red, yellow, and green—and the poop came out the same color.

Barbie

While we skipped ahead to the 1970s to mention milestones in the baby doll arena, you may have thought we were forgetting the most famous doll of all. Never!

An American icon, Barbie is not just a doll—she defined the postwar generation of little girls (and a few boys). For once, children could play with dolls without being mommy—they could dress them and imagine grown-up glamour, careers, and exciting evenings.

But as you've no doubt noted, the teenaged fashion model doll was not really a bolt out of the blue for Mattel, but rather a fairly logical progression from dolls that were becoming less babyish and downright chic.

Ruth Handler, creator of Barbie and cofounder of Mattel, said she got the idea for the doll while watching her daughter Barbara play with one-dimensional, flat paper dolls. To the child, the paper images had exciting lives and things to do. A light-bulb went on in Handler's head.

Interestingly, Ruth Handler never played with dolls as a girl. But she threw herself into the design of Barbie, using a chesty German doll she'd bought in Switzerland as a model. That doll was a Bild Lilli doll.

Bild was the name of a German comic strip featuring a gold-digging sexpot: Lilli. The Lilli doll was not intended for children (think stag parties and gag gifts). Mattel designed their own version of Lilli, exactly the same size, and when it took off, Mattel quietly bought the rights to the Lilli doll, and possibly the molds.

Doubtful? Go ahead, Google a picture of the Bild Lilli doll. It's impossible not to see a more-than-striking resemblance to early Barbie.

The original Barbie of 1959 had a ponytail, black and white bathing suit, hoop earrings, and holes on the soles of her vinyl feet that fit onto prongs. In other words, she was always posing, as befits a "teen age fashion model."

This might be a good time to mention that those original $3 dolls in their black and white bathing suits have gone for as much as $25,000 at auction. That's in mint condition, of course.

By 1960, Mattel proclaimed Barbie a "Busy Gal" and a fashion designer with a portfolio by day; in the evenings, she purred into her own microphone as a hot chanteuse. During that first decade, there were nurse and stewardess uniforms, and even an astronaut costume. Today, Barbie's had anywhere from 80 to 120 careers, depending on who's doing the counting, and those include presidential candidate and Olympic gold medalist.

And about that design . . . for decades, credit for Barbie's look and measurements have been debated. Jack Ryan held some of the early patents for Barbie, but Mattel has downplayed his role. (Ryan was a colorful character—you can read more about him in the Mattel section of Toy Companies.)

To contain costs, Mattel contracted with a Japanese firm to make Barbie of vinyl, using new and sophisticated technologies. They sent a Lilli doll overseas to show what they wanted, and then molds were made and sent back to Mattel headquarters. The molds came with tiny nipples on the breasts because the Lilli doll had them, so Jack Ryan used a delicate Swiss watchmakers' file to rub them off and sent the prototype back.

Another Mattel employee who had a lot to do with Barbie's look was Charlotte Johnson. Mattel hired her away from a teaching job in an art institute and sent her to live in Japan for a year. From the Imperial Hotel in Tokyo (the hotel designed by Frank Lloyd Wright that inspired his son to create Lincoln Logs), Johnson designed and oversaw the manufacture of the doll's 22 original ensembles.

Imagine ordering up tens of thousands of tiny zippers and minuscule buttons before anyone had heard of Barbie, and you can understand why Charlotte Johnson had to stay in Tokyo for a whole year. Once the designs were set and factories had cut the fabrics, outfits were farmed out to hundreds of home-workers all over Japan, some sewing on buttons and appliqués, others attaching the completed clothes to cardboard backing.

Back in the states, Ruth Handler worried. She knew girls would love Barbie; their parents, though, might take some convincing. Ruth's concern led her to hire a famous marketing psychologist, Ernest Dichter, to help design a campaign that would make the doll more

The very first Barbie had hoop earrings, no blue eyeshadow, and holes in her feet.

palatable to parents. Mattel paid Dichter $12,000 for six months of work, and he delivered. Finding that mothers did, indeed, hate the busty doll while their daughters loved it, Dichter suggested that Mattel present the doll as a poised, polished role model for girls. They heeded his advice, and that's how Barbie became the "Genuine Teen Age Fashion Model," as it said on the box. That's also one reason why Mattel has always referred to Barbie as *her*, never *it*.

By that time, factories in Japan were turning out 20,000 Barbies a week. But when Mattel introduced Barbie at the New York Toy Fair in March 1959, disaster struck: toy buyers and sales*men* (in those days, the sales force was almost all male) ignored the doll. As a result, Mattel cut back on production.

Ruth was distracted by the impending wedding of her real daughter Barbara to pay much attention to the apparent setback. And good that she didn't because by summer of the same year, every girl in America wanted a Barbie doll. No one knows why; it just happened. The toy world has never been the same.

The ever-changing Barbie can be dated by things like hair styles and eye makeup. Case in point: Ponytails were sold through 1966, with "bubblecut" coiffures introduced in 1961, then wigs and eventually Color Magic hair. Blinking eyes were available in 1964. Twist and turn bodies followed bendable legs, and by 1968, Barbie could even talk. Not till 1971, though, did Barbie drop the sideways glance that some found so flirtatious, and start looking straight ahead.

Ken made his debut back in 1961 (take a wild guess what the name of Ruth Handler's son was). In 1962, Mattel signed with the Irwin Company to produce sports cars for both Ken and Barbie. The car was an orange Austin-Healey 3000 MKII, about 18 inches long. There were other colors, like pink and aqua, but those are extremely rare (and by now, you realize that rare, in Boomer toy talk, is a synonym for valuable). Barbie's Dream House then came along in 1963, which by the 1980s, evolved from the original cardboard house into a molded plastic three-story pink palace, with an elevator and swimming pool.

And is there any Boomer girl who doesn't remember hearing a version of "That doll dresses better than I do!"

ICEBREAKER
(without doll) #942
Red velveteen skating skirt
topped with flurry, white jacket.
Red knit leotard with turtleneck
and long sleeves, long stockings
and skates complete the set. $3.00

RED FLARE
(without doll) #939
Luscious red velvet ensemble.
Flared coat with bell sleeves
and white satin lining.
Matching pillbox hat, handbag,
long, white gloves and
Red shoes. $3.00

Which of these did you or your sister own?

Charlotte Johnson continued to outfit Barbie with chic clothes and accessories through the doll's first two decades. The fact that the clothes were made in Japan became a selling point, and it was highlighted in ads. Each outfit had a name like "Sweet Dreams," "Golden Splendor," and "Solo in the Spotlight"—a torch singer ensemble that came with a microphone. The fabrics sparkled; the stitches were tiny. My personal favorite was "Silken Flame," a red velvet strapless bodice attached to a full white satin skirt that was simple yet elegant.

At this late date, some of those early doll clothes can fetch hundreds of dollars, but beware: many outfits were reissued in later years for collectors, so if you find a like-new pink satin "Enchanted Evening" gown with pearls and stole, it may be a 1990s creation, not a 1960 original.

Mattel went all out, showcasing more than half of Barbie's original outfits for the doll's first commercial, aired during a break on *The Mickey Mouse Club*. It started with a song, sung not in a child's voice but in that of a grown woman:

Barbie, you're beautiful!
You make me feel
My Barbie doll is really real!
Barbie's small and so petite,
Her clothes and figure look so neat.
Her dazzling outfit rings a bell.
At parties she will cast a spell.
Purses, hats, and gloves galore,
And all the gadgets gals adore!

After the male announcer mentioned the price, the song went on:

Someday, I'm gonna be
'xactly like you.
Till then, I know just what I'll do.
Barbie, beautiful Barbie,
I'll make believe that I am you!

Then the man comes back to intone: "You can tell it's Mattel, it's swell."

After the British Invasion (remember Mary Quant, miniskirts, and go-go boots?), fashions changed dramatically. Rather than alter Barbie, however, Mattel came up with a British friend for her: Francie, with fashions from swinging London. Over the years, Midge, her best friend, and Skipper, her little sister, were introduced into Barbie's world too.

Although they were always tweaking the doll, in 1967 Mattel did a complete makeover of the classic Barbie, giving her straight long hair and a new wardrobe. More marketing genius ensued when Mattel offered a trade-in program to encourage girls to get the new Barbie—your old Barbie plus $1.50 got you the new model. The result? Over 1.2 million dolls were traded in for the new style in one month.

Let's face it: Barbie's pretty impressive, and we're not talking about those standout ta-tas. Here are the real measurements that put Barbie in the Toy Hall of Fame:

- After introducing Barbie at the New York Toy Fair in 1959, Mattel sold over 300,000 of the dolls that first year at $3 each.

- In the first eight years of production, Mattel sold half a billion dollars worth of Barbie dolls and accessories.

- In the 21st century, Barbie is a two million dollar a year industry.

- Over a billion dolls were sold by 2002.

 *Barbie Imitators*

To no one's surprise (cheap imitations were its hallmark), the Marx Toy Company came out with a ponytailed doll in 1961 named Miss Seventeen. At 15 inches high, she stood taller than Barbie, but she had an unmistakable resemblance. The following year, Marx produced Miss Bonnie, exactly the same size as Barbie—or rather to be more accurate, exactly the same size as Lilli—because Marx had bought the rights to make the Lilli doll in the US and immediately sued Mattel for patent infringement. Counter-accusations involving more and more toys—including the Burp Gun—ensued, and after two years a judge dismissed the case, ordering each side to pay their own dang legal fees.

Why hasn't anyone ever made a movie about these shenanigans? Mattel later bought the rights to Lilli so that they'd never fight that battle again.

Not to be outdone by Marx, Ideal Toy Company came out with the Tammy doll in 1962. Based on the Debbie Reynolds character from the movie *Tammy and the Bachelor*, the doll had a more babyish face and body, although she did have breasts. You could buy Tammy's Mom and Tammy's Dad dolls too, as well as clothes for all of them; an endless stream of brothers and sisters and a boyfriend followed. As the 1960s progressed, Tammy got slimmer and more coquettish, but her run ended in 1966.

American Character Doll Company brought out the Tressy doll to compete with Barbie—her big selling point being hair that grew. Little girls would squeeze a button and pull the hair to make it long, then twist the button to retract the hair. Except for the hair, Tressy imitated Barbie in size (11.5 inches tall), look (her painted eyes glanced sideways like Barbie), and arched feet that came with plastic, open-toed heels, just like you-know-who.

Besides the fashionable wardrobe, Tressy also came with brushes and combs, curlers, and setting solutions. Barbie got a dream house? Well, Tressy had a beauty salon! She even had a little sister, Cricket. However, none of that competed seriously with the staying power of Barbie. American Character Doll Company went out of business in the late 1960s, and Tressy was no more.

Ideal brought out a larger doll with "hair that grows" in 1969, just after American Character Doll Company—makers of Tressy—went out of business. Ideal bought some of their patents as the company liquidated, including the mechanism for growing hair. They called their new doll Crissy, and at 18 inches tall, she was clearly not meant to compete with Barbie.

Big childish eyes and a fairly flat chest also made Crissy quite different, but she was not a baby or child—she was probably what we call a Tween today. Over the years Crissy swiveled, talked, looked around, was marketed with friends (including one called Tressy), and acquired curling machines, braids, beads, and extensions. Ideal continued making these dolls into the 1980s.

There were more, of course, but these are the most memorable. So check your attic, your old boxes, and the back of the linen closet—if you find an intact doll, boxed and pristine, maybe you'll hit the jackpot. Remember the $25,000 Barbie?

But windfall aside for those mint-condition treasures, isn't it sad to think that one little girl didn't have that doll to play with? After all, dolls aren't made to sit in unopened boxes.

Chapter Eleven

Bikes and Outdoor Toys

Bicycles

A new bike! For many, it was the ultimate Christmas present. A bike dwarfed all other gifts under the tree; it may have also kept your parents up till 4am if they had to assemble it. For those who never received a bike on Christmas morning . . . gosh, I'm sorry. That sucks, but that's what therapy's for. You may want to skip the next few pages.

Bikes for kids were introduced after World War I, way back in our grandparents' era. Before that, cycling was strictly a grown-up activity. Believe it or not, the world of serious cycling considers the Boomer years a slow, inactive time; high-tech racing bikes and their complex innovations didn't start happening until the 1980s.

A popular poster of Annette Funicello on a Schwinn in the late 1950s.

Boomers beg to differ. After World War II, the market for bicycles switched dramatically to children, and by the mid-1950s, those children were receiving two to three million bikes a year. To us, those bikes were anything but "slow and inactive"—they were exciting, shiny, and fast!

Manufacturers quickly caught on to the fact that modifying bike styles each year generated more sales, so as bikes evolved, accessories like fancy horns, reflectors, speedometers, and headlights were in high demand.

In 1949, Schwinn came out with the Black Phantom, and it was even shinier than its predecessors. Why? Because it had chrome! Chrome fenders, chrome rims . . . ahh how it shone. As with cars of the era, chrome was flashy, modern, and very *in*. The success of the Black Phantom in the 1950s spawned siblings—a Green Phantom and a Red Phantom—giving Schwinn dominance over the US bicycle industry.

In case you didn't know, Schwinn was not a newcomer to the Boomer era—the company had actually been a player in the bike market since the 1890s. For the first half of the 20th century, Schwinn sold most of their bikes to giant retail chains like Sears & Roebuck and Montgomery Ward, and the store name—not Schwinn—appeared on the bikes. It was only in 1950 that Schwinn decided to grow their own brand by insisting that *their* name be on all their bikes. Once that decision was made, they began selling them everywhere: department stores, sporting good stores, even hardware stores—any retail outlet where the Schwinn name was prominently displayed.

Schwinn used celebrities like Bing Crosby, Lana Turner, and even Ronald Reagan in its ads, and in 1958 the company started advertising on *Captain Kangaroo.*

So why—on a toddlers' show—would a company run commercials for two-wheel bicycles that their main audience couldn't even ride? Because Schwinn was brilliant: they realized that the ten million toddlers watching *Captain Kangaroo* would be asking their parents for bicycles in just a few short years, and they wanted all ten million of those kids to demand a Schwinn for Christmas.

For decades, up into the 1950s, American bikes were built heavy. Customers could buy imported European bikes instead; besides being lighter and faster, they were cheaper in those days and began to gobble up a bigger share of the market. By 1955, over one-third of the bikes sold in the US were imported from Europe. To compete, Schwinn and other companies started making what they called "middleweight" bikes: not as light as the European models, but far lighter and narrower in design than older American bicycles. Suddenly, that's what everyone wanted, and other bicycle companies jumped on board.

Here are some bikes of the era you might remember:

Donald Duck

Shelby produced the Donald Duck bicycle starting in 1949. It was popular for years: a bright bike with 24-inch wheels that made a quacking sound and had Donald's face mounted on the base of the handlebars. The fenders, both front and back, curled up gracefully at the end like a duck's tail.

Corvette

Schwinn designed its Corvette a year after the sports car of the same name debuted. It featured handbrakes and a 3-speed rear hub with other Euro features. The Corvette bike went out to dealers in 1955 and Schwinn dominated one-fourth of all the US bike sales that year.

Whizzer

Whizzer Motor Company started making this model that featured an engine mounted on the bike in the early 1940s, but they proved popular after the war too. The engine turned the bike into a motor vehicle in some states, so it fell victim to local regulations and laws, disappearing around the mid-1950s.

Radiobike

Huffy's Radiobike came out in 1955, possibly the most ill-timed bike innovation ever. Why? Transistor radios hit the shelves in 1956, and the Radiobike—with its big radio set mounted just in front of the seat—suddenly looked clunky.

Cowboy Bikes

Rollfast made a Hopalong Cassidy bike, and Monark came out with a Gene Autry model. These bikes had toy pistols set in a holster attached to a fringed saddlebag.

Spaceliner and Spacelander

These came out at the end of the 1950s: bikes for the Space Age from two different manufacturers. Sears sold the Spaceliner, with slim contours and lots of chrome, while the Spacelander was made of fiberglass and won awards for design in Great Britain.

Varsity

The bridge to the 1960s was the Varsity, another offering from Schwinn. It debuted as an 8-speed bike and quickly went into production as a 10-speed. The Varsity answered the growing demand for speed, but it was durable and soon featured an all-steel derailleur. With derailleurs, the state-of-the-art transmission system for bikes, riders could increase performance by using hand controls to shift the bike's chain from one sprocket (or gear) to another.

Sting-Ray

The hottest bike of the '60s. Two features made this beauty unique: its chopper-style handlebars and a banana—or polo—seat. The bike style started as a fad in California, where kids were stripping down 20-inch bike frames and adding the long seat and high handlebars for no apparent reason other than they liked them. They called them Pig Bikes, and Pig Bikes were great for doing wheelies.

A 1964 Sting-Ray.

Remember wheelies? You leaned back and yanked the handlebars up and for a few great seconds, you coasted on the back wheel alone. Kind of like the Lone Ranger on Silver, when the horse lifted his front legs and whinnied.

To keep the history lively, there are two stories about the development of wheelie bikes and Sting-Rays:

In the Schwinn version, a company sales rep reported to headquarters that out in Orange County, California, kids were customizing bikes like crazy with polo seats and high handlebars. Frank W. Schwinn, son of the company's founder, was gravely ill and his vice president was running Schwinn. The VP went into the factory and dummied up the first Sting-Ray prototype based on what that sales rep told him.

When Mr. Schwinn died and all the company executives came to Chicago for his funeral, they stopped by the plant and saw the Sting-Ray prototypes. They weren't sold on the look, but they *loved* riding the bikes.

The other story behind the Sting Ray-style bike concerned a guy named Peter Mole who noticed the custom bike craze in San Diego in 1962. He worked for a bicycle parts distributor that could not keep polo seats or high handlebars in stock, because all the kids were buying them to add to their bikes. Peter Mole contacted Huffy, a Los Angeles-area bike maker, about designing such a bike for mass production. Huffy was hesitant, so to seal the deal Mole promised to buy all the special parts back from Huffy if the bike flopped. The result was the Huffy Penguin, so named because the frame was painted black and the long seat was white.

The Penguin came out in early 1963 and sales were brisk—even after Schwinn introduced their Sting-Ray many months later. Huffy came out with new models, including the Dragster series, but they started selling their bike through discount stores and cut Peter Mole out of the deal.

Mole's mistake, as he later said, was that he did not have an exclusive contract with Huffy. In the end, it didn't matter much; Schwinn—who supplied all the big bike shops and retailers—soon controlled the market for those wheelie bikes.

Schwinn sold 45,000 Sting-Rays that first year. The demand was actually higher, but the supplier ran out of 20-inch wheels. In the coming years, however, Schwinn was shrewd. They added new features, such as a 16-inch front wheel, as well as new colors and models (Orange Krates and Pea Pickers, etc.), so there was always a reason to want the latest model. In 1968, the year that the first Krate was introduced, five million Sting-Rays were sold.

Huffy declared bankruptcy in 2004, a victim to both shady accounting and competition from China. But the Huffy Penguins—those first few hundred bikes—are rare and valuable these days.

As for Schwinn . . .

Well, the Sting-Ray was its last big hit. Except for that bike, the company seemed to lose its savvy after Frank W. Schwinn's 1963 death, even when his son took over—the third Schwinn to run the company. When the BMX bike craze got popular, Schwinn as a company didn't seem to notice; ditto with mountain bikes. Schwinn simply kept making the same bikes it had in the 1960s, ignoring the demand for lighter bikes and new innovations until it was too late.

Schwinn declared bankruptcy in 1992 and the family sold its interest in the company. Several more sales followed, and today Schwinn is owned by Nautilus, Inc, the maker of Bowflex and Stairmaster.

Raleigh, another maker of wheelie bikes, introduced the Raleigh Chopper in 1969. The Chopper had an even longer seat that bent up in back, a tall sissy bar, and wider tires. A British company, Raleigh has been sold several times and rights to use its name were held by Huffy for awhile. Today, it's split into a couple of companies, both owned by different Dutch groups.

 *Skateboards*

The historical jury is out on exactly when these made it into middle-class use, because the skateboard evolved from homemade contraptions. In fact, the first theory of skateboarding is that it was developed by surfers who basically fitted small surfboards with roller skate wheels.

A second theory is that early skateboards were homemade scooters. When the handle broke off, kids improvised and voilà—a skateboard.

Whichever it was, skateboarding became urban, modern, and cool. You needed sidewalks, not paths or dirt; you relished parking lots, not fields. Essentially, skateboarding is a 20th century (and beyond) sport celebrating individual skill and daring.

The first skateboard was officially sold in 1959, and it was called the Roller Derby. A few years later the early skateboard maker, surfer Hobie Alter of California, managed to get Johnny Carson to ride a skateboard down his studio hallway in 1964. Soon after, the Vita Pak Juice Company was looking for new product lines when an employee suggested using old orange-crate wood for a platform and fastening it to wheels. They approached Hobie Alter with their idea, and Hobie agreed to design the board. He dropped the orange crate in favor of fiberglass, and Vita Pak went into the skateboard business with their "Hobie" board.

A very early wooden Hobie Super Surfer Board and Wheels from Vita Pac, courtesy KrauseHaus.

Other manufacturers had names like Makah, Surf Skater, and Bun Buster—the last company sold 50,000 boards in 1965. Skateboarding soon became a national pastime, with competitions along the California coastline and on college campuses in the East.

The mid-'60s was the high point of the early skateboard phase. In 1965, skateboarding was even covered by *Newsweek* in an article that described its popularity as "a national tidal wave."

At that time, you could buy wood and fiberglass skateboard models that were between 26 and 35 inches long, with ball bearing clay wheels. The opaque fiberglass (which yellowed over the years) was molded around a polished wood core. Those sidewalk surfboards started at $1.25 and went up to $15—or even $50 if you got one with a motor attached. As a result of the craze, the sales figures put out by different companies are astronomical: 50 million boards sold in 1965 alone. Skateboarding, for one brief shining moment, was considered a $100 million a year industry.

So what happened after 1965?

Basically, skateboarders hit a brick wall—not the kind that most mothers worried about, but the kind that kept enthusiasts from getting better and pushing the sport to extremes. Blame it on the steel or clay wheels, which didn't allow for tricks. With steel, a rough patch of sidewalk or an unexpected rock or pit would throw a rider onto a nearby lawn—if they were lucky. And turns had to be wide, with plenty of room—more like guiding a boat than a board. Once you mastered that, what else was there to do?

Hobie Alter, the surfer-turned-manufacturer, had developed clay wheels in the late 1950s (the clay was actually plastic, paper, and ground walnut shells). And although they allowed more maneuverability, they didn't last very long—a few days at best.

So right about the time that cities started prohibiting skateboards because of broken bones and noggins, kids stopped using them. New companies that had cropped up to make skateboards found themselves with product and no buyers. In short, the industry went from $100 million in one year to zip. The rumor went round that Vita Pak alone was stuck with four warehouses full of 200,000 Hobies.

Not until 1970 did someone come up with synthetic rubber wheels. Actually, those amber polyurethane wheels, made for roller skates, were about to be thrown in the trash. A Baby Boomer and former skateboarder named Frank Nasworthy saw them, took a few home, and tinkered with an old skateboard. He tested the polyurethane wheels on the hills and parking structures of Columbia Pike in Virginia.

Nasworthy soared. Those wheels provided the traction and durability that earlier skateboard wheels lacked. But Nasworthy was very young and not your typical entrepreneur. He took his new board to California where he simply used it for himself instead of trying to market it. Three years passed before he sank $700 into a new company called Cadillac Wheels. After that, Nasworthy became the man credited with reviving the sport.

Although skateboarding lay dormant for a decade, it re-emerged with a vengeance in 1975 —pretty much after the Boomer era. It took off again mainly because the technology caught up with the sport, thanks to Frank Nasworthy. The spark was the Zephyr team of Venice, who skateboarded to cultish fame at a freestyle competition in Del Mar, California. What followed made a great story; in fact, it's twice been made into movies in *The Lords of Dogtown* and *Dogtown and the Z-Boys*, the latter being a documentary.

 *Frisbee*

Back in 1937, a teenager named Fred Morrison and his soon-to-be wife Lucile Nay tossed a popcorn can lid back and forth at a Thanksgiving party. Later, they switched to pie pans, then cake pans, becoming the first to recognize the cake pan's superior aerodynamic capabilities. They were playing their pan-toss game on the beach in Santa Monica one day when someone offered them a quarter for the toy.

"A light came on," Morrison wrote many years later. Not a big light—not a "we can change the world" or even a "we can get filthy rich" light. No, this little light of Morrison's reminded him that cake pans cost a nickel. "A drive-in hamburger cost nineteen cents. If we could sell two pans, we could both have a burger and split an order of fries."[26]

Empires have rarely been built on less.

The couple started buying cake pans in bulk from a local hardware store and hit the beaches, selling the pans for a quarter until World War II intervened. Morrison became a P-47 pilot and briefly a prisoner of war, but he survived and came home to Lu, their two daughters, and Southern California.

In his spare time he redesigned his toy, calling it the Whirlo-Way (after a famous racehorse, Whirlaway). With a partner named Warren Franscioni, he checked out plastic manufacturers and had some prototypes made. Flying saucers were in the news thanks to that little dust-up at Roswell, so he renamed the toy the Flyin-Saucer.

Fred Morrison selling his Pluto Platter in the 1950s.

Morrison and Franscioni found that the discs were a big hit at the Los Angeles County Fair in 1948. The pair would start playing with one, and pretty soon fairgoers were queuing up to buy them for a dollar. A marketing strategy developed: demonstrate the toy and sell it at fairs.

That plan proved exhausting, and after two years, the partners shook hands and parted ways.

Morrison went to work in construction, but when he had time he tweaked his flying disc. A new plastic—polyethylene—made an even better Flyin-Saucer, so Morrison ordered thousands and went back to working fairs, this time with family members helping out. By 1956, the Flyin-Saucer income was such that construction jobs became a secondary occupation, carrying the family through winter till fair season started. Morrison sold 15,000 Pluto Platters—the new name—for a buck each at the Iowa State Fair alone. Life was good, and getting better.

At some point a stranger suggested that Morrison talk to "the boys at Wham-O." At that time, Wham-O was a mail-order company selling slingshots out of a Southern California office. The Morrisons were skeptical, but then the boys from Wham-O sought them out at the Los Angeles County Fair. After several meetings, the Morrisons decided to sign over the rights to make and market their Pluto Platter to Wham-O.

Mr. Melin and Mr. Knerr—the boys at Wham-O—prepared TV commercials, designed packaging, and secured a patent, while Morrison went back to the fairs. That was fine with Wham-O. In fact, since Lu and Fred Morrison were going to the fair anyway, would they mind bringing a few wooden hoops along and demoing them as well? Morrison agreed to do their market research, but thought the hoops—prototypes of the Hula Hoop, of course—were a waste of time.

Vintage Frisbee, courtesy MollyFinds.

Six months later, Wham-O rolled out the Frisbee, a name Morrison hated. He might have been wrong about those hoops, he admitted (by then, Hula Hoops had become the national craze). But about calling his own flying disc a Frisbee? "I sure as hell knew I was right!" he wrote nearly fifty years later, saying it was a "stupid idea!" Not only that, "I thought the name stunk!" So there! "Frisbee? . . . GAWD!"[27]

Needless to say, in 2005 Morrison wrote that rant with tongue firmly in cheek. By the time the Wham-O boys retired, Morrison had received over $2 million in Frisbee royalties from the company.

So how did Wham-O come up with the name Frisbee? One story says that Rich Knerr remembered a bakery in Connecticut called the Frisbie Pie Company, and that students used to toss their pie tins around, much like the original cake pans Fred and Lucile tossed. Knerr himself, in an interview, claimed that was just a coincidence and that the toy's name was inspired by a cartoon character named Mr. Frisbee.

When the Frisbee took off in 1957, Gay Talese, writing for the *New York Times* in August of that year, observed that "Hundreds of thousands of them have been sold this summer." According to him, the fad first caught on at Princeton and other Ivy League schools. Talese even talked to someone at the Frisbie Pie Company (the one in Connecticut) who claimed that the craze was not a new thing. Five thousand Frisbie pie tins had gone missing, they said, after an earlier Frisbee-style fad right after World War II.

In 1967, Wham-O hired marketing genius Ed Headrick and he restyled the Frisbee. He added rings (actually, ridges) and a racing stripe to the surface. Dodger pitcher Sandy Koufax endorsed it, and a new, aggressive, and successful ad campaign began that promoted Frisbee throwing as a competitive sport. One game, Guts, had been around for awhile and even had tournaments in the late '50s, but other games—like Frisbee Golf, Frisbee Football, and Ultimate —came out in the next decade, leading up to 1974's World Frisbee Disc Championship at the Rose Bowl in Pasadena.

By the time Fred Morrison died at age 90, Wham-O had sold over 200 million Frisbees, and Morrison got a royalty for every one of them, through all the permutations of Wham-O ownership.

 *Hula Hoop*

Myths about the Hula Hoop are legion: While hoops have been around forever, did Wham-O develop this toy independently, deciding on polyethylene over bamboo or wood—or did they borrow the idea from an Australian company, making a donation to a Sidney children's hospital as payment?

One story says that Wham-O sought out Australian entrepreneur Alex Tolmer, who sold an exercise ring made of bamboo. Tolmer ran Toltoys, an innovative toy company from down under, and experimented with different types of plastic—like polyethylene. Using that flexible material, Toltoys sold 400,000 hoops, and Wham-O took notice.

Spud Melin claimed that a friend from down under did indeed tell them about the fad. And Tolmer sold Wham-O toys in Australia, so while the details may be fuzzy, there was definitely a relationship between Tolmer and the boys from Wham-O.

By the end of 1957, Wham-O had tried out names like Twirl-A-Hoop, Whoopee Hoop, and Swing-a-Hoop as they tried to interest people in the toy. Like other big fads of the '50s (Frisbee and Slinky come to mind), the toy had to be seen in action to be appreciated. Starting with Spud Melin's daughter's school, Wham-O reps would take the hoop to local grammar schools and parks, and once kids saw it— Boom! They had a hit. Sales took off into the stratosphere when the Hoop was featured on TV's *The Dinah Shore Chevy Show.*

At $1.98 each, the demand shocked the company—they sold 25 million in the first few months. Other companies, quick to manufacture copycat versions, sold dozens of millions more. Wham-O shut down all other manufacturing to make more Hula Hoops. They turned out 20,000 per day, which wasn't enough. So Wham-O contracted with plants in Johannesburg, Tokyo, Paris, and other locales to make and ship 20,000 hoops a day. Customers bought five or ten at a time to see how many they could swing around at once.

Red Skelton posed with a Hula Hoop for the October 5, 1958 cover of Parade.

Here's a bit of cultural trivia: Hula Hoops made previously taboo hip-swinging and gyrating acceptable. Wham-O's VP of Marketing Bob Payne pointed out that Hula Hoops cleared the way for television to start showing teenagers doing the Twist. In fact, Payne said, before the Hula Hoop, *"The Ed Sullivan Show* never showed the original bump-and-grinder, Elvis Presley, below the waist. It was only after the Hula Hoop craze swept the country that Sullivan suddenly decided it would be all right for the camera to dip below Elvis's belt line."[28]

In the celebrity circle, Red Skelton posed with the hoop on the cover of *Parade Magazine*; Art Linkletter and Debbie Reynolds were Hoop users; and when Jane Russell competed in a New York Hula Hoop contest at Sardi's East, her picture made the front page. No one knows the exact figure, but at least 70 million—and maybe as many as 100 million—Hula Hoops and imitations were sold during the craze.

And then suddenly, the orders stopped. "It was born in January and dead as a doornail by October," Rich Knerr recalled for Tim Walsh in *The Wham-O Superbook: Celebrating 60 Years Inside the Fun Factory.*

No one can say exactly why, but Wham-O accumulated a warehouse full of returned hoops. The world simply got tired of hula-hooping.[29]

More trivia: Remember Fred Morrison, inventor of the Frisbee? Sales were really starting to move on that toy when Morrison developed and tested another idea: a Popsicle Machine. It wasn't really a machine, just an eight-pack mold into which people could pour Hawaiian Punch or fruit juice. The set went into the freezer and presto—popsicles! Morrison's design included a Cups 'n Sticks mold that fitted over the top of the juice mold.

Wham-O and Morrison signed another contract for these Popsicle Machines just as the Hula Hoop tanked. So the Wham-O boys thought: why not grind up and melt down the unwanted hoops—which were bright colored plastic—to make the Cups 'n Sticks part?

It was a brilliant idea, except that workers forgot to remove the staples and wooden dowels that held the Hula Hoops together. When splinters and metal clogged the hot plastic injector mechanisms, "it took days to remove the hardened plastic from the mold and clear the orifice," Morrison remembered. "After a couple of contaminated plastic cloggings, the Boys gave up on the Popsicle Machines."[30]

Wham-O survived, though just barely. In 1965 they brought out a new version of the toy, the Shoop-Shoop Hula Hoop, with a ball bearing inside. Though sales have been modest, they've been steady and reliable ever since. In fact, when Rich Knerr and Spud Melin retired in 1982, Wham-O was still selling about 1.5 million Hula Hoops each year.

BB Guns

The BB gun has a surprisingly long history—if you don't include ancient blow guns, you can trace them back to the 16th century when bellows air guns shot darts, or to the 17th century when pneumatic air guns were created in France. Though these weren't toys, their design was similar to the BB gun (the term BB refers to ball bearing, by the way).

In the US, the Plymouth Iron Windmill Company of Michigan set up an air rifle division to make wooden air guns during the 1880s. That product evolved into a steel gun. According to company lore, the general manager tried out the gun and said, "Boy, that's a daisy!"

Dwight Burdette took this sad photo of the Daisy Factory's lone wall, still standing in Plymouth, Michigan (the company moved to Arkansas in 1958).

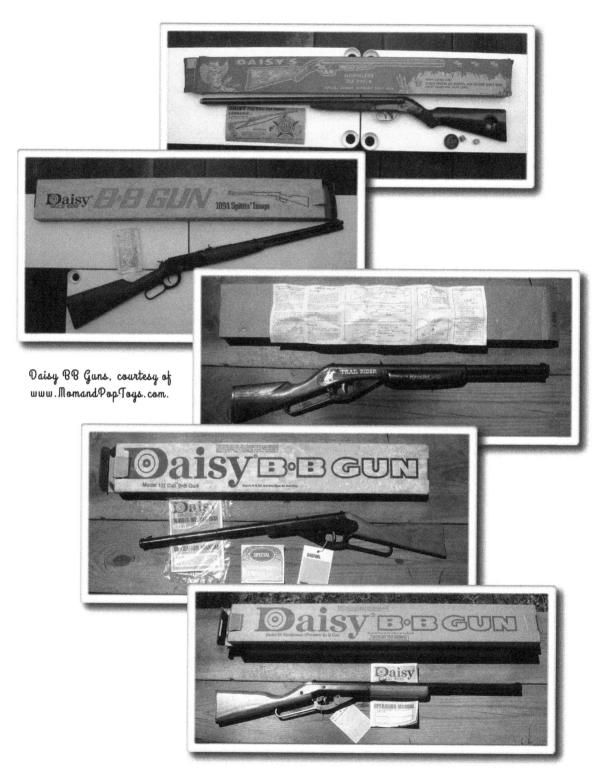

Daisy BB Guns, courtesy of www.MomandPopToys.com.

The gun was so successful that the company changed its name, dropped its previous business (windmills), and bought out its competitors. It became Daisy, and it was Daisy who hit on the idea of naming the guns after Western heroes, decades before the 1950s. And as you probably know, the Red Ryder BB Gun—named for a comic book hero and licensed by Red Ryder's creator, Fred Harman—became its most popular model to that point. By 1949, a million Red Ryders were sold each year.

While traditional BB guns use air to propel a projectile, Daisy's most popular model was the 960 Noisemaker of 1953—a great gun that had no projectiles. It just made noise, and that was enough to make it the best-selling toy of the year.

In the 1960s, Daisy introduced the Spittin' Image line, BB guns designed to replicate famous guns in every detail except fire power, like the .45 Colt Frontier revolver and the Winchester 94 carbine of 1894.

In 1958 the company moved from Plymouth, Michigan, to Rogers, Arkansas, and maintains an Airgun Museum there. The staff and curators spend much of their time answering questions about BB guns, though they do not do appraisals. Check them out online at DaisyMuseum.com.

And if you still have your Daisy Air Gun? Go ahead, you can admit you still bring it out on occasion and pretend you're an outlaw.

Chapter Twelve

Non-Toys

ot all gifts were toys, not even when we were small—but who wants to talk about clothes (other than Hopalong Cassiday outfits, of course)? This section stretches into the '70s for a few awkward, "you're not a kid anymore" gifts that could be cool, funny, and all-too-quickly passé.

 Macramé

Is it a toy or a gift? Enough of us got macramé craft kits to warrant including them here, but we gave some as gifts too: hanging plant hammocks to Mom, toilet paper holders to Auntie Grizelda, hippie-looking shoulder bags to our friends. Well, scratch that last one. Even in the

'70s, we knew better than to give a macramé bag to a friend.

Simply ornamental knot work, macramé dates back centuries to the Middle East, but it was the hippies in the 1960s who made it popular as a craft. They carried bags woven and knotted out of hemp or (less suggestively) jute, twine, sisal, or any rope-like material, preferably earth toned. For a brief period, vests, hats, bracelets, and belts were quite the rage at concerts and "happenings," and then they went middle class.

When the '70s dawned, Grandma handed out macramé craft kits as Christmas gifts so we could make ourselves pouches like the counterculture had used for marijuana. How groovy—and ironic—was that?

Macrame owl looking for love on Etsy.com, courtesy of RetroPhit.

 # Lava Lamps

Lava lamps did not provide much light, nor were they filled with lava. But they were unquestionably cool, and everybody wanted one for awhile. And as with so many things retro, lava lamps are in high demand again.

The lamps were invented in England by a man named Edward Craven Walker. A former RAF pilot, Craven Walker (no hyphen, but he used both names as his surname) wandered into a pub one evening and saw a martini shaker with a glob of wax in it. The pub owner told him that it was an egg timer. The shaker went into the boiling water next to the egg, and when the heat melted the wax, the egg was cooked.

A vintage 1960s Lava Lamp, courtesy Bridgett Gartman.

That planted the seed. When he wasn't working on other projects—producing films celebrating nudity or helping to found a naturist[31] retreat near his home in Dorset—Craven Walker played with the melting wax idea. He knew he could make something of it as a novelty to ornament a room and set a mood.

Eventually he came up with a formula that to this day remains a proprietary secret and creates the soothing movement of the lava lamp. Basically, two substances swirl around inside a glass container but never mix. The wax is weighted with the solvent carbon tetrachloride so that it doesn't just stay at the top of the container. Instead, once the wax is heated by an element at the base of the lamp, it expands, rises, cools a bit and congeals, then sinks. Wowwwww.

Production started in 1963 when Craven Walker founded the company Crestworth Limited to produce his new Astro Lamps. Two years later, he took them to a convention in Hamburg and they attracted the attention of a couple of American entrepreneurs. That same year—1965—the Lava Brand Century Motion Lamp Company of Chicago began producing Lava Lites.

By the later 1960s, seven million lava lamps a year were sold worldwide. They became the rage as they were sleek in design, with the contours of a rocket ship. But as Professor Stephen Horner pointed out in *Smithsonian* Magazine, they created a mood by evoking our primal days, eons ago, when we gazed into the fire every evening.

Lava lamps were featured in TV shows like *The Avengers* and *Prisoner* and even a James Bond flick, where four lava lamps served as bedposts. In the 1970s, demand dropped but the novelty lights never went out of production. When sales fell to about 100,000 a year globally, Haggerty Enterprises acquired the US license for lava lamps, which today are assembled in China. At the time, Crestworth Limited continued to supply the rest of the world.

In 1989 Craven Walker allowed a couple with the last name Grainger to become partners in his company, and they changed the name to Mathmos two years later. Craven Walker remained on board, though, right up to his death in 2000. Mathmos still makes the lamps today—in fact, they still sell replacement bulbs for the 1965 Astro lamps.

Mood Rings

Nineteen seventy-five was the year that every one of us grown-up—or nearly grown-up—Boomers had to have a Mood Ring (especially if you were female). One of several people claiming to be the genius behind the fad was Marv Wernick, who bought some "liquid crystals" after reading an article about them in a magazine—or after seeing a doctor use them to measure temperature in the hospital (stories vary). Wernick watched the material change colors when touched and wondered, *"What* can I do with this?"

Having been in the jewelry business for over twenty years—half of that time spent designing his own jewelry—he set out mulling and tinkering with the substance. Before Mood Rings, he created Rainbow Ropes, long loops of wooden beads in bright colors, that were displayed and sold alongside clothing so customers could buy an outfit and the jewelry to match. That was a first for the '60s—Wernick was quite the innovator.

He then put the liquid crystals into glass or quartz pendants and rings and took his new creation to trade shows, calling them "Magic Pendants." He never patented his idea—patenting jewelry probably never occurred to him—and imitations proliferated. Someone in New York called it "Mood Jewelry" and the name stuck; in fact, it turned the items into a fad.

Two other people are sometimes credited for the Mood Ring invention: Joshua Reynolds and Maris Ambats, who sold the Mood Ring in New York for $45 to $250 each. But even though many rings were sold, neither Reynolds, Ambats, nor Wernick got rich. There were simply too many imitations from numerous manufacturers.

So just how *do* the rings change color with temperature?

The thermotropic liquid crystals inside the hollow glass actually twist, changing their molecular structure, which in turn alters the light wavelengths (the color) that are either absorbed or reflected back. Hence, color changes with temperature. The same principle is used in today's digital thermometers—the kind that simply lie across your forehead—and if Wernick did indeed see such a strip measuring fever in a hospital, it may have been an early prototype.

The deep blue or green default colors were the shades that indicated you were calm and relaxed, according to most charts. If the ring turned yellow, you had tensed up, meaning something was exciting you. Nervous tension or anxiety would turn the ring brown, but the best color to see was pink or purple. That meant you were very happy, and probably in love.

Like all fads it eventually ended, and the 1975 Mood Ring bonanza fizzled out over one weekend, leaving stores and their customers saturated with product. Wernick expected that, as he knew he was selling a novelty item—once everyone had a Mood Ring, it was no longer a novelty.

Let's face it: how many times can you make someone smile by saying, "I see you're in the mood"? As a pick up line, it got old fast.

The initial Mood Ring fad ended in November 1975, and stores became desperate to unload them. This was why many a doting Auntie bought Mood Rings for her nieces as Christmas presents, since the prices were slashed and "this is what all the kids are wearing, right?"

Today, it's common to see cheap Mood Rings at fairs and flea markets, but the style is different. Instead of one big jewel, the ring is flat with a strip of the liquid crystals set over a metal band. The strip changes color as the metal conducts body heat to it. They're still cool, but we Boomers know that there's nothing like an original.

Pet Rocks[32]

Finally—the perfect toy for grown-ups!

In 1975, the only Christmas present worth giving or receiving was the Pet Rock.

Like other pets, they came in a ventilated carrying crate. "PET ROCK" was printed on it in faux stenciling, along with an assurance that the rock was pedigreed, an important distinction given all the inferior imitations that flooded the market later. Inside, the stone rested in a bed of excelsior.

In the excitement of giving and receiving, many new owners missed the small print on the box, warning them NOT to remove the new pet before reading the instructions. Fortunately, the rocks—perhaps forced into hibernation by wrapping paper or the scent of Christmas potpourri—proved docile and downright lazy once the crate was opened. None were reported missing, and few ran away.

The 32-page owner's manual advised new caretakers to let their Pet Rock acclimate gently to its surroundings by leaving it in its own "special place" for three days, with a ticking alarm clock nearby to soothe it, and old newspapers spread around the crate in case the rock got excited.

With headings such as "Your PET ROCK and you," and pictures showing packs of wild rocks (which were "surly, vicious, and unpredictable . . . nearly impossible to domesticate"), the manual, titled *The Care and Training of Your PET ROCK,* was arguably a bestseller in 1975—right up there with *Shogun.* Yup, over a million copies were sold. Owners were instructed in rock training, from basic obedience to more advanced tricks. Two sessions a day, 15 minutes each, worked best; rocks, surprisingly, had a short attention span.

According to the book, commands such as "Sit" and "Stay" were not difficult skills for the pet to master. With a little practice, rocks would obey a hand gesture alone. A recalcitrant (not to be confused with calciferous, a different breed of stone entirely) rock might occasionally need to be told "Bad Rock! Bad!" but would learn the commands eventually. Teaching a rock to come when called required "extraordinary patience." "Be gentle," owners were cautioned, and as with other commands, "reward obedience with praise."

Advanced tricks were problematic. Most Pet Rocks took quite well to playing dead, and when placed on a hill they quickly learned to roll over. In fact, Pet Rocks usually didn't tire of this trick until they reached the bottom of the hill. They could even be taught to skip over water, although they were notoriously bad swimmers. Some tricks were beyond their skills, however. As the manual said, "Don't be ridiculous. You can't teach a rock to shake hands."

While not normally aggressive, Pet Rocks could also be taught to attack. When confronted by a mugger, owners were instructed to grasp their rocks firmly, shout the command, "Attack!" and with Pet Rock in hand, "bash the mugger's head in."

Because "a healthy rock is a happy rock," the manual offered some tips on Pet Rock health hazards as well, along with pictures that showed rocks in various stages of deterioration. If blood comes out of the stone, for example, the manual advised calling the Internal Revenue Service immediately. It may not help the rock, but the IRS had been "attempting to do this very thing for years."

Pet Rocks and their training guide emerged from the fertile (and possibly inebriated) imagination of advertising copywriter Gary Dahl while he joked with friends and coworkers at a neighborhood bar. After listening to others run through a litany of pet problems, Dahl announced, "I have a pet rock," and an advertising legend was born. Over the next months, Dahl wrote the manual, hired a designer, got financial backing from a former employer, and arranged to haul two-and-a-half tons of rocks from Rosarita Beach in Baja, California, (where, he declared later, each rock was individually tested for obedience before being selected). His Pet Rocks debuted at autumn gift shows and became the must-have gift for Christmas.

Pocketing 95 cents on every rock sold at $3.95, Dahl became a millionaire three weeks before Christmas. His explanation for the phenomenal success of Pet Rocks? "You might say we've packaged a sense of humor."

Sadly, however, the season quickly passed. The public's attention span was apparently as fleeting as a rock's. By Valentine's Day, Pet Rocks were being abandoned like . . . well . . . Mood Rings. They ended up—as Dahl plaintively wailed—in "the attic, the back corner of dresser drawers, and in extreme cases, in landfill and obscure piles of rubble."

You may be comforted to know that once domesticated, Pet Rocks seldom reverted to a wild state, even when abandoned. Their slavish obedience would put Shakespeare's Kate to shame: those told, "Stay!" forty-some years ago have never moved a muscle. Just as well, because in 1975 Dahl cautioned ominously, "The world is already overcrowded with discarded, unwanted rocks and millions must be destroyed each year. These poor, unfortunate rocks meet brutal ends in roadbeds, cement mixers, or as land fill."

For a while, burial-at-sea services or quiet rest at a Pet Rock sanitarium were options for disenchanted owners, but the companies providing these services have moved on. Some Pet Rocks, however, have attained positions of honor, stability, and even fame. One, for example, has journeyed as far as the South Pole to sit faithfully on the bookcase of the McMurdo Station Cosmic Ray Observatory in Antarctica, its nesting straw unsoiled.

As for Gary Dahl, he's weathered the vicissitudes of fortune rather well. After making his million and becoming a textbook example of marketing innovation, he bought a big house, opened a pub, won the 2000 Bulwer Lytton Fiction Contest (for intentionally bad prose), and wrote a book: *Advertising for Dummies* (who better?). For years he's owned his own advertising agency, and word is that he's working on a book: *The Saga of the Pet Rock.*

Boomers as Gift-Giving Parents

Pet Rocks appealed to an adult audience in the 1970s and were pretty much the last big Christmas fad catering to the kid in Boomers. By those years, many of us were parents, or at least doting aunts and uncles. Christmas came to a new generation, but Boomers footed the bill. Cabbage Patch Kids, My Pretty Pony, Transformers, He-Man, and Trivial Pursuit are all worthy of nostalgic prose, but theirs is another story, to be told another time.

References

CHAPTER ONE

[1] The process was described in an interview with a 92-year-old former employee, in the book *Seasons Gleamings: The Art of the Aluminum Christmas Tree,* by J. Shimon and J. Lindemann.

[2] The reporter was named William Croffut, and he wrote for the *Detroit Post and Tribune.*

CHAPTER TWO

[3] The cookbook, a wonderful overview of American meals (with recipes, of course) is *Square Meals*, written by Jane and Michael Stern (Knopf, NY: 1984).

[4] Reilly quoted in Chief Marketer Network ezine, Promo|Direct section: "Campbell's Family Tradition," Nov. 1, 2003; online at: http://www.chiefmarketer.com/special-reports-chief-marketer/campbells-family-tradition-01112003#

[5] In case corporate histories thrill you: Carl Gilbert Swanson partnered with John Jerpe and Frank Ellison in the 19th century to run a dairy products firm called Jerpe Commission Company. Poultry, butter, and eggs were their business. Swanson bought out his partners in the 1920s but waited till after World War II to change the name of his company to Swanson and Sons. Gilbert and Clarke, his sons, took over the firm in 1949. They ran it successfully for six years, then sold their 20 plants to Campbell Soup and went out and started a new venture, Butternut Foods, which eventually got absorbed by Coca Cola.

[6] This is not to suggest that women's feelings weren't complicated, or that they lacked ambition. The war had been terrible, the Depression before it also traumatic. The entire country craved a return to safety and normalcy, and the stereotyped family unit, with Mom in the kitchen, represented that.

CHAPTER THREE

[7] Lee, Brenda. *Little Miss Dynamite.* NY: Hyperion Books, 2002. pp. 78–79.

CHAPTER FOUR

[8] Mendelson, Lee. *A Charlie Brown Christmas: The Making of a Tradition.* HarperCollins, 2000.

[9] The critics' words were in Russian, of course, not English. Jennifer Fisher reprinted these translations in her 2003 book, *Nutcracker Nation.* Yale U Press, 2003.

CHAPTER FIVE

[10] Yup. It had nothing to do with his work, but the elder Wright was not paying his son. Finally, the younger man claimed his wages by deducting them from a payment he picked up to deliver to Dad—and got fired.

CHAPTER SIX

[11] Actually, Richard returned to the US once, in the early sixties, after announcing he wanted to take three of his six children back to Bolivia with him—but not which three. Betty had detectives watching Richard, terrified that he'd rip her family apart again. After a few months he finally left—and that really was the last she heard from him. For more details. see Shook, Robert L. *Why Didn't I Think of That!* NY: New American Library. 1982.

CHAPTER SEVEN

[12] Kaye, Marvin. *A Toy Is Born.* NY: Stein & Day, 1973.

[13] Walsh, Tim. *The Wham-O Superbook: Celebrating 60 Years Inside the Fun Factory.* Chronicle Books, 2008.

CHAPTER NINE

[14] Kaye, Marvin. *A Toy Is Born.*

[15] Kaye, Marvin. *A Toy Is Born.*

[16] Wyden, Peter. "The Troubled King of Toys." *Saturday Evening Post,* March 5, 1960.

[17] Wyden, Peter. "The Troubled King of Toys."

[18] Kaye, Marvin. *A Toy Is Born.*

[19] In his well-researched book *Timeless Toys : Classic Toys & the Playmakers Who Created Them.* (KC, MO: Andrews McMeel Pub, 2003), Tim Walsh identifies Parl Chaze as the toy's developer, and Chaze's employer Arthur Grandjean as the inventor. Other sources say the French inventor was Arthur Granjean or Grandjean or Paul Chaze, but the Ohio Arts website gives his name as Andre Cassagnes—and we hope they know best.

[20] Oppenheimer, Jerry. *Toy Monster.* Hoboken, NJ: Wiley & Sons, 2009.

[21] Oppenheimer, Jerry. *Toy Monster.*

CHAPTER TEN

[22] Flubber, tremendously popular at first, generated over 1600 complaints of skin rashes and had to be recalled. Read about it in Chapter 7: "Boy oh Boy, It's a Hasbro Toy!"

[23] We now call them action figures—a term that was first used to promote the James Bond figure designed by Marvin Glass a year after GI Joe's debut.

[24] The associate marketing director was Fredric C. Behling, quoted in Marvin Kaye's *A Toy Is Born.*

[25] Quotes from Neil Estern, interviewed by Chris Johnson for the article "The Ideal Face of the 1960s." *Doll Reader*, May 1997.

CHAPTER 11

[26] Morrison, Fred, and Phil Kennedy. *Flat Flip Flies Straight!* Wethersfield, CT: Wormhole Publishers, 2006.

[27] Morrison, pp. 119–120.

[28] Kaye, Marvin. *A Toy Is Born.*

[29] An alternate reality version of the Hula Hoop phenomenon was presented in a 1994 film, *The Hudsucker Proxy*. Tim Robbins played a hapless mail room clerk who is promoted to run the company, but the scheming, evil manager played by Paul Newman wants him to ruin the place, so that Newman and his cronies can cheaply buy up the stock, then take over again. The Coen Brothers needed a wacky toy that no one expected to catch on to fit their movie plot, so they "borrowed" the Hula Hoop. Most moviegoers remembered what a huge hit Hula Hoops had been, but the rest of the story was Hollywood fiction, filtered through the producers' imaginations. A disclaimer appeared at the end of the movie, just in case anyone was fooled. The one thing true about *The Hudsucker Proxy* was that those hoops were phenomenally successful.

[30] Morrison, Fred, and Phil Kennedy. *Flat Flip Flies Straight!* pp. 123–125. But Morrison's memory may be foggy, since Tim Walsh—author of *Wham-O Superbook: Celebrating 60 Years Inside the Fun Factory*—featured a 1962 ad for a 98-cent "Frozen Sucker Mold," the same type of popsicle maker Morrison described.

CHAPTER 12

[31] Naturist being the British term for nudist.

[32] A version of this article was originally published in "Americana: Pet Rocks," *American History Magazine*, June 2005.

Index

S

Acknowledgements

I have many people to thank for each separate bit of this book, but I'll start with the one person who deserves thanks for every part of it:

Stacey Aaronson—who edited and designed *The Boomer Book of Christmas Memories*, creating the clever chapter headings and so much more—contributed pictures as well. Who knew that the perfect book editor also had vintage Madame Alexander Dolls and the 1960 Life game, that her father held onto his Spirograph and that her grandmother made keepsake Raggedy Ann and Andy dolls for her favorite grandchild? Thank you, Stacey, for sharing your photos and for all your hard work on this book.

In fact, thank you to everyone who shared their pictures!

First and foremost, my brother Robert Von Gerichten provided the cover photo, even though it exposed his more vulnerable side. Robert also dug into his record album collection, Christmas train photos, and even found and set up his plastic army men for the camera (although I suspect he enjoyed that last part way too much).

I'm indebted to several food companies that allowed me to use their old ads and pictures, and their employees were a pleasure to work with—specifically, Corporate Archivists Susan Wakefield of General Mills and Jonathan Thorn of Campbell Soup Co., and Chris Spina of Pinnacle Foods for the Swanson's TV dinner ads. David Walbert rounds out this list of food contributors for his Christmas cookie photo.

Others—old friends and new—came forward with personal photographs. I'd like to thank Susan Strother Carrier, the exuberant toddler who introduces the toy section (also the two-year-old with a coonskin hat); Cheryl Riggs Gardner, who got a Chatty Cathy for Christmas in '61 and shared other pictures as well; Dan Wheeler for loaning me his executive Slinky; my high school friend Beverly for the photo of her brother, Gentleman George Wheeler (and thank you George, for being a good sport about it!); Mary Watkins for letting me burrow through her closets and boxes of sheet music to find the ultimate treasure: Dam Trolls! Flo Selfman shared pictures of her Toni and Nancy Ann dolls, Debra Ann Pawlak her View-Master, and Valerie Myers shared Suzette.

Thank you to all the online vendors and collectors who allowed me to use their pictures, especially George Mauler of MomandPopToys.com. George took fresh photos of models, costumes, aliens, toy guns, and BB guns just because he is a Great Guy. Other generous folks are Rick of SuperBalls.com, the PaintByNumbersMuseum.com, MisterToast, Mark A. Wright of tibranch.com, who contributed the GI Joe photos, and Etsy vendors KrauseHaus, MollyFinds, BridgettsGadgets, and RetroPhit.

And thanks also to various Presidential Libraries and to all selfless souls who put pictures up on the Commons pages of Flickr and Wikipedia. From the Children's Museum of Indianapolis to Jon "ShakataGaNat" Davis—I can't say you'll never be forgotten, but your pictures are appreciated.

As for books, there were times that I felt as if I read every book written in the last half of the 20th century about holidays and toys—and loved all of them. But a couple of authors really must be mentioned, as anyone who enjoyed this book will probably enjoy theirs:

Tim Walsh, author of *Timeless Toys: Classic Toys and the Playmakers Who Created Them* as well as *Wham-O Superbook: Celebrating 60 Years Inside the Fun Factory*, is first on the list. Both of his books are full of personal interviews, pictures, and great stories. Professor Karal Ann Marling collected tons of information about 20th-century Christmas celebrations in her book, *Merry Christmas!* And of all the books about the toy industry, both lurid or factual, my favorite was *Toy Wars: The Epic Struggle Between GI Joe, Barbie, and the Companies That Made Them.* It balanced memoir, facts, and action as the authors followed Hasbro's moves in the early '90s.

A more complete list of books and sources can be found at the book's website, http://www.BoomerBookofChristmas.com, and I am grateful to all of them. Mistakes, I've made a few, but then again . . . I apologize in advance.

*V*ickey Kall was born a Boomer in the halcyon spring of '54. Like so many of her —or any—generation, she thought she would never grow old.

One day in the 1980s, she learned that her boss was younger than she. A week later, her nephew announced that he was studying the Vietnam War in history class. A cloud obscured the sun, and reports of an impending apocalypse began to spread.

She had not saved her old Archie comic books. Her short-sighted parents had not stockpiled virgin Barbies or first editions of *A Canticle for Leibowitz*. As a child, she played with the toys she was given, rather than preserving them, unopened, in the closet. Foolish girl! How was she to pay for retirement?

She returned to college, thinking she could write for a living. Newspapers folded, cloud sourcing replaced investigative journalism, and the End of Days loomed ever nearer.

"Write what you know," Papa Hemingway is often quoted as saying. And so she did, but no one was interested in the memoirs of a former Executive Assistant Network Account Coordinating Administrator—no matter how many ways the title could be arranged—who spent her lunch hours reading Ursula LeGuin novels.

And so, in the end, she resorted to research about Christmases of yore, when TVs were new and bulky, clocks looked like starbursts, and nothing was on or open 24 hours except hospital emergency rooms.

This book is the fruit of that effort.

Buy it, please. Help keep Vickey off the streets.

The Boomer Book of Christmas Memories is on the web at:

http://www.BoomerBookofChristmas.com

and you can follow Vickey on Twitter (@VKHistory) or Facebook (Vickey Kall)

CPSIA information can be obtained
at www.ICGtesting.com
Printed in the USA
LVHW071615241220
675097LV00015B/1685

9 780985 397340